Decomposed

Decomposed

The Political Ecology of Music

Kyle Devine

The MIT Press
Cambridge, Massachusetts
London, England

© 2019 Massachusetts Institute of Technology

All rights reserved. No part of this book may be reproduced in any form by any electronic or mechanical means (including photocopying, recording, or information storage and retrieval) without permission in writing from the publisher.

This book was set in Stone Serif and Stone Sans by Westchester Publishing Services. Printed and bound in the United States of America.

Library of Congress Cataloging-in-Publication Data

Names: Devine, Kyle, author.
Title: Decomposed : the political ecology of music / Kyle Devine.
Description: Cambridge, MA : The MIT Press, [2019] |
Includes bibliographical references and index.
Identifiers: LCCN 2019005613 | ISBN 9780262537780
(pbk. : alk. paper)
Subjects: LCSH: Music--Environmental aspects. | Sound recordings--
Environmental aspects.
Classification: LCC ML3916 .D5 2019 | DDC 621.389/32--dc23
LC record available at https://lccn.loc.gov/2019005613

10 9 8 7 6 5 4 3 2 1

Contents

Preface, Acknowledgments, and Notes to Readers

When he was about my age, my dad started building signs for a living. You know the ones. Think flickering neon letters in a diner window, or blinking bulbs chasing themselves around a marquee. Think fluorescent tubes and backlit lightboxes at malls and gas stations. Think LEDs and jumbotrons, Times Square and Shibuya. Think Vegas.

At the outset, my dad had never built a sign. To figure out how, he decamped late one night, climbed a freestanding sign, unscrewed the thing, and peeked inside. The anatomy of an electronic sign, it turns out, is not so complicated. But it takes a lot to put one together and keep it glowing.

I've worked in the sign business—albeit occasionally and part-time, to earn some pocket money when I was in school. I helped build signs in the shop. I remember the sheet metal breaks and huge spools of plastic, the smell of hot steel and spray paint, the impossibly bright blue flashes and strangely robotic gurgles of the arc welder. I also worked on the cranes, installing new signs and fixing fried filaments. And I spent time in the office. There I learned about international materials shipments and industry suppliers; about national systems of classification and certification; about local permits and electricity grids; about municipal variance meetings where urban planners and sign manufacturers brawled over their divergent visions of the cityscape; about tensions between the sign industry's main goal (to get your attention) and government traffic safety regulations (drivers must not be distracted). Knowing something about all the people and things that had to align in order for a sign to exist, and seeing that signs were everywhere, it intrigued me that other people hardly seemed to notice them. Even though electronic signs are advertising media, and so nothing if not visible, somehow they also fade into the background of the everyday.

Through college and university, I kept working at the sign company from time to time. When I wasn't sweeping the shop floor, changing lightbulbs around town, or updating databases in the office, I was in the classroom learning about notes and chords. As the curriculum advanced, I also learned to see music as a cultural phenomenon that reflected and inflected bigger social issues. With the right musicological tools and the right interpretive know-how, it was possible to show that tonality signified capitalism, atonality signaled revolution, symphonies symbolized sexism, fugues figured philosophy, noise represented society, and so on. Music became more than notes and chords. It was something much more significant.

This new, critical approach to music was eye-opening. And it was of obvious political importance. Yet my time with signs meant that, whatever music might have symbolized, I couldn't help but wonder about all the things and activities that must have been required to fill the classroom with pianos, scores, recordings, playback equipment—all the things we needed to study music, let alone to make music and listen to it more generally. In the same way that signs tend toward invisibility despite their prevalence and regardless of all the human and material resources that go into them, I sensed that a lot of what makes music possible was inaudible. What were all these LPs and CDs made of? Where did they come from? Who assembled the turntables and CD players? And what happened to all this stuff when it wore out or broke down, became unwanted or obsolete?

In retrospect, my dual apprenticeship in signage and solfege is the core of this book. It was around then that I started to think about music less like a symbol, and more like a sign. So this book is dedicated to my dad, for introducing me to the world of signs. And for being so reliably my dad.

Acknowledgments

If the convention of dedication is ancient, it is less clear when it became customary for authors to begin their books with lists of acknowledgments. Still, it is a custom I embrace. I have to start by thanking Tom Everrett. I wouldn't have come to this topic without him, and the end result wouldn't be the same without his wisdom and friendship. Patrick Valiquet is another close friend and sharp mind. A lot of the ideas that underpin this book were fine-tuned in conversation with him. Georgina Born, Simon Frith, John Shepherd, Jonathan Sterne, and Paul Théberge saw the beginnings of this project and eventually read the manuscript, too. Their encouragement has been a tonic. Their input has been invaluable.

Over the years, I have also received many more welcome words, helping hands, and smart suggestions that made lasting impressions on this book. Thanks to Aaron Allen, Melissa Avdeeff, Geoffrey Baker, Darin Barney, Alyssa Beaton, David Berry, Alexandrine Boudreault-Fournier, Matt Brennan, Ainslie

Coghill, Aditi Deo, Vebhuti Duggal, Andrew Eisenberg, Simon Gadir, Kyle Gipson, Lydia Goehr, Katie Helke, Piers Hemmingsen, Christopher Johns, Laura Keeler, Caleb Kelly, Gabrielle Kielich, Murray Leeder, Steven Maddock, Alexander Magoun, Franny Nudelman, Richard Osborne, Vibodh Parthasarathi, Benjamin Piekut, Nick Prior, Elodie Roy, Luis Sanchez, Michael Sims, Gavin Steingo, Arnar Eggert Thoroddsen, Steve Waksman, Tom Western, and Eric Weisbard. Special thanks to my coworkers and students at the University of Oslo, as well as my previous coworkers and students at the University of Oxford and the City University of London, all of whom have helped in all kinds of ways. It goes without saying that I'm enormously thankful for the support of family and friends both near and far.

In researching the history of what recordings have been made of, and what happens to those recordings when they are disposed of, there is no one archive or fieldwork site. Accordingly, the research for this book is a patchwork. It takes a page from Harold Innis in being a study of materials as well as documents, of people themselves as living documents, of necessarily multisite archival research and essential fieldwork (to paraphrase from Robin Winks's foreword to *The Fur Trade in Canada*). I am grateful for the help and advice offered by a variety of librarians, archivists, and organizations—even in those cases where our best efforts turned up more haystack than needle. Thanks to Jonathan Hiam and the New York Public Library for the Performing Arts, Ashley Augustyniak and the Chemical Heritage Foundation's Othmer Library of Chemical History, Nicolette Dobrowolski at the Syracuse University Libraries, the library and curatorial staff at the Canada Science and Technology Museum, Ivar Håkon Eikje at the National Library of Norway, Barbara Truesdell at Indiana University's Center for the Study of History and Memory, Lucas Clawson at the Hagley Museum and Library, and Anja Borck at the Emile Berliner Sound and Image Archive. I would also like to thank a few others who will go unnamed: interviewees, tour guides, and representatives at pressing facilities, streaming services, and in other corners of the recording industry.

I have presented parts of this research on several occasions, and I'm grateful for all the discussion in those contexts. Bits of this book have appeared in *Popular Music*, *Où va la musique? Numérimorphose et nouvelles experiences d'écoute*, *On Popular Music and Its Unruly Entanglements*, and a Canada Science and Technology Museum report. Those bits are used here with permission. Full citations can be found in the bibliography.

Notes to Readers

Numerous quantitative dimensions of recorded music appear this book. All such figures represent my most careful estimates and extrapolations based on the sources I have been able to find. Nevertheless, these numbers should be treated with an inclination toward cross-examination. Sales figures for recordings are notoriously patchy, especially before the First World War, while recording industry statistics are generally problematic and should be taken with a grain of salt. Further up the supply chain, things are even more scattered, uncertain, secretive. And it is impossible to know exactly how many music recordings and playback devices have ended up in the garbage. Even so, it is clear that we are dealing with millions and millions of kilograms of materials, billions and billions of recordings and devices. Finding out that some of my quantities are off by a thousand or even a million would not change the book's overall message. The amounts are huge and the issues ought to be reckoned with.

It is also worth noting that I have encountered these figures in various currencies (American dollars, British pounds, Indian rupees) and various measurements (pounds, kilograms, short tons, long tons, maunds). Currency figures are in US dollars unless otherwise indicated. All weight measurements, including tonnage, have been converted to the metric system unless otherwise indicated. In keeping with the use of US spelling conventions in this book, the word "ton" thus implies the 1000-kilogram metric ton and not the 2000-pound imperial ton. Basic rounding rules apply.

Introduction: Political Ecology and Recorded Music

Somewhere off the highway, on the edge of town, there is a sea of star-spangled big rigs, parking lots, and loading docks. The building itself is mostly windowless and concrete, a low-rise about the length of a city block with a footprint the size of 250 one-bedroom apartments. It may not be a sight to behold. But this is where records come from.

After plenty of cold calls, cold shoulders, and cold feet, I had arrived on the doorstep of the one pressing plant that welcomed me for a research visit. Inside, my guide greeted me with a smile and a nondisclosure agreement. We started the tour in the mastering studio, followed by the packaging department, before stepping onto the pressing floor. Dozens of hydraulic machines run all day and night. They look like relics, because they are. The basic technological principles of record pressing have not changed for a century, and the machines themselves are decades old.[1] These contraptions fill the place with hissing and clanking as well as the sweet-and-sour notes of warm grease and melted plastic. There are containers called hoppers at each pressing station, full of the lentil-like polymer pellets that get funneled down into the machinery, heated and fused to form larger biscuits

Figure 0.1
Anonymized record pressing plant, somewhere in the United States

that resemble hockey pucks, and squashed to make records. I was not allowed to see the separate warehouse where this company stockpiles its plastic. Still, the empty fridge-sized cardboard boxes on the pressing floor hinted at their origin. They were marked with big red letters proclaiming "vinyl compound" and "Product of Thailand."[2] I didn't catch the name of the company that made this plastic, and I was not told by my guide. Vinyl suppliers agree not to mention their wholesale customers, and wholesale vinyl customers agree not to mention their suppliers.

While vinyl pellets are shipped in large boxes, it takes only a handful to make a typical record.[3] United States–based petrochemical corporations such as Tenneco and Keysor-Century supplied much of this raw material until the LP market dried up after 1990 and, consequently, the US supply chain also evaporated. Nowadays, with the stylus back in style, the ingredients of LPs are manufactured offshore. As much as 90 percent of the polyvinyl chloride (PVC) used by today's US record manufacturers is made by the Thai Plastic and Chemicals Public Company Limited (TPC), headquartered in Bangkok.[4] TPC has produced

PVC for a wide variety of applications since 1971. But the company's connection to the recording industry was established only around 2007, when US manufacturers sought a new supplier that could provide the high-grade plastic needed to meet the exacting standards of record pressing and the increasing demand for LPs.

Thai Plastic and Chemicals makes this specialized compound on the banks of the Chao Phraya River, about a half-hour's drive south of Bangkok. After a year of unanswered emails and weeks of being hung-up on, I finally got a tentative invitation to tour TPC's facilities and boarded the next flight to Thailand. Shortly after touching down at Suvarnabhumi Airport, and moments after checking into my hotel, by coincidence the first person I met in Bangkok was a retired Belgian petrochemical engineer. Samuel (not his real name) had worked mainly in plastic food packaging, though he had some knowledge of PVC. He was surprised when I told him not only that vinyl record sales were on the rise but that that the recording industry still used what he saw as a grimy and outmoded material. Sam lived hard. He told stories of discos hidden beneath the palaces of Saudi princes, and I lost count of the number of stiff drinks he ordered before breakfast on a Sunday. For his part, he couldn't remember what his own doctoral thesis was about. But Sam knew one thing for sure: TPC was not going to let me see how PVC is made. He was right.

If southbound traffic was surprisingly light on Bangkok's Industrial Ring Road Bridge, security was unsurprisingly tight at the TPC facility. After some confusion about who I was and what exactly I was doing there, TPC's guards ultimately refused me at the gate. Speaking through an app on his phone, my cab driver delivered the badly translated bad news: "This is not the case.

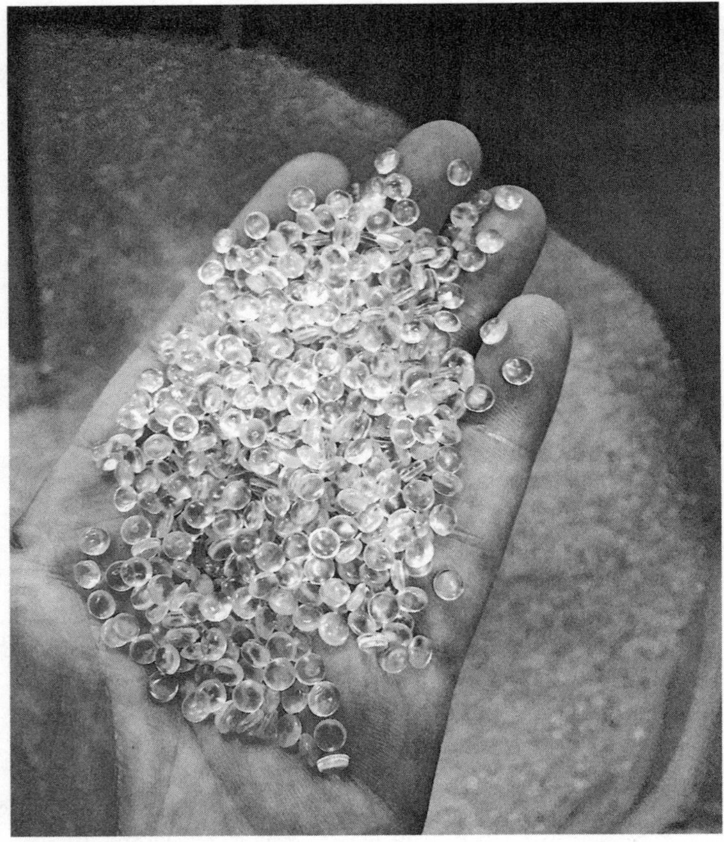

Figure 0.2
A handful of plastic pellets, similar to those used in record pressing

Figure 0.3
At the gate of Thai Plastic and Chemicals, just south of Bangkok

You are not allowed to view the links." I was told the company would need a month to do the relevant paperwork and to prepare the plant for a visit from an outsider. Instead, a representative from SCG Chemicals (TPC's parent corporation and one of the largest petrochemical manufacturers in Asia) agreed to meet at my hotel to discuss their business and to explain how vinyl is made.[5]

The process of producing PVC compound, which TPC does at a rate of 500 kilograms every hour, is complicated. There are numerous phases, a campus of buildings, tall silos and taller cranes, deep vats, and busy and noisy machines, as well as many workers in hardhats and hairnets and safety glasses. But the basic principles are easy to imagine. Think of a Play-Doh Fun Factory. If you have ever rolled some Play-Doh in your hands, placed it in one end of a garlic-press-like gadget and squeezed it out the other—then you know how PVC compound is made. In other words, once PVC has been synthesized from its constituent chemicals, the raw resin is then mixed with a variety of additives, heated to form a molten plastic compound, forced like spaghetti strands through a die, and chopped into pellets. TPC employees are quick to explain the complicated sciences, the high levels of industrial expertise, and the thorough quality-control checks needed to produce this high-grade vinyl compound. They do so in ways that are meant to impress vinyl lovers.

One topic that TPC avoids, and one that vinyl lovers do not broach, is that the polymerization of polyvinyl chloride uses carcinogenic chemicals that can harm its handlers, while the operation produces toxic wastewater that the company has been known to pour into the Chao Phraya River.[6] Indeed, TPC has "a history of environmental abuses" going back to the early 1990s.[7] And then there is ethylene, a hydrocarbon that is essential to the production of PVC resin and which is produced by processing a natural gas called ethane.[8] TPC and SCG carry out this work in refineries at the Map Ta Phut Industrial Estate of Rayong Province, southeast of Bangkok on the Gulf of Thailand. Rayong Province may be known for its beautiful beaches, but Map Ta Phut is one of "Thailand's most toxic hot spots with a well-documented history of air and water pollution, industrial accidents, illegal hazardous waste dumping, and pollution-related health impacts including cancer and birth deformities."[9] We cannot know how much of the effluent in the Chao Phraya or how many of the transgressions of the Map Ta Phut Estate are directly linked to the production of LPs. One thing, though, is certain: this is where vinyl comes from.

From here, the trail goes cold. Tracing a record to its pressing plant is not so difficult. Tracing that pressing plant's vinyl pellets to the facilities where the PVC compounds and resins were likely produced is also possible. Finding out which barrel contained the crude, which tankers and pipelines carried the petroleum, which derrick coaxed the oil from underground—this is all hidden from the public. Even if the specifics of such processes are kept under wraps, the occupational hazards of oil drilling, the planetary problems of petroleum, and the political plights of petrocapitalism are known: people suffer, communities scatter, oils spill, environments suffocate, wars storm, empires soar.[10] These are the conditions that define the production of petroleum, and they spiral into existence every time a needle glides through a groove.

If this mini-travelogue from oil drop to needle drop speaks to the troubling beginnings of a record, the ends of vinyl are just as problematic. Vinyl records are tough stuff, both materially and socially. They are strong but supple, bending but rarely breaking—characteristics that lend records physical longevity. In fact, the physical life of an LP long outlasts its social life. This is the case even though vinyl records are known to be difficult to part with. When particular listeners do eventually lose interest in particular albums, LPs circulate almost endlessly in secondhand economies: record shops, flea markets, thrift stores, garage sales. But records do wear out. They do, eventually, die. From this perspective, secondhand economies only prolong the inevitable. When vinyl records finally meet their ends, some are turned into speed bumps and traffic cones. Others become kitschy bowls

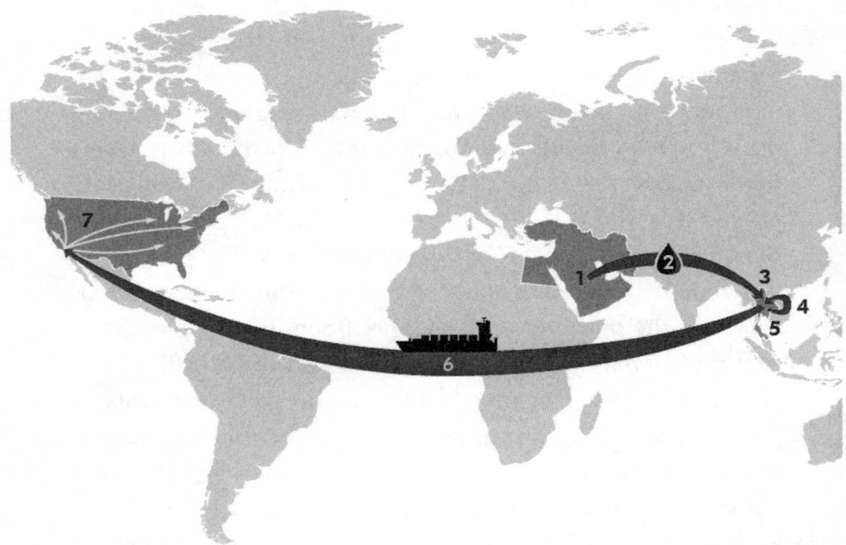

Figure 0.4
One possible supply chain of contemporary vinyl record production: (1) oil extraction somewhere (probably the Middle East); (2) oil shipment to Rayong Province, Thailand; (3) oil refinement and creation of PVC resin; (4) PVC resin shipped to TPC, near Bangkok; (5) PVC resin combined with additives to create PVC compound; (6) PVC compound bulk shipments to distribution centers in the United States; (7) PVC distribution to record pressing plants. (Graphics designed by Scott Bodaly)

and hip eyeglasses.[11] The majority, though, are not upcycled or downcycled or recycled. They are sent to landfills, where they leach cancer-causing chemicals into the ground. And they are sent to incinerators, where they become toxic smoke. Of the billions of vinyl records that have been pressed since the 1950s, most will end up buried or burned.

The World in a Piece of Plastic

Petroleum and plastic, interment and incineration. These are not the issues that normally spring to mind when spinning a record. Musicians and fans are more likely to describe the ways that vinyl itself sounds special, looks special, feels special. And they are particularly likely to say these things when comparing LPs to digital audio files, offering their remarks as explanations for the recent resurgence in vinyl sales—the so-called vinyl revival.[12] The discourse is everywhere. Writing for the *Guardian*, one journalist claims that listening to an LP is "a more enveloping experience than hearing Spotify through your laptop."[13] A writer for the *New York Times* registers something similar: "The reasons cited [to explain the vinyl revival] are usually a fuller, warmer sound from vinyl's analog grooves and the tactile power of a well-made record at a time when music has become ephemeral."[14] Similar statements appear in reportage from Australia, Brazil, Canada, India, Jamaica, Japan, the Philippines, South Africa, South Korea, throughout Europe, and elsewhere—not to mention the trade papers of the plastics industry itself.[15]

The so-called vinyl revival does not just mean that listeners are digging up and dusting off used records with renewed passion. Fans also want new vinyl. Musicians again want to release vinyl. Accordingly, record companies are pressing fresh vinyl. Those few pressing facilities that managed to stay afloat while vinyl sales sank through the 1980s and 1990s are now increasing their production. Others that were closed are being reopened. And new facilities are popping up around the world. Some writers treat this anachronistic regrowth of vinyl sales as a symptom of (and potential antidote to) a wider cultural nostalgia that defines our digital age—a condition that has been diagnosed as retromania.[16] Whether the explanations are framed in terms of romance and audiophilia or nostalgia and retromania, the underlying assumption is that the revival of vinyl is "a logical consequence of the digital revolution in the music industry," which is to say that this so-called revolution has spawned an "antithesis in the form of the vinyl boom."[17] These same feelings and rationales are applied to the recent renaissance of the cassette—and even, in a retrospectively predictable development, the potential resurrection of the CD.[18]

This book, by contrast, has nothing to say for or against the sounds and experiences of vinyl. It asks readers to set aside their convictions about the aesthetics and phenomenologies of formats. Nor does this book explain *why* vinyl sales have been steadily rising in the first decades of the twenty-first century.[19] To the extent that the vinyl revival is covered here at all, it is more in terms of consequences than causes (although the question of why the recording industry turned away from earlier materials and first started using vinyl is addressed in chapter 2). Nor is the immediate goal to challenge the mistaken idea that music has become more ephemeral or less material with the rise of digital file storage and transfer (although I do take exception to this notion throughout, and especially in chapter 3).

Rather, the purpose of beginning this book's century-long material history of recording with the contemporary vinyl revival is to underline the fact that sound reproduction is social reproduction. The rise in musician and listener demand for LPs (as well as cassettes and CDs) is a rise in musician and listener demand for plastic—which is equally a rise in demand for the products of petrochemicals and the politics of petrocapitalism. From the perspectives of both audiophilic and nostalgic attachments to plastic recording formats, musical culture's addiction to its own past means perpetuating and compounding our broader cultural addiction to oil. Whereas the typical lament of retromania's critics is that our world is symbolically recycling its cultural resources at an ever-increasing pace in the context of digitalization (the worry here being that there is nothing new under the sun), the revival of vinyl is part of a bigger picture where our world is materially depleting its natural resources at an ever-increasing pace in the context of capitalism run amok (the worry here being that there may eventually be nothing at all under the sun). If retromania is petromania, then revivalism is recidivism.

As much as this book is emphatically not a love letter to the LP, neither is it intended as hate mail.[20] Guilt is not the goal. Rather, it is understanding. The point is to reanimate the inglorious conditions of the vinyl record—conditions that not only echo throughout every format in the history of recorded sound but which are concealed in the widespread glorification of these seemingly inanimate objects. Seeing the world in a piece of plastic, though, poses special challenges. Its readymade convenience masks a variety of other realities:

> The practice of considering plastic objects "as they are," rather than as the product of a non-plastic substance, is deeply ingrained in us. When looking at a wooden table, it is easy enough to perceive and comprehend the trees from which it was constructed. Yet, when we gaze at food packaging [such as an ice cream container], few of us will visualize the crude oil and gas within it.…The average citizen does not have ready access to the geopolitics within these plastic boxes.[21]

The basic insight here is long-established but nevertheless disarming. We tend to treat the things we buy only as finished and purchasable products, forgetting all the hard work and raw materials that go into them. Although it can be unsettling to find out that something as delicious as ice cream or something as delightful as a vinyl record is inseparable from a variety of invisible and inaudible but nevertheless disturbing realities, confronting those realities is the first step toward understanding them—and maybe improving them.[22]

Staple Commodities and Supporting Casts

Music researchers can help. They are going back to work. They are, in a sense, returning to foundational questions about music as a cultural commodity and cultural industry—to critiques of music and capitalism.[23] The goal is to understand how musicians earn a living in uncertain times, to understand how they (and those around them) make money by making music, and to understand the shifting consumption patterns and experiential possibilities offered by these arrangements. Some of these researchers have noticed that a monolithic idea of "the music industry" has widespread currency in scholarship and everyday conversation, and that this idea misrepresents what is actually going on. When people say "the music industry," they usually mean the *recording* industry. Instead, the phrase "music industries" better represents the diverse forms of music's commodification and divisions of labor: not just recording but also publishing, copyright, concerts, merchandising, the instrument trades, and so on.[24] This is a necessary corrective. But it can be pushed further.

Even this expanded notion of the music industries does not address the full range of activities that define the selling and buying of musical commodities. In widening our conception of the music industries to include those assorted areas just mentioned, the assumption is still that our primary concern lays with the ways that musicians earn (and fans spend) money in ever-changing capitalist social formations. A fuller conception and critique of the music industries would need to understand not only the conditions of making and hearing music *as music* (musicians of all sorts selling their services to record labels, publishing houses, and concert promotors; fans of all stripes exchanging their money for songs, scores, and tickets).[25] It would also need to include a conception and critique of the conditions surrounding all the other efforts and substances that go into making, moving, and unmaking the objects that constitute music's material culture. The idea here is not just an expanded conception of the music industries that nevertheless remains focused on the "musicians–audiences–recordings nexus." It is the idea that there is no music industry. There are instead "many industries with many relationships to music."[26]

Although existing work on musical commodities and musical labor directs our attention toward a fairly broad set of music's economic and cultural contexts, thereby dispelling some of the mystery surrounding the circumstances in which music is made and heard, there is a highly intoxicating form of mystification at work in the ideology of musical culture more generally, and it discourages us from thinking about the conditions of music at their most expansive. This is a form of mystification that breeds discourses of exceptionalism whereby music, supposedly more so than other cultural activities such as film or food, sport or sex, is seen as a special pursuit that somehow transcends the conditions of its production and "expresses the human creativity, intelligence and emotional depth that, we think, almost lifts our animal selves to equality with the gods."[27] Even if the extremes of such myths have been discredited, there are still many people (scholars included) who want to believe, at least in some qualified form, in the purity and goodness of music—in some form of musical exceptionalism. The commodity fetishism that builds up around the products of musical labor is thus compounded by a quasi-religious fetishism that is attached to music as such.[28] For these reasons, critical interventions into music's commodity status require not only demystification but also deflation.[29]

In certain ways, cultural commodities may indeed be special compared to utilitarian goods, while cultural industries may sometimes work differently than run-of-the-mill manufacturing. It has been important to develop conceptual models that articulate those differences.[30] For example, cultural commodities such as LPs and books are arguably produced and consumed in ways that differ from potato chips, partly because of differentials in sales potential. That is, whereas an LP or a book can be purchased once but consumed over and again, a bag of chips needs to be purchased every time it is enjoyed. Additionally, cultural commodities are said to garner special levels of symbolic investment and to generate particular forms of attachment and pleasure. This makes cultural commodities remarkably strong resources for social action and identity construction.[31] The forms of work and contractual obligations that define musical production and authorship are also seen as special or unique. Recording musicians, for example, are said to work in conditions of both extreme independence and extreme exploitation. Such conditions are seen to be "without a precise equivalent in other areas of cultural production."[32] Whatever the specificities of music as a cultural commodity or cultural industry, the deflationary mode suggests that we can learn a lot from examining the ways that music exists in more or less the same conditions as any other commodity or industry.

Transactions of exchange surrounding finished products, acts of consumption, forms of attachment, the symbolically meaningful paths of cultural artifacts, the labor of musicians themselves—all of this is preceded by and dependent on a variety of other materials and actions; all of it is outlasted by and inseparable from disposal and decomposition. Here, the social life of things becomes necessarily tied to the social death of things.[33] As such, if music research has in some sense rediscovered its voice as a critique of capitalism, then a fuller-throated version of this critique "must extend beyond the *usually named* music industries, to broadband, consumer electronics, computers and software, and a range of other related fields."[34] Examples of those other related fields include the raw materials, supply chains, waste streams, and working conditions that precede and exceed the commodity phase in which a cultural artifact circulates as a finished and meaningful product. In these senses, an attempt to understand what music is, how it works, and why it matters need not rush toward the specialness of music's cultural commodities and working conditions. It may also linger on the ordinariness of music's staple commodities and supporting casts.

The staple commodities in this book are shellac, plastic, and data. Together, these three forms of materiality have defined the history of commercial recording since 1900. Between 1900 and 1950, the dominant recorded music format was the 78 rpm disc, which was made of an insect-derived resin called shellac. Between 1950 and 2000, the most common music formats were LPs, 45s, cassettes, and CDs—all of which are made from petrochemical plastic. And since the year 2000, downloading and streaming audio files have taken over as the most common means of listening to recordings, which exist as digital data. This is obviously a basic scheme. On inspection, it breaks down on several levels.

For example, each of the three time periods bounded by my chapters actually overlap in different ways. Plastic was first developed and used in the shellac era. The digitalization of music began in the plastic era. And plastic remains prominent in the digital era. The tidy material uniformities suggested by my three chapter titles also conceal a messier set of realities. Certainly, 78 rpm discs contain shellac. But they also consist of many other materials (mostly crushed rocks), while wax cylinders also sold well in the first decade of the twentieth century. LPs, 45s, cassettes, and CDs are indeed all made of plastic. But they are each made of different kinds of plastic, and they make use of other materials in both their inscriptions and their packaging. Digital audio formats definitely exist as data. But those data come in many different configurations of algorithmic origami (MP3 being the most iconic). And no data can exist, let alone become meaningful, unless they are stored on a hard drive or server, transmitted through overground and underground and undersea cables (not to mention satellites), processed by local access networks and computers and phones, and finally transformed into sound by loudspeakers and earbuds. Indeed, while recorded music has always been tied to the devices and media systems that are necessary to play various formats, listening to music as data requires that special attention be given to the seemingly nonmusical infrastructures and accessory technologies needed to store, transmit, receive, and hear that data. These complexities (and more) are addressed in the book's individual chapters. Yet as a blueprint for the history of recording, the shellac–plastic–data scheme does describe the overarching cultural and commercial formations of this industry since 1900.

To organize this book around staple commodities is not to suggest that people are irrelevant.[35] On the contrary, it is to highlight that a much wider range of people and a much broader range of experiences have played much more central roles in the history of recorded music than is normally recognized. For example, although shellac records would neither exist nor matter without musicians and listeners, such records would equally not exist without the women and children that harvested and processed insect resin in colonial India. Nor would they exist without the women and men that worked to quarry rocks in Indiana in order to provide a foundation for these recordings, nor without the scientists that pulled all-nighters as they raced to develop the most suitable formulas for these discs. Plastic formats could not exist without the drillers and toolpushers that pumped oil from the ground or the chemical engineers and material scientists that cracked hydrocarbons and developed polymer compounds to the specifications demanded by the recording industry and its customers. Nor would they exist without the women and men that pressed these records in factories. Data files could not be stored or transferred without the software engineers that develop algorithms or the IT workers who build and maintain internet infrastructures. Such files could not be accessed without miners in places such as the Democratic Republic of the Congo, who extract the rare minerals and metals that make up our listening devices. Nor could those files be heard without the solderers and line-workers who assemble these accessory electronics in places such as China. Moreover, all recording formats and listening devices need dump sites and communities willing or willed to absorb these technologies as they break down and obsolesce. Such workers are not typically thought of as musicians. Indeed, they are not usually thought of at all. At best, they might be considered support personnel.[36] Yet their labors are essential parts of the musical world.

Combining these perspectives on staple commodities and supporting casts, it is necessary to see consumer desire, resource extraction, and commodity manufacturing as coefficients of disinterest, disposal, and decomposition. There is no separation here between the apparently musical and the supposedly nonmusical, nor between the so-called human and the purportedly nonhuman. In fact, these ostensibly nonmusical actions and nonhuman materials constitute the grounds upon which more obviously musical cultures are built. It is for this reason that an effective critique of music's commodification must come face-to-face with its entire material culture and its place within the entire capitalist world system—the web of life.[37] This is a project of demystification and deflation, an analysis of staple commodities and supporting casts. In these ways, a critique of political economy becomes a critique of political ecology.[38]

Political Ecology: Mediatic Musicology without Music

Political ecology is multifaceted and difficult to summarize.[39] At a basic level, though, the field is defined by critical attention to the principles of action and the forms of social order that link material environments and human cultures. Political ecologists demonstrate a particular interest in the stresses on natural and human resources that surround materials extraction and processing as well as product manufacturing, consumption, and disposal. From this perspective, the political ecology of music is straightforwardly about how the stuff of musical culture is made and possessed, dispossessed and unmade.

The entire musical world could be viewed through the lens of political ecology: songsheet publishing, instrument manufacturing, concertgoing, and so on.[40] I have chosen to focus on recording formats, on the material forms that contain musical information, despite recent realizations that the historiography of music (especially popular music) has been written as a history of records—and that this bias has come at the expense of understanding the history of music as a concert tradition and performance practice.[41] Placing recordings at the center of this book is not meant to re-inscribe them at the center of music's historiography. Rather, it is to continue troubling and expanding those existing understandings by revising that history from the inside. If the turn toward performance in music research emphasizes that music is not a thing but an activity, the lesson here is that things are activities too.

Even within the world of recording, political ecology is expansive. For example, political ecology is not limited to any particular music genre. As a set of generalized conditions, it defines the whole of recorded musical culture. Political ecology even extends beyond recorded music, encompassing other forms of sound recording such as audiobooks. Yet the world of popular music shoulders a special burden in relation to political ecology. This is because popular music has made up the bulk of record sales since 1900. Other forms of recorded music and sound are nevertheless implicit and complicit in the dynamics of making and unmaking, possession and dispossession, that animate this history.

On the side of making and possession, a critique of music's political ecology focuses on all the people that must harvest, extract, process, manufacture, and move all the various substances that are needed before a recording can be bought or sold or listened to. There is a global web of raw materials and supply chains that undergirds what is traditionally called the recording industry. This web is able to mobilize, synchronize, and aggregate massive contingents of people and materials, intertwining numerous governments, economies, populations, and environments. While such processes and materials may seem peripheral or unmusical, they are actually central to what the recording industry is and how it works.

On the side of unmaking and dispossession, a critique of music's political ecology focuses on how even our favorite recordings, like all good things, must come to an end. That is, recordings eventually enter into circuits of dispossession.[42] Here, one mode of accumulation (as an expression of fandom) gives way to another (as a measure of disinterest): where we once collected records, our records now collect dust. And when the value of billions of such recordings is finally exhausted, the questions become: where do they go and what happens to them? Political ecology is here interested in waste, in the sense of both the ravages of production and the remnants of consumption.

The issues for the political ecologist thus extend beyond who is making and listening to music, or buying and selling it—and even beyond what that music sounds like, how it feels, or what it means. Political ecology underlies all those situations. But this perspective is not an invitation to extol the importance of objects as against straw figures of textualism or constructionism. It does more than merely and merrily assert the materiality of music. A critique of political ecology also questions the presumptions that guide certain ways of thinking about the relationship between musical culture and the material world. While the central aim of this book is to describe (and critique) the conditions of music's political ecology, a parallel aim is to critique (and describe) a particular conception of music that encourages us to take those conditions for granted in the first place.[43] The two perspectives require each other. Together, they suggest the need for a musicology without "music."

The phrase *musicology without music* is not a call to abandon music or music research. Rather, it is a call to expand and multiply those domains by insisting that they are not only tied to but constituted by a variety of distributed and ostensibly nonmusical people, things, and conditions. To downplay or neglect those people, things, and conditions is to subscribe to a definition of "music" whereby preconceptions about what music is determine the parameters of what musicologists should do. This is a definition of music that says musicians and fans are what *really* matter in musical culture. It is a definition that supports hierarchies about what counts as a creative act and what counts as a musical practice. It is a definition that persists in limited focuses on authorship and celebrity as well as the consumption of cultural artifacts as finished products. It is a definition of music that ignores where the materials of musical culture come from, who makes them for us, how they get to us, and what happens when we no longer want them. In short, common understandings of music tend to exclude a lot of the sweat and stuff that musical cultures rely on.

Taking a cue from genre researchers, it is possible to understand "music" as a performative category—a meta-generic political apparatus that upholds ideological distinctions between obviously musical things and practices, on the one hand, and seemingly nonmusical things and practices, on the other.[44] A musicology without music suggests that researchers should not be so sure that they know in advance what counts as a "properly" musical practice or a "properly" musicological object of study. The word "without," then, connotes less its everyday prepositional meaning as *lack* than its older adverbial meaning as *outside*—although the latter (musicology that begins from a position that is exterior to "music") authorizes the former (musicology that proceeds in the absence of "music"). The point is to develop a version of music research that does not begin as a musicology *of* music—that does not begin in a tautology where the force of preconstructed definitions of music delimit what musical culture can be or where music researchers should focus their attention.[45] A critique of political ecology unfolds these categorical presuppositions and opens up their exclusions. Such a perspective is therefore measured not in losses but in gains. It attempts to understand the farthest-flung material conditions for storing, processing, and transmitting information that are always already anterior, posterior, interior, exterior—and therefore fundamental—to any meaningful engagement with musical forms or practices. The goal is to describe and improve the messy associations of biology, geology, capital, and culture that define our collective musical life on this planet.

Approaching music in this way means understanding it in mediatic terms.[46] It is to describe the situations in which something called "music" can come to be as it is in the first place. From this perspective, music can be dispersed not just into discursive constellations but into those things we need to make and hear it. Those things can be further dispersed into consumer electronics industries and information technology infrastructures as well as their nuts and bolts, circuits and volts. Those sectors and infrastructures can in turn be dispersed into the industries that extract and process raw materials. And all of this can eventually be dispersed into planetary forces and geological timespans. The scale of analysis, the number of layers we peel back, depends on what we want to illustrate—on the types of knowledge we wish to produce, the sorts of critical interventions we wish to make. A critique of music's political ecology happens to proceed at a level of dispersion where any musical contents or meaningful encounters with a recording can be understood as surface effects of more general mediatic conditions.

Of all the frenzied activity at the buffet of renewed materialisms that nourishes today's cultural research, saying that political ecology promotes a mediatic perspective on music is to specify which of those materialist appetites most energize this book—and why. I have drawn freely on various ideas from various new materialist discourses, which may be summarized in terms of a broad non- or posthuman turn in the social sciences and humanities. Yet my primary interest here is in the materialities of communication as they have been understood in the Anglophone reception of so-called German media theories, as well as the ways that such ideas have been cross-pollinated with seemingly French actor-network-theories.[47] I use the phrase *Anglophone reception* deliberately. I am engaging with that reception advisedly. There is good reason to think that seeing Friedrich Kittler as a straightforward champion of media materialism, which is common enough in the Anglophone literature, is to downplay his commitment to symbolic forms and stop short of his proximity to philosophical idealism. There is also good reason to think that seeing Bruno Latour as a straightforward champion of thing theory, another common position in Anglophone scholarship, is to downplay his commitment to textual exegesis and stop short of his distance from historical materialism.[48] Rather than simply insisting on hardware or objects, Kittler and Latour are extending poststructuralist theories of writing. They are ultimately thinkers of the systems and devices of inscription that define the production of knowledge and the maintenance of the symbolic order.[49] Yet the goal I have set for myself is not to follow German media theory or French network theory to the letter. Like all translation effects, the Anglophone reception of these ideas has been productive in its own ways. The mediatic point here is that every system of inscription is tied to a system of extraction. Every discourse network is a resource network. If this book sympathizes with today's material turns, it is less for the fun and the fashion than to forge a focused intervention into musical culture and music research based on a particular critique of political ecology.[50]

To speak of the political ecology of music is not to say that research in this vein begins with music and then connects that phenomenon with its environmental conditions or technological mediation. Rather, it is to say that political ecology is a precondition of music, a key part of its mediatic situation. This means that a critique of political ecology should not be confused with environmentalism as such. One reason is that political ecology attends to divisions of labor and conditions of production that are not strictly matters for eco-criticism.[51] Another reason is that, in its everyday sense, environmentalism is often framed in terms of a foundational division between human cultures and the natural world, meaning that such a division always already subtends the interrelation of politics and ecology. But these understandings of culture and nature are historically specific, and they actually interfere with the work of political ecology.[52] Culture and nature, music and environment, do not preexist or happen *to* one another. They *are* one another. The challenge is to understand their emulsion.

In the same way that organizing this book around staple commodities is not to write an anonymous history in which supporting casts are irrelevant, saying that political ecology underwrites the situation of music (whether we know it or not and regardless of any meaningful production or consumption practices) is not necessarily to strip the musical population of its agency. It is, though, to focus on agency at a particular level of generality. Here, "the tactics of calculating subjects become minor variables within authorless processes by which fields and relationships are made and transformed."[53] The LP can again serve as an example. Musicians and listeners may slow records down and speed them up, play them in reverse or scratch them back and forth. Still, this does not change the fact that vinyl records are made of plastic, or that those musicians exert their creative agency in a petro-capitalist political ecology. Musicians may incorporate vinyl's signature crackle into their tracks in order to signify authenticity or nostalgia. But this does not change the fact that the crackle of vinyl is also the form of meaningless background radiation that defines all music that has ever been released on this format—and that this crackle exists regardless of what music a given LP contains, who bought it, or what it means to them.

The potential contribution of political ecology seems twofold. Analytically, a critique of political ecology offers an expanded conception of the musical world. It highlights more fully the global reach and power of the industries of music. It insists that the aesthetic and industrial circulations of musical culture hinge on the material and economic circulations of resource networks. It considers dispossession not merely as an afterthought or an adjunct to ironically linear models of product lifecycles but, rather, as part of a topology of musical materiality in which the question of disposal is immanent in desire and manufacturing, in which "afterlife ... is anticipated before exchange."[54] If studies of consumption and possession have revealed much about music as an agent in social life, then so can rituals of disposal and dispossession reveal various social logics and inform our understanding of musical culture.[55] Together, these ways of looking at musical culture call for "a change in focus, from the 'objectness' of things to the material flows and formative processes wherein they come into being"—and wherein they cease to be.[56]

Implicit in the above is a second potential contribution of political ecology: a particular avenue for critical social engagement and transformative social commentary. Cultural policy is an established and increasingly important topic in music research.[57] Such work rightly focuses on difficult questions of cultural value and attendant arts funding issues in the face of the continued hardening of market-driven economic philosophies. A critique of political ecology may add to the public relevance of music research by spurring scholars to look at those places where music's economic and cultural significances encounter its environmental and human consequences, thus opening the door to interventions at the intersections of music, media, and environmental policies.[58] The issue is one of making us more aware—and more accountable—as scholars, musicians, and listeners.

In examining the political ecology of music, we may not always like what we see. Music will always be about special concerts and compositions, genuine connection and community. It will continue to serve as a site of subcultural subversion, a resource for radical resistance, a path toward healing and coping. But music can also be brutal. It can be damaging. Indeed, numerous studies have demonstrated music's capacity for harm in contexts ranging from representational wrongdoing and social exclusion to the weaponization of sound in social control and torture.[59] If such studies show how music can function as a direct and instantaneous means of violence, the material history of sound reproduction encapsulates a variety of indirect and longitudinal assaults on laborers, cultures, and environments that are bound up with legacies of inequality, dominion, and extraction. These broader conditions of sound recording are functions of our fondness for music. But these conditions are diffuse. They are distant from most musicians and fans, and therefore largely inaudible to them. Even so, such conditions are intensely present in the lives of those who manage and process the materials that our musical propensities depend on. Such conditions have also left their marks on the regions to which the destructive effects of harvesting and processing these materials have been outsourced. To engage in a critique of music's political ecology is thus to highlight that our aesthetic investments have material effects—and that these effects, while distributed, nevertheless coordinate what we might call the slow violence of music.[60]

Political ecology therefore de-ontologizes the question of what music is, clarifying the power of "music" to naturalize and sustain perceptions of musical cultures that are annexed from their material conditions. It de-essentializes the question of how music works, interrogating the politics of musical analyses that would focus only on those formal features and functional attributes that constitute the distinctiveness of music as an aesthetic object, sensual experience, or identificatory matrix. By refusing to consign the people and practices that fall outside the conventional remits of music and musicology to the categories of the nonmusical or the amusical, political ecology also de-parochializes the question of why music matters. The ethical obligations of musical culture reach beyond its spectacular texts and contexts, even beyond the music professions as such. The point is to open up additional avenues of attention, intention, and care in the musical world. These avenues would consider, not just music and musicians, but all those ways of life in all those places that find themselves on the opposite sides of the normative divisions that are reproduced by prevailing understandings of what music is, as well as established emphases on how it works. It is true that music would not have values or effects, neither positive nor negative, if we didn't already love it—if it didn't already matter. But this is precisely why those who most believe in music's positive values should be most concerned about its negative consequences. It is why those who love music best should be the first to welcome a critique of its political ecology.

Thinking in these ways introduces important ambivalences and ambiguities into musical politics. David Hesmondhalgh argues that, while music has the potential to contribute to "human flourishing," music researchers have tended to "overestimate people's freedom to use music, and to understate ways in which music is tied up with social problems such as inequality and suffering."[61] Whereas Hesmondhalgh proceeds at the level of musical listening and performance as resources for building personal and communal identities, his point is amplified—and the stakes are raised—in accounting for music's political ecology. If we want to join Hesmondhalgh in believing "that music's most valuable contribution to collective human life might be to advance political struggles for a better distribution of flourishing," then we should also reckon with the social inequalities and material degradations that are distributed throughout music's political ecology—many of which are found long before music's production and long after its consumption.

Digitalization ≠ Dematerialization

When music fans, journalists, and scholars alike describe the history of recorded music, they frequently adopt a narrative of dematerialization. Here, for example, is Philip Auslander: "To look at the progression of the material forms of music media—from shellac or vinyl discs to CDs to direct downloading from the Internet or the Celestial Jukebox—is to witness the progressive dematerialization of the musical object."[62] This understanding of recorded music's history has only become more entrenched with the rise of digital streaming, which seems self-evidently insubstantial. But digital infrastructures and devices are absolutely material, and they require a lot of energy, while digital files are themselves also material (albeit microscopically so).[63] As a historical thesis, dematerialization is an ineffective description of the political ecology of recording.

Another narrative of dematerialization surrounding the history of recording is more accurate, in one sense, but also falters at the level of political ecology. Record company profits are nowadays organized less around making things than exploiting rights. This has arguably been the case since the 1980s, when "the monopoly privileges of musical copyright holders" became "centrally important for the entertainment corporations' profits":

> Because of music's peculiar ability to enhance the value of other goods, directly (films, videos, television programmes) and indirectly (in advertisements, shopping malls, etc), it doesn't have to be sold to the public at all. The musical commodity can circulate within the media, generating income from the exploitation of performing rights alone.[64]

This industry shift has also become entrenched by digitalization. Increasingly significant portions of major label profits (and in some cases musicians' livelihoods) come from licensing both new songs and back catalogues to streaming services and advertising firms, while digitalization also makes it easier to track down and collect on rights royalties.[65] But, again, digital licensing fees and digital rights royalties can only exist within a larger digital media system, meaning that any shift in business model from making musical things to managing musical rights is nevertheless inseparable from the technological objects, economic cycles, labor practices, material resources, and energy sources of many other sectors.[66]

Together, these material realities lead to a counterintuitive argument about the history of recording. While the political *economy* of music may follow a path of abstraction, from the solidity of manufacturing to the airiness of rights agreements, the same cannot be said of the political *ecology* of music. What might seem like a story of progressive dematerialization and eco-friendliness—an evolution from sticky resins and fuming factories to pristine data streams and unworldly cloud networks—is just the opposite.

This argument does not rest solely on the fact that digital media systems are undeniably and intensively material. Nor does this argument rest on the idea that online, data-based musical materialities simply represent a step in the wrong direction: from the use of raw materials that are relatively renewable (shellac) and commodities that are readily recycled in secondhand economies (LPs), to delivery infrastructures that weigh heavily on the environment (server farms) and musical commodities with short life expectancies (accessory electronics) as well as ambiguous afterlives (data files). There is some explanatory power in that argument. But it is an oversimplification (see chapter 3). While the difficulties of storing and transmitting music as a digital file are real, the recyclability of LPs and the renewability of shellac are not as uniformly positive as they might seem. Most vinyl records will someday become exhausted and will eventually perish (see chapter 2). And the renewability of shellac is offset by a variety of other concerns surrounding colonialism, extractivism, and sweated labor (see chapter 1). The political ecology of recording is more problematic today than ever before, not only because of the material weight of digital culture, but because the history of recording does not amount to a straightforward story of progress and obsolescence in which formats replace one another with definite finalities and dynastic singularities, like successors in a royal family.

At every moment in the history of recording, a variety of formats coexist and overlap in different ways. A particular format may dominate the market and generate the most advertising ink at a given time, but new formats are always emerging, while older formats continue to circulate residually among listeners of particular dispositions and demographics.[67] The years around 1980 illustrate this point. If LPs and cassettes were the dominant formats, the CD was emerging, while the 78 lingered residually in attics and archives, was still perhaps favored by certain listeners (either because they preferred the sound of shellac or because they never updated their record collections) and was still actively manufactured for listeners in some places (78 rpm recordings were mass produced in India until the mid 1970s).[68]

What seems to differentiate things today, in the context of online digital music commodities, is that formats such as LPs do not just exist as anachronistic antiques, retro residues, audiophile amusements, or "zombie media" from an earlier moment.[69] Rather, LPs are being actively revived. Although genre revivals are commonplace in music history, the discourses and practices of *format* revivals seem particular to the twenty-first century. From this perspective, the vinyl record today sits somewhere between an archaic medium ("that which is wholly recognized as an element of the past, to be observed, to be examined, or even on occasion to be consciously 'revived'") and a residual medium (that which "has been effectively formed in the past, but [which] is still active in the cultural process, not only and often not at all as an element of the past, but as an effective element of the present").[70] A format that may have been described as archaic or residual through the 1990s has in a sense become both, thereby transforming into a renewed medium through cultural and economic processes of revival.

There are some good explanations for why the proliferation of the public internet has coincided with "reinvigoration[s] of earlier forms of material culture," which may also help explain why music today is characterized by a variety of coterminous and overlapping formats and modes of consumption.[71] As Raphaël Nowak finds: "the reception of music is currently characterised by a multiplication and coexistence of various music artefacts that all possess their own features and characteristic forms of appeal for listeners."[72] Or, in Elodie Roy's words: "Different musical media, far from erasing each other, interminably coexist and intersect, creating a heterogeneous technological ecology" that is "a characteristic part of the contemporary musical world."[73] Rather than proceeding to the level of explanations and causes, though, it is worth staying on the level of consequences and effects. Although digital music media certainly pose their own political-ecological questions, the addition of format revivals to existing cultural logics of dominance, emergence, and residue also contributes to the possibility that the contemporary political ecology of music is more taxing nowadays than in previous times. An old economic principle can help illustrate this new media problem.

The Jevons Effect

It would be reasonable to expect that squeezing more energy out of a given resource should make for less overall consumption of that resource. Yet the opposite is usually true. This is the Jevons effect: greater efficiency in resource usage is actually followed by greater consumption of that resource.[74] Greater consumption then leads to a need for increased efficiency, which in turn leads to more consumption, which subsequently requires greater efficiency, and so on. For example, we might expect that the improved fuel efficiency of modern cars—driving farther per liter of gas—would lead to a decrease in the amount of petroleum we pump and, further up the supply chain, the amount of oil we extract from the earth. Actually, though, highly efficient gasoline engines have been paralleled by an increase in the overall amount of fuel we consume.

The same thing happens in situations where resource usage not only becomes more efficient but where, in principle, a given resource becomes unnecessary. Take office paper, for instance. While digital document storage, transmission, and retrieval could hypothetically eliminate the need for office paper, in reality digital documents generate at least as many printed pages as those earlier businesses and bureaucracies that relied solely on paper files, memos, and letters.[75] People prefer to supplement the provisions of digital documents (tapping keys, clicking mice, swiping screens) with those of the printed page (folding up, stapling together, thumbing through)—paper cuts and all. This is another instance where media formats do not simply replace one another but where dominant, emergent, and residual technologies and techniques become mixed, complementary, and interdependent. Thus, digital mediation does not just lead to more printed pages as well as continued reliance on paper's supply chains and waste streams. It also introduces new questions. In storing and sending digital documents, we also need the resources to construct and maintain digital infrastructures, the devices to access those infrastructures, and the forms of energy that power the digital world. Digitalization amplifies the Jevons effect. As Vaclav Smil notes:

> In an overwhelming majority of cases, these complex, dynamic interactions of cheaper energy, less expensive raw materials, and cheaper manufacture have resulted in such ubiquitous ownership of an increasing range of products and more frequent use of a widening array of services that even the most impressive relative weight reductions accompanying these consumption increases could not be translated into any absolute cuts in the overall use of materials.[76]

In other words, the miniaturization of digital documents and devices is offset by a massification of material production and consumption (not to mention disposal and waste).

Digital music is no different. In the same way that computers and email have not straightforwardly replaced office paper, the rise of downloading and streaming have not eliminated previous recording formats or led to a decrease in the number of listening devices that we purchase. The forms of music's digitalization in the twenty-first century do not represent a revolutionary rupture with previous formats. They represent overlaps, continuations, and proliferations of them. We increasingly listen to music across multiple media systems. Like digital documents, listeners today supplement the sounds and experiences of online music with those of other formats. We stream MP3s *and* we spin LPs. We crave computers *and* cassettes. The unequal but worldwide rises of music downloading and streaming have resulted, not in the elimination of earlier recorded music commodities but, rather, in an expansion of formats, devices, and means of consumption—as well as the forms of materiality and energy required to make and power those devices, and the spaces necessary to dispose of them. Under advanced consumer capitalism, the possibility of less means the reality of more. Take Radiohead, for example.

When I started writing this book, I lived near Radiohead's hometown. One morning on my way to work, my bus trundled past Thom Yorke. He was driving a fuel-efficient little car. It was green, literally and figuratively. "That makes sense," I said to myself: Radiohead was known for their environmentalism, especially since commissioning carbon audits of their 2003 and 2006 North American tours. But it also got me thinking. Back in 2007, the same year the audit was published, had I not mail-ordered the deluxe version of their latest album, *In Rainbows*? Was this album not elaborately packaged in a thick cardboard box and slipcase, stuffed with inky inserts, and wrapped in plastic? Wasn't it pressed onto two heavyweight twelve-inch 45 rpm vinyl discs, even though the music would have easily fit on one standard LP? Didn't this special edition also include a CD version of the album, plus an additional CD of bonus material? And didn't I also get a download code? Hadn't a hundred thousand other people placed the same order?[77]

Most of the hype and controversy surrounding *In Rainbows* focused on its experimental pay-what-you-want model of music consumption. While listeners like me may have shelled out for the deluxe version, anybody with a good enough internet connection and a big enough hard drive was able to pay whatever they felt the album was worth—which included the option of downloading it for free. Jeremy Morris summarizes how the

Radiohead experiment crystallized real questions about the future of the recording industry in an era of online piracy, about the cultural and economic value of music in a new and uncertain commodity form, about what the digital music commodity might be and how it might function.[78] Downloading magnified the question of what fans were actually paying for when they spent their money on an album, and it raised the issue of whether recording-oriented musicians could make a living through album sales. Ultimately, the debate was about the politics of online music, about who holds the power in the twenty-first-century musical world: fans, musicians, or the record industry?

Yet Radiohead's *In Rainbows* also offers a prominent example of what Morris calls the splintering of the recorded music commodity in an age of digitalization. In addition to storing and streaming digital audio files, musicians and fans search for ways to add familiar values and material properties to online music. They transpose whatever aesthetic, experiential, and material dimensions that they feel disappear into the digital onto additional formats and other products, thereby supplementing the ways that digital music is sold, bought, and made meaningful. Aspects of recorded music that have been micromaterialized have been re-materialized in other ways.[79] Morris's critical engagement with the political economy of the digital music commodity therefore opens up a further critical engagement with music's political ecology. From this perspective, the most remarkable thing about *In Rainbows* is not that it prototyped a new model of music consumption but, rather, that it encapsulates an established principle of capitalist production. *In Rainbows* exemplifies the Jevons effect, and it illustrates the core argument of this book.

The digitalization of music is not the dematerialization of music. Rather, the digitalization of music represents a splintering and proliferation of music's commodity forms—and therefore a massification of music's material bases, even if some of music's digital materialities are microscopic. Recorded music has of course always relied on a tremendous number of people and materials that are typically invisible and inaudible to most listeners—the histories and effects of which are covered in this book's individual chapters. Yet if there is a single takeaway here, it is this: Because of the particular cultural formations of musical listening that have taken shape in the twenty-first century, music's political ecology is an even more serious concern than ever before.

Conclusion

The industrialization of music, which is to say the mass production and mass consumption of recordings, has been debated as an ideological problem, while issues of life and death have been productive laboratories for cultural theory.[80] Political ecology invokes a complementary and literally grounded range of critical issues. It shows that, just as "the modern process of consumption ... is as much about dispossession as possession," so is the history of recorded music as much about decomposition as composition.[81] It shows that, whereas the phenomenon of recording sparks passionate debates about whether inscription divides the liveness of performance from the deadness of mediation, so does recording rely on divisions of labor that can be matters of life and death for those who interact with the materials that form the bases of those formats, experiences, and arguments. Political ecology also shows that whereas the phrase "music industry" typically "describes a complex network of rights-owners and licensed users, a continual flow of rights income which seems inexhaustible and sometimes, indeed, quite random," the phrase "music industry" equally describes a complex network of laborious materials extraction and processing, a continual flow of exhaustible resources and exhausted commodities, as well as patterns of accumulation and dispossession that have discernible and describable logics—not to mention observable material and human consequences.[82]

If unrelenting processes of industrialization, consumption, and waste have strained our planet and its people to the point of crisis, then music is part of the problem. A critique of music's political ecology addresses the troubling supply chains of 78s, the poisonous petrochemicals used to manufacture LPs, the nonbiodegradable plastics in CDs, the energy-guzzling server farms that power streaming audio files, and the toxic graveyards of obsolete consumer electronics around the world. If we are accustomed to the accusation that certain types of music are disposable, we should also think about what happens to recordings when they are actually disposed of. And if commonsense tells us that the music industry is in the business of making records, we should also address what those recordings are actually made of. Questions about the material composition and decomposition of the recorded music commodity—about what happens to music before production and after consumption—need to be asked and answered. Political ecology encourages us to confront the relationship between music's cultural and economic value, on the one hand, and its human and environmental cost, on the other.

Looking at the political ecology of recorded music is not merely an exercise in quirky eccentricity (*78s are made of bugs?!*)

or irksome provocation (*musicology without music?!*). It is an ethical position. If we are serious about understanding the character and extent of music's involvement in the circumstances of thriving and suffering in this world, and if we truly want to intervene in those circumstances, it is not enough to research the political economies and cultural policies that surround unmistakably musical forms of labor and leisure. Nor is it enough to analyze the politics of representation and identity in obviously musical texts and recognizably musical contexts. It goes without saying that such tasks are essential. But the consequences of music reach far beyond those realms that we normally consider to be musical. Although research into music's political ecology may seem to take us far from our treasured object of study, it does so in the service of bringing us closer to understanding the full constitutional force of music's role in the dynamics of human relatedness.

1 Shellac (1900–1950)

In the early days of sound reproduction, recordings came in all shapes and sizes, spun at various speeds, and were made from all sorts of stuff—from household tinfoil to high-tech Condensite, beeswax to beef fat, celluloid to spermaceti.[1] One company made edible novelty records out of chocolate, and there was even some question as to whether cheese was ever used as a key ingredient in records.[2] As early as 1895, though, the race to efficiently mass duplicate recordings led Emile Berliner to develop a composite disc recipe that featured a natural resin called shellac. The combination of the disc format and the shellac formula was preferred, not only to Thomas Edison's cylindrical phonograph recordings, which at the time were predominantly made of vulnerable wax, but also to the hard vulcanite rubber then used in pressing discs, which was prone to blistering and warping.[3] Disc sales overtook cylinder sales after 1910. With the arrival of electrically powered turntables in the 1920s, the speed of recordings was standardized at 78 revolutions per minute.[4] In these ways, the shellac 78 rpm disc became the standard material form of recorded sound for nearly half the history of commercial sound reproduction.

Although shellac was the industry standard between about 1900 and 1950, the composition of these records never stood still. No two batches of compound were exactly the same. Record labels constantly adjusted their formulas through this period, in response to various market pressures and in search of higher-definition sound (a search that both influenced and responded to consumer demand).[5] Early record pressing plants were thus chemistry labs as much as anything else, and the early recording industry was a chemical industry as much as anything else. What is more, recording was an especially demanding application of the chemical and material sciences, pushing those fields harder than other industries and contributing lasting innovations to them. The story of recorded music during this time is one of secret recipes and materials sciences—as well as their global supply chains and divisions of labor. Because it is unusual to think of music in these terms, an example from another cultural form is instructive.

Philip Ball has shown how the histories of art and chemistry share a bond. The sciences of color and pigment have influenced how painters paint, what their paintings look like, and how artworks portray meaning (not least because colors fade and, anyway, the symbolism of color changes as a function of history and culture).[6] Throughout history, many artists have worked closely with chemists and other technical advisors to ensure they were using the latest high-tech colors. (J.M.W. Turner, for example, had a pigment advisor in Michael Faraday.) If the look of paint has always existed in a symbiotic relationship with the science of chemistry, by the end of the nineteenth century the history of art and the *industry* of chemistry were inseparable. As Ball writes: "The modern chemicals industry was spawned and nurtured largely by the demand for colour.... Many of the world's major chemicals companies ... began as manufacturers of synthetic dyes."[7]

Disclosing this relationship has implications for how we normally prefer to think about art. "It is a challenge to the imagination," Ball says, "to connect these ugly factories and alien or unsettling names—cadmium, arsenic, antimony—with the stuff that, smeared over canvas, leaves us breathless in art galleries. Can such a villain (and the chemical industry's transgressions are not at all imaginary) be responsible for this beauty?"[8] Rooting the glory of art in the inglorious conditions of commerce, applied science, smoky labs, and dirty chemicals may appear to demote this cultural form from the virtuous to the vulgar, leaving it humiliated and undignified. Yet this is art's reality. Whatever beauty of technique or depth of meaning we may find in a particular painting, the conditions of its political ecology are right there on the surface, hidden in plain sight, awaiting no close reading and caught in no hermeneutic circle. Similarly, the recording industry has always been tied to basic sciences and substances, as well as wider economies and ecologies—none of which is normally considered musical. But they are. And we can hear them. This has implications for how we typically think about music.

It is of course possible (sometimes even advisable) to marvel at the music contained in the grooved surfaces of a 78 rpm disc. Take for example Blind Lemon Jefferson's "Mosquito Moan," released by Paramount in 1930.[9] In a straightforward sense, this is a song about bugs:

> I'm sittin' in my kitchen, mosquitoes all around my screen
> I'm sittin' in my kitchen, mosquitoes all around my screen
> I'm about all ready to get a mosquito bomb, I'll be seldom seen

In a more imaginative sense, we could contextualize the mosquito as "a trickster, an animal figure often used in African-American story and song of the time to allude to cunning, humor, and deceit to obtain personal gain." And in a figurative sense, we might interpret mosquitoes as "metaphors for human tormentors, constantly dogging Jefferson as he tries to live his life in early twentieth-century America." Such a reading is suggested by the song's second-last verse:

> Mosquitoes all around me, mosquitoes everywhere I go
> Mosquitoes all around me, mosquitoes everywhere I go
> No matter where I go, they sticks their bill in me

From here, it would be possible to associate "Mosquito Moan" with a broader cultural history of early-twentieth-century blues songs about insects—bedbugs, bees, boll weevils—and perhaps to write a book about these quirky earworms.

Moving from the lyrics to the instruments of their expression, we could note the "moaning" tone of Jefferson's voice, which has been described as "not strident, but high enough to carry above street noises."[10] And from vocal tone we could extend outward to broader musical and generic characteristics such as Jefferson's "complicated, dense, free-form guitar style," which owed more to jazz and swing than other blues guitarists of his day.[11] All of this, and more, might culminate in a kind of stylistic genealogy of Jefferson's role in establishing the Texas blues and influencing contemporaries such as Lead Belly as well as a later constellation of rock guitarists including Eric Clapton. Yet regardless of the musical developments that may have influenced or arisen from Jefferson, regardless of any blues subgenre about bugs and, indeed, regardless of what Jefferson's song about insects is actually "about"—there is a sense in which *all* music recorded during the shellac era *is* bugs. That is, to listen to any 78 rpm shellac disc is to encounter insects (among other things). Literally.

The story of the lac beetle, from which shellac resin is derived, will be told below. For now, the important thing to note is that no stylistic genealogy or close reading of the musical content inscribed in the grooves of a shellac recording can access the preconditions of its mediality. Rather, it is the materiality of the grooves themselves—the characteristic surface noise of the 78 rpm disc as a format—that serves as an ever-present reminder of its political ecology. For music lovers and musicologists, though, surface noise is usually heard as a distraction. Some commentators say that shellac records sound like "frying bacon by the side of Niagara."[12] Amanda Petrusich, in her book on 78 collectors, writes that these records have "a high and persistent background hiss. The melody might be fully obscured by a staticky sizzle that feels otherworldly and distant, like the song had been buried in the backyard and was now being broadcast from beneath six solid feet of dirt."[13] Of course, afflictions like static and sizzle can equally become objects of affection, just as the crackle of an LP has taken on nostalgic characteristics and become musically meaningful in its own right. But sizzles and crackles are equally textures that exist at the level of formats, over and above any specific musical text or generic form. In other words, while surface noise can both obscure content and become content, the 78's sizzle exists no matter if the music on disc is Blind Lemon Jefferson singing about bugs or anyone else singing about any other topic (or indeed whether a piece of music features lyrics at all). The surface noise is there whether the disc was released by Paramount or any other label. And the surface noise persists no matter how many people heard that disc or what it might have meant to them. This is one level at which political ecology works as aesthetic analysis—albeit a mode of aesthetic analysis that is less concerned with the hermeneutics or poetics of particular musical texts than the overarching media morphologies of formatted musical textures.[14]

It is through the materiality of the grooves themselves—their characteristic surface noise—that we can access a history of recorded music that is about rising chemical corporations and pressing plants, global supply chains, exploitative labor regimes, and environmental harm as much as it is about the circulation of musical aesthetics and experiences as conventionally understood. It may not be very comforting to think of music in this way. Music can obviously be compositionally interesting and experientially uplifting. It can obviously contribute positively to formations of personal and collective identity. Yet a critique of political ecology shows that music is equally a matter of beetles, shellac shipments, hard labor, pollution, and material decomposition—as well as a range of other effects that are not typically understood as musical, and which are far from uplifting or positive. What's more, this was not an awkward early phase in the industrialization of recorded music, one that was subsequently grown out of in favor of more stable materials or responsible practices. Although the details of substance and practice change throughout this history—changes that are tied up with important shifts in music's aesthetics and ethics, industries and ecologies—the basic patterns are established in the shellac era.

Better Listening Through Chemistry: Formats and Formulas

Somewhere in the aisles of teeth and bones, amongst the shelves of feathers and quills that he stockpiled in his labs, Thomas Edison also stored "an interminable collection of chemicals."[15]

Edison is usually thought of as an innovator in electric light, electric power, and electric media. Yet many of his early fascinations and ongoing activities were founded in chemistry, which is to say studies of the properties, compositions, and reactions of compounds. This includes several of Edison's celebrated telegraph innovations. For example, the electricity required to transmit a telegram's dots and dashes between a tapped key at one end and a clicking sounder at the other was, for a time, provided by batteries. Batteries are chemical reactions, and significant parts of Edison's efforts to innovate and industrialize the telegraph involved improvements in battery chemistry. Indeed, since he was a child Edison had experimented in many aspects of both the chemical and material sciences. His work in recording was no exception.

Even that most iconic early recording material, tinfoil, was an object of constant experimentation and refinement. Edison never settled on a standard tinfoil thickness or composition (it ranged from 8 to 28 percent tin). Such variations were partly due to the fact that Edison was beholden to his metal suppliers, meaning that shifts in the format's composition followed shifts in the price and availability of raw materials.[16] The biggest limitations of tinfoil, though, were that it was difficult to attach to the cylinder base, that it was too soft to withstand repeated playback, and that detaching it from the cylinder base would destroy any chance of listening to the recording at a later time. Indeed, Edison was never truly satisfied with tinfoil and, around the invention of his phonograph in 1877, he experimented continuously with other substances, including copper and iron.

After a period when other media commanded more of his time and energy (telegraphs, telephones, lightbulbs), when Edison returned to the phonograph in 1888 his attention shifted from tinfoil to "wax."[17] This was largely because wax was harder than tinfoil, meaning that cylinders could withstand repeated playback. He also hired two chemists around this time: Franz Schulze-Berge, who came in on a recommendation from none other than Herman von Helmholtz, and Jonas Aylsworth. Schulze-Berg mainly tested record duplication. Aylsworth studied the playback surface. Both were key processes.

Mastering and molding, the means by which an original recording is transformed into stampers that can press hundreds and thousands of duplicates, have commanded more attention in the history of sound recording. True, these were especially challenging and interesting processes, involving advanced chemistry and material-scientific know-how: gold-plating and nickel-bathing, electroplating and acid-etching. As such, the processes used untold amounts of various metals and chemicals—all of which connect the recording industry to political ecologies of mineral extraction and chemical synthesis, not to mention the question of how the used materials and hazardous waste were disposed of.[18] However, because the materials used to produce records themselves were consumed in such greater quantities than those of mastering and molding (making millions of records and not just thousands of stampers), for the purposes of this investigation the surface is where the action is.

Aylsworth worked with Edison for about thirty years, both as an employee and as a consultant. He was instrumental in Edison's transition to wax during this early period. One formula that they developed, which was used around 1896 and mixed in 400-kilogram batches, was based in materials and methods related to modern cosmetics and candles—which is to say soapified animal fats such as beef tallow and processed paraffins such as coal-based "stench wax" (ozocerite).[19] Although some of these waxy ingredients may have smelled bad on their own, together they sounded pretty good. Still, there were production problems. Manufacturing of wax cylinders was tricky, and mass-producing them was especially so. What's more, given that listeners typically stored and played their cylinders in household parlors, which could be very hot in summers and very cold in winters, wax cylinders melted and cracked with the seasons and were prone to become moldy. The switch in 1908 to cylinders that played for four minutes, rather than the earlier two minutes, had extremely fine grooves. This necessitated a harder wax compound, which proved to be brittle and even more fragile.

In late 1912, Edison's search for a more effective cylinder surface resulted in a shift from wax to celluloid. These cylinders sold relatively well, partly because they had a bigger dynamic range and a wider frequency spectrum than the wax cylinders.[20] Still, the clear market trend toward disc recordings in the early 1900s led Aylsworth and his colleagues to develop a different material, at first in secret, and later with Edison's approval: phenolic resin. Phenolic resin, which went by the trade name Condensite, was synthesized using a combination of formaldehyde and a weak acid called phenol (also known as carbolic acid). This resin was spread like a varnish onto a blank core made from wood flour and clay. Although Edison long favored the cylinder, the promise phenolic resin was such that he was compelled to enter a new recording market and introduce a format that he had previously shunned: a disc phonograph.[21]

The success of the Edison discs was such that, by 1914, his company was using about a ton of synthetic phenolic resin every day, making Edison "the largest individual user in the United States of carbolic acid (for making phonograph records)."[22] Yet the coincidence of the boom in the disc business and the beginning of the First World War posed a problem for Edison. Because most of the United States's phenol acid supply came from Britain, and because Britain had stopped exporting the acid as a result of its use as a precursor for explosives such as TNT, the supply had dried up. Faced with the prospect of shutting down his record presses, Edison began synthesizing his own phenol in a factory that took less than three weeks to build and which, a month later, was producing several tons of phenol per day—much more than Edison needed for Condensite. The excess became caught up in a conspiracy known as the Great Phenol Plot.

Edison sold his extra phenol to a variety of interests, including the Bayer pharmaceutical corporation of Germany. Like Edison, Bayer was short on the phenol it needed to make one of its key products: aspirin. For a time, Bayer was buying nearly all of Edison's excess phenol. Because the United States was not yet officially involved in the War, the Trading with the Enemy Act was not yet in force and Edison was free to do business with a German company. Yet the dealings between Edison and Bayer were secretive and underhanded, involving a front corporation established and funded by the German government. This caused public outcry over the question of whether Bayer was purchasing Edison's phenol as a way of diverting the supply into aspirin—thereby preventing the acid from being used in Allied explosives. Edison was shamed and eventually ended the deal, supplying future excess phenol to the US military.[23]

Edison's ventures and misadventures in chemistry during this period position the recording industry as an early innovator in rheology (the science of flow) and as one of the earliest large-scale manufacturers of synthetic plastic. As Oliver Read and Walter Welch note: "The extensive and important research made by Edison and his associates in the field of chemistry of plastic materials at this time … marked the beginning of our modern synthetic thermo-setting plastics industry."[24] In other words, the recording industry has, since its beginning, been a materials science and a chemical industry—and not just a consumer of trivial amounts of chemicals that were originally developed by, and used primarily in, other trades. As the phenol story shows, the record industry was actually an innovator and supplier of key chemicals to other industries. Yet this is not a straightforward cause for celebration, neither of Edison's ingenuity nor the revolutionary scientific contributions of music recording. For example, unlike later chemical and material innovations in the recording industry, such as the plastic V-Discs for which the recording industry was saluted for offering US troops some musical comforts of home during the Second World War (when shellac was in short supply), the Great Phenol Plot offers a case in which the recording industry was not only tightly bound with chemical and pharmaceutical industries (which have their own dark histories and practices) but directly involved in the conspiracies and atrocities of battle.[25]

It is ironic that, for all his success in other enterprises, Edison remained stubbornly committed to recording formats and formulas that met with limited commercial success.[26] In the same way that he stood behind the cylinder in the face of the disc's success, Edison did not use shellac as a main ingredient in his recordings until just before he left the record business in 1929. As such, although the story of Edison does place the recording industry at the forefront of ushering in the plastic age, the magnitude of which is sometimes compared with other epochal material transitions in human history such as the Stone Age and the Bronze Age, the majority of the recordings made and sold during this period continued to use a natural resin, and the recording industry's broad shift to synthetic plastic would wait until after 1950.[27] Indeed, most of the recording industry put its money on a technically inferior format (discs) and a formula whose supply chain was even less predictable than wax or phenol (shellac).

Emile Berliner was one of the foremost pioneers of discs and shellac. In his earliest disc formulas, he had tried several other solutions. Celluloid, which worked well enough for Edison's phonograms and discs, "was not quite hard enough for the gramophone system," while hard rubber produced records that "were imperfectly pressed and showed flat places." Vulcanized rubber was especially promising, despite certain flaws, but the rubber company to which Berliner had subcontracted his pressing "was unable to correct this part of their work and furnish a reliable output."[28] He called this situation—the inability of several materials sciences and industries to meet the demands of recorded sound—an "emergency." Something else was needed. Thinking back to his time at the Bell Telephone Company, where Bell had used "a shellac composition" instead of rubber in their hand-pieces, Berliner decided to solve the problem internally.[29] His nephew, Joseph Sanders, was right for the job.

Sanders is most often remembered as the employee that Berliner sent to Germany to establish a European arm of his operation. Indeed, the resulting label and its recordings are renowned to this day: Deutsche Grammophon. The reason Berliner chose Sanders, though, was not as a talent scout or recording engineer but as a materials scientist who knew his way around a pressing plant and who knew how to whip up a batch of shellac. Sanders wrote numerous diary entries about the materials used in recordings—and the amount of work it took to get the mixture right. On 2 April 1906, for example, around the time he bought his wife Hannah a new Stanley steam-engine car, Sanders scribbled that he was "very busy with patent matters as well as experiments on discs and materials." He "frequently worked all night" on these projects.[30] Sanders was still keeping these hours as of New Year's Day, 1907: "Have been working till late at night most every night and getting there anywhere from 7:00 to 8:30 in morning."[31] His work paid off, eventually resulting in shellac discs that "showed remarkable uniformity, and, moreover, because the material was harder than hard rubber, the reproduced sound was louder and more crisp."[32] Although the work of Sanders and Berliner was foundational, similar studies were carried out at many other recording companies, and similar formulas became the standard across the industry.

Berliner recognized the hard work of arriving at effective shellac formulas. In a reflection on the problems of materials in the phonograph business, delivered in 1913 at the Franklin Institute in Philadelphia, he wrote:

> Few people have a conception of the untiring efforts which have been made year after year, and still continue, in order to obtain a composition which will answer all the necessary requirements for resisting the wear of the needle or prevent the latter from being ground blunt too fast.... Shellac is much adulterated and the mineral and fibrous substances which are added require careful selection and this whole department is in the hands of experts who do nothing else all the year around but test the substances and the mixing processes which are employed for producing record material.[33]

As Sanders and Berliner make clear, the recording industry required especially exacting standards from the chemical and materials sciences. The purity, consistency, and durability of shellac mattered more in records than in other applications. Looking back on this period of intense and ongoing experimentation, RCA's B.F. Aldridge noted: "It is easy to understand, accordingly, that as satisfactory formulae were developed, they became valuable properties and 'top-drawer' secrets.... This critical area soon became a field in itself. The skillful mixing of wax and shellac with other materials quickly established such internationally known experts."[34]

Names like Jonas Aylsworth and Joseph Sanders are not well known in history of sound reproduction. Without wishing to glorify these figures, it is no exaggeration to say that their roles in defining the sound of this era are just as important as, say, Fred Gaisberg's recordings of Enrico Caruso. Were it not for the ongoing work of various scientists, and the correspondingly intimate relationships between the recording industry and the rising chemicals corporations, all the music that was recorded during this period would sound different.

Still, this history is not only about elite US and European men or their businesses, be they household names like Edison and Berliner or unsung protagonists like Aylsworth and Sanders. The story of recorded music during the shellac era is equally about millions of unnamed laborers in the Global South (including many women and children), thousands of unknown miners and factory workers, tons of filler materials, and innumerable insects—all of which played defining roles, not in the history of musical forms, but in the general media morphology and political ecology of the 78 rpm format.

Beetle Juice

Shellac is a resin made from lac, the sappy secretion of a beetle that is native to southern and eastern Asia. Twice a year these insects swarm "like blood-red dust" in the forests of India, and twice a year the twigs that they encrust with lac are harvested, crushed, washed, dried, melted, and "made into thin sheets which are broken into the familiar flakes of the shellac of commerce."[35] Although shellac was established as one of the earliest transnational commodities in the seventeenth century, and while the modern shellac trade began in the nineteenth century (owing to its use in everything from hats and poker chips to furniture varnish and electronics components), it was the popularity of the phonograph record that fueled the explosion of the shellac industry after 1900.[36]

The tremendous demand for shellac during these years was such that the quality of the supply was uneven: "Often it was loaded with impurities such as grass, weeds, gravel, plain dirt, and it seemed, anything else that would add weight to the shipment."[37] Indeed, the resin was a continuous source of uncertainty among record manufacturers. Like all crops, shellac yields were unpredictable and monitored closely in industry trade papers such as *Talking Machine World*. Shellac crops that produced 4 million kilograms of resin in one season might give only 1 million the next.[38] Record manufacturers were at the mercy of bugs, soil, and weather patterns. Some commentators, though, blamed the individuals who harvested shellac:

> India is the chief source of supply and here we run up against the difficulties of production. The human factor in the equation here causes all the trouble. The native of India has no ambition to make money. He goes out and makes a few baskets of shellac and sells these for enough money to satisfy his simple wants. To go out and gather twice the number of baskets and earn twice as much money never even occurs to him. There are here and there a few enterprising natives with some business sense, but the great majority are supremely indifferent.[39]

Racist stereotypes about the inefficiency and indifference of Indian laborers were widespread—and of course exaggerated.

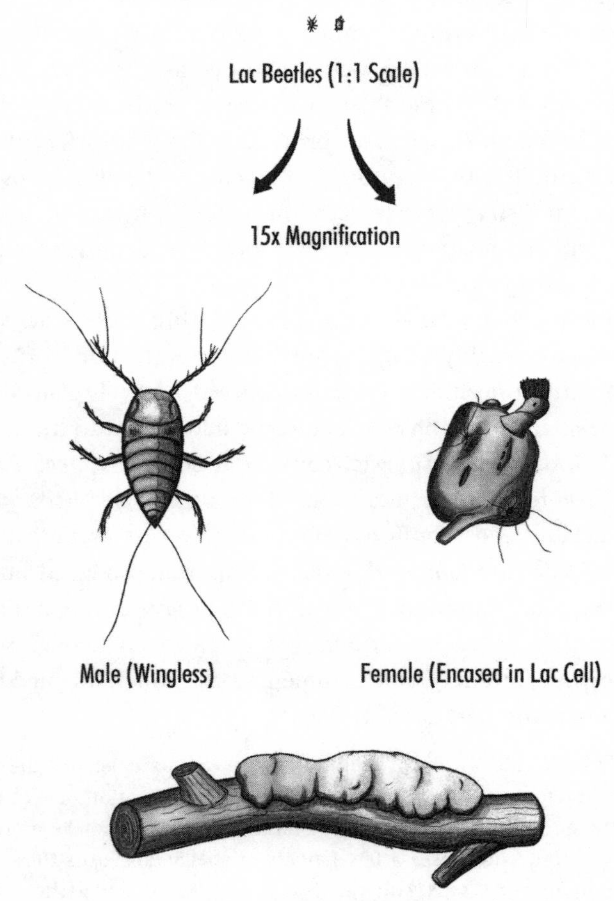

Figure 1.1
Lac beetle reproduction cycle. (Graphics designed by Scott Bodaly)

"Numerous comparisons are often attempted such as that an average Lancashire girl in a weaving shed can do the work of six Indian cotton mill operatives," in the words of one labor report. "Such opinions usually emanate from individual employers who desire to sweat their labour.... The efficiency of the Indian labour generally is no less than that of workers in most other countries. Not only this, but... the skill of the Indian labourer has been demonstrated to be even superior in some cases to that of his prototypes in foreign countries."[40]

Stereotypes notwithstanding, the unpredictability of shellac crops was cause for concern and motivated the recording industry's search for alternative materials. According to the manager of one record label, there was "one prospect" that could be an especially "great deterrent" to the industry's financial well-being: "It is the rapidly advancing price of one of the principal materials of which gramophone records are manufactured, and for which, up to now, no substitute has been found, although many attempts have been made by experimentalists to produce one. That commodity is shellac." One of the "dominating features" in the minds of the industry, said this manager, was therefore "whether supplies of shellac will fail, and if so, whether some substitute will be discovered and upon this to a very great extent depends the abounding continuance of the gramophone and record trade."[41]

Import taxes posed another problem. Industry representative Marion Dorian fought the US Committee of Ways and Means in the House of Congress:

> He pointed out to the committee that both of these commodities are of foreign origin; cannot be produced in this country [sic], and are indispensable in many American industries, including the talking machine industry. That American manufacturers are in close

> competition with foreign manufacturers for foreign markets on products where these ingredients form an important part, and that the foreign manufacturer already enjoys an advantage over the American because of his closer proximity to the source of supply, cheaper transportation rates and cheaper labor. That the imposition of a duty upon these hitherto free raw materials will constitute discrimination against the American manufacturer in favor of his foreign competitor, and either result in closing these foreign markets to him or compel him to shift such portion of his manufacture as is meant for foreign consumption to a foreign country, thus depriving American labor of an opportunity to retain for its benefit work it has formerly exclusively enjoyed.[42]

The risk of this so-called "useless tax," in other words, was that foreign record manufacturers in Germany and Britain would inadvertently gain a competitive advantage because they were closer to the origin of the shellac supply chain.

Although Dorian managed to keep the tax at bay, wartime restrictions and attendant cost inflations caused the most serious difficulties.[43] Shellac was scarce as a result of its use in anticorrosive paint for Naval ships and various other munitions. What is more, the First World War and its aftermath saw the UK price of shellac jump from a prewar £50 per ton to nearly £900 per ton in early 1920, settling below £500 by the end of 1921.[44] Indeed, in comparing the pre- and postwar importation of shellac into Britain, one commentator found that the amount of available shellac in 1920 had fallen to roughly half of that imported in 1913, while the price had increased by over 1,000 percent.[45] As a result, record compositions varied, prices yo-yoed, consumers complained about variable quality, and the industry searched restlessly for a new material more or less since the moment it had "settled" on shellac. The upshot of this scarcity and inflation was that the record industry used lower quality shellac, less virgin shellac, and less total shellac per disc, which resulted in rougher records (both in terms of acoustic definition and needle wear-and-tear). Still, the postwar boom in consumer demand was enough to offset the overall rise in price and the variable sound quality, and shellac maintained its centrality until about 1950.[46] By then, shellac production in India peaked at 40 million kilograms per year—the majority of which went to record companies.[47]

The Victor Talking Machine Company's stockpiles of shellac during the interwar years averaged between 10,000 and 20,000 bags, each of which weighed about 75 kilograms. Victor was constantly ordering more, at a rate of 500 to 1,000 bags per week, and using a total of about 4 million kilograms of shellac in a year.[48] Their main suppliers were the Ralli Brothers, an India-based exporter, and the Rogers-Pyatt Shellac Company, a major US-based importer. Both companies found themselves in and out of trouble in the courts and the media. The Ralli Brothers were suspected of cornering the market and artificially driving up shellac prices, while Rogers-Pyatt was charged with shorting customers, accused of tax evasion, and indebted to creditors.[49] Rogers-Pyatt also stirred up controversy in Rhinebeck, New York, where the company was based for a time. Rogers-Pyatt was evidently polluting the local stream, thereby poisoning the cows that drank from it and killing the trout that swam in it. Their backyard was a mess and the stench of the operation offended nearby residents.[50]

While millions of kilograms of resin could go a long way in the recording industry, yielding many more millions of discs, it took innumerable beetles about a year to produce a single kilogram of the substance.[51] Given average shellac yields, that level of production would have required a forest the size of Los Angeles.

Protecting those crops could involve the use of toxic pesticides to keep away hungry ants, birds, and monkeys.[52] Additionally, the process of producing resin is a "feast of death" in which a tremendous number of lac beetles die.[53] Although this macabre process constitutes the species' natural reproductive cycle, committed vegans who avoid shellac-coated jelly beans (as well as those whose protests led Starbucks to stop using the cochineal insect to dye some of its products red) will also want to skip these records. Nevertheless, the rapid lifecycle of the lac beetle is such that shellac itself is a renewable resource. Shellac records are also biodegradable, leading some commentators to call for a return to the format. Even if that were possible, the cultivation, harvesting, and production of shellac complicate this notion. The arboreal hosts of lac beetles offer one such complexity.

Lac beetles infect trees; lac resin is "a disease of the host."[54] One of the trees that affords the highest shellac yields is the kusum, or Ceylon oak. A kusum tree grows more slowly and reproduces less easily than other species, and is "affected very strongly by the attacks of the lac insect and requires several years to recover its vitality."[55] Only 2 percent of India's lac production during this period came from "government forests," with an additional 5 percent from larger commercial interests. "The rest is entirely in the hands of uneducated villagers, cultivating a few trees each."[56] In this unregulated majority of the industry, it was uncommon for cultivators and harvesters to observe the rotation patterns necessary to sustain tree crops. And, even though there were cultivators with the specific task of attending to the health of the trees, neglect was ordinary, while harvesting techniques (which basically involve sawing, striking, and scraping tree branches) were often "gross and ravenous."[57] This could lead to the death of host trees. Moreover, given the erratic shellac market, such workers were as likely to cut down kusum trees and sell them as firewood as they were to cultivate them carefully as lac producers.[58] When we consider that billions of discs were manufactured during the half-century long shellac era, the political ecology of these practices comes into focus.[59] Our aesthetic investments weigh on material environments, in ways that parallel other histories of music's entanglements with indigenous forest communities and supply-chain capitalism.[60]

Before shellac was shipped out to record pressing plants across the world, it was processed and refined in various factories around India. According to an Indian government labor investigation, commissioned in 1943 and published in 1946, shellac factories employed an estimated 30,000 laborers.[61] Such workers had one of five main jobs: there were melters, crushers, *kamins* (women who winnowed seedlac), *khalifas* (those who made cloth bags for shipping), and coolies (general unskilled laborers). The working conditions were horrible. Unlike larger industries such as textiles, shellac processing was mainly unregulated and, even in cases where certain regulations did apply, they were often "flagrantly disregarded," in the words of the report. Laborers worked from dawn till dusk, every day of the week, in factories that were "ill-ventilated, ill-lighted, congested and positively dirty." These factories were dangerous (machines did not have proper guards) and foul (drains were not cleaned regularly). The toil took its toll: fingers cramped from repetitive and monotonous tasks, feet swelled and bled from crushing lac, ears rang and lungs filled with dust from grinding materials, and eyesight faded from heat exposure.

The wages paid for such work were the lowest in India, and the salaries of unskilled laborers and women were particularly out-of-step with increases in the overall cost of living. Although the Employment of Children (Amendment) Act prohibited the services of workers under twelve years of age, the act was "disregarded quite openly" and child labor was "freely employed on low wages and sweated practically everywhere." What is more, because shellac was a seasonal commodity, these workers had neither "security of tenure" nor access to other basic rights and benefits. When workers needed money to support themselves and their families in the offseason, they became indebted to their employers, who lent rupees at interest rates of 600 percent. For these reasons, shellac processing was singled out as one of the most deplorable industries in India.[62]

Companies such as RCA Victor, which was formed when the Radio Corporation of America purchased the Victor Talking Machine Company in 1929, were frequently keen to point out that a "turbaned man raising bugs in India and the leader of a symphony orchestra or jazz band [each] have a share in producing the phonograph records of today."[63] Yet such companies were consistently silent on the ways that shellac cultivation, harvesting, and processing also shared in the controversies that mark the extractive colonial industries surrounding forestry, agribusiness, and sweatshops writ large.

Vibodh Parthasarathi's work helps to situate such issues in relation to India's wider early twentieth-century musical cultures and media industries. He outlines a tripartite logic of extractive capitalism, which both fed off and furthered a broader colonial enterprise. Two of these logics are familiar to music scholars. There was financial extraction, which involved the recording industry of the Global North expanding its territory to the Global South, both in terms of selling foreign records in India as well as working to establish local markets for local musics (with the majority of the profits kept by the parent labels). And there was symbolic extraction, which involved northern composers and recordists appropriating the aesthetic traditions of the Global South, using those traditions to revitalize their own practices and markets (usually without attribution or remuneration). The third logic of extraction, less discussed in music research but equally problematic, was material. It involved the colonialist assumption that the products of Indian lands and hands were simply for the taking.[64] If financial and symbolic extraction can be heard in the grooves of particular records, the political ecology of material extraction is enfolded in the grooves of every record pressed during this period.

Filler

Central as shellac was to the political ecology of early recorded music, the resin was actually a minority ingredient in disc records. The majority of these records—up to 85 percent—consisted of filler, a mixture of minerals, fibers, and lubricants in which shellac acted as a binding agent. The chief fillers were crushed slate and limestone, mixed in equal parts. Limestone was particularly important, not only because it was inexpensive (so was slate) but because it was smooth. In other words, limestone sounded good. It flowed well under the needle. As such, in the same way that the industry's drive for higher-definition sound existed in a symbiotic relationship with materials science and chemistry as well as an extractive relationship with insects and laborers, musical preferences had additional material consequences for the industry's political ecology. To value the aesthetics of limestone was to make other claims on communities and environments.

The best and, therefore, the majority of the US recording industry's limestone came from Indiana. Ever since the railway connected Indiana to the rest of the country in 1853, the region had supplied the vast majority of limestone in the United States—including, by the 1930s, three-quarters of the limestone used in US-made records. Partly for this reason, in 1940 RCA Victor moved a significant portion of its production facilities from the rust belt (Camden) to the stone belt (Bloomington). Columbia, the second-largest record company after RCA Victor, was not far behind. In the words of RCA engineer Warren Rex Isom, "the advantages of being near the source of the best filler ... showed up larger than was expected on the bottom line of the balance sheet."[65] For a business that manufactured tens of millions of records every year, where even a small reduction in the size of paper record labels could save tens of thousands of dollars per annum, it seems reasonable that the corporation would have saved significantly by eliminating long-haul limestone shipments from its production chain.[66] But RCA had ulterior motives. They smelled even bigger profits.

The situation in Indiana following the Depression was not good. The local furniture industry had collapsed, while the need for trees in that industry gave way to harsh winds that made it difficult for farmers to cultivate crops in the region's agricultural economy. Likewise, the limestone industry had declined to a tenth of its former size (from 5,000 laborers to 500).[67] None of Indiana's industries showed signs of recovery. The unemployment rate in the region was above 40 percent and, moreover, the local workforce had very little experience with organized labor unions. It was a perfect storm: "The limited industrial culture, low levels of unionization, and, most important, the destruction of the local economy made Bloomington a dream town for a capitalist in search of workers for labor-intensive electronics production."[68] Although this situation did provide RCA with a reserve army of male labor, both in terms of stonecutting and heavy lifting in factories, "the corporation chose Bloomington because it had 'a large field' of 'high class feminine labor' to fill the assembly lines."[69]

Women comprised approximately 80 percent of the workforce in RCA's Bloomington factory and about 75 percent in its earlier Camden plant. The politics of women's labor in the communications and electronics industries, of which recording is a part, is steeped in contradictions. On the one hand, the feminization of such labor was marked by forms of discrimination (women were paid lower wages than men) as well as regulation and patronization: "Management's standard explanation for its preference for young female workers typically rested on the idea that women's mental and physical characteristics made them peculiarly suited to the intricacies of electrical assembly work."[70] Women were inexpensive and supposedly docile employees, with deft and nimble fingers, according to a widespread trope in industry discourse. Of course, such stereotypes of women workers "had less to do with any traits inherent in women than with the type of workers the company sought for the manufacture of particularly competitive goods."[71] Forms of sex-typing and exploitation abounded in the industry. Yet, on the other hand, women also found value and meaning in these factories. They found senses of purpose and community in their work, not least through their involvement in improving working conditions and organizing labor unions. Similar tensions between exploitation and empowerment in women's media labor actually go back to the incorporation of women in telephone exchanges in the late 1800s, and forward through various other forms of electronics manufacturing and assembly in the twentieth century.[72] As with Alejandra Bronfman's history of feminized labor in mica mines (which were also key to the recording industry during this period), the point here is "not to overstate either the exploitation or the freedom and independence" of women workers but, rather, to signal the foundational role of such women (and the problematic construction of gendered labor) in the history of recorded music.[73]

When RCA eventually pulled out of Bloomington, moving its facilities to Mexico at the end of the century, it left behind "environmental hazards, widespread economic displacement, and land use issues that the city continues to wrestle with."[74] Isom could not have foreseen such fallout, and his cost–benefit assessment does not mention that the move to be near the best filler was part of this longer history whereby RCA (and others) moved into downturned cities and developing countries in order to keep material and labor costs down. Nor does Isom consider the environmental implications of limestone extraction, which is infamously destructive of landscape, habitat, and water supplies—issues that mark the region to this day. From this perspective, the critical ecosystems for 78s were as much the quarries of Indiana as the forests of India.

In addition to processed bug resin (shellac) and petrified aquatic organisms (limestone), 78s contain a variety of other materials: from asbestos to asphalt, caustic soda to cement, flour to formaldehyde.[75] Carbon black, a sooty powder that results from incompletely burning petroleum products, was a particularly important component. It was used as a pigment to dye records black, as a filler to smooth out the surface of records, and as a kind of lotion to reduce the friction between the needle and the groove.[76] Recipes varied by company and were often trade secrets.

One thing that was not secret, though, was the widespread use of scrap in these records: "Almost any amount of scrap could be—and was—used in the shellac compound."[77] Technically, "scrap" was defined as defective records and pressing excess that could be reground and reused. Scrap material constituted up to 70 percent of a given batch of recording compound. But scrap batches also included dust that had been swept off the factory floor, as well as pieces of stone, soda bottles, and other garbage. Isom explains why: "Boxes labelled 'scrap' around the presses, in the warehouses, and wherever invited their use for the disposal of waste material.... Years of dedicated attention to changing the labels on the scrap boxes to read 'used compound' and to label the waste cans 'waste' or 'trash' was wasted effort."[78]

Although the confusion of scrap bins and waste bins "always caused those who were quality conscious to cringe a bit," as a result of the increased surface noise contributed by such materials, "no real harm was ever found to result from this practice." In fact, there was a benefit: "surface noise was a partial blessing for it masked many of the other faults. Shellac records were full of blisters and unfilled grooves which produced ticks and pops in the sound. The hard particles from the impurities in the raw shellac, from the trash in the scrap and from thermal decomposition of the uncontrolled fusing of the ingredients all were present. A shellac record without surface noise to mask these faults would have been intolerable."[79] Regrinding paper labels, though, was a different story: "True, the paper that was left was no worse than the bark from the trees or dirt from the tropical groves. It did, however, add to it."

The heterogeneity of shellac records, both in and of themselves as well as within particular companies and across various brands, highlights that using "shellac" as a shorthand for the recordings made in this period is something of a misnomer. The chemists that struggled to develop a material base of the disc format that could be pressed uniformly, shipped without breakage, and listened to with pleasure, as much as the laborers that worked to provide the materials for them to do so, point to a wider political ecology. These other staple commodities and supporting casts, dismissively referred to as filler, are in their own ways central to the history of recorded sound.

Cakes, Biscuits, and Waffle Irons: Pressing Records in the Shellac Era

The various constituent materials of 78s converged, mixed, and took shape in pressing plants. With their smokestacks, assembly lines, and heavy-duty machinery, these plants were obvious sites of standardization, mass production, and industrialization. Although recording was not the first instance of musical mass production (precedents include the sheet music and instrument trades) there is a sense in which music had not been seen as an "industry" before sound recording.[80] Once it was recognized as an industry, though, music recording attracted the same mixture of wonder and scorn that marked industrialization as a whole. Indeed, pressing plants were usually part of much bigger operations. The recording industry during this period was, first, a hardware manufacturer (record players) and, second, a software provider (records themselves). The shift to an industry that contracted and marketed musicians on record, primarily selling rights and outsourcing hardware manufacturing and record pressing, took shape later.[81] While this earlier phase of industry integration has been a target of criticism, record companies and the general public were more impressed by the operations than they were depressed by big business.

Figure 1.2
Bird's-eye view of the Victor factories, 1911. (Courtesy of Hagley Museum and Library)

In 1924, Victor wrote a letter to its dealers and distributors, proudly describing its Camden plant. The campus employed roughly 10,000 people. It had an internal standard-gauge railroad and trucking service as well as its own printing facilities for record catalogs and promotional material. It had its own fire department, police force, and hospital, as well as its own symphony orchestra and restaurant. Victor boasted of a raw materials inventory totaling $8 million at any given time, of a 6.5-hectare hardwood lumberyard, of burning 60,000 tons of coal each year to feed the 18,000-horsepower machines required to run the place, and of a dedicated water plant to quench the daily 60-million-liter thirst of its production facilities. The mailer

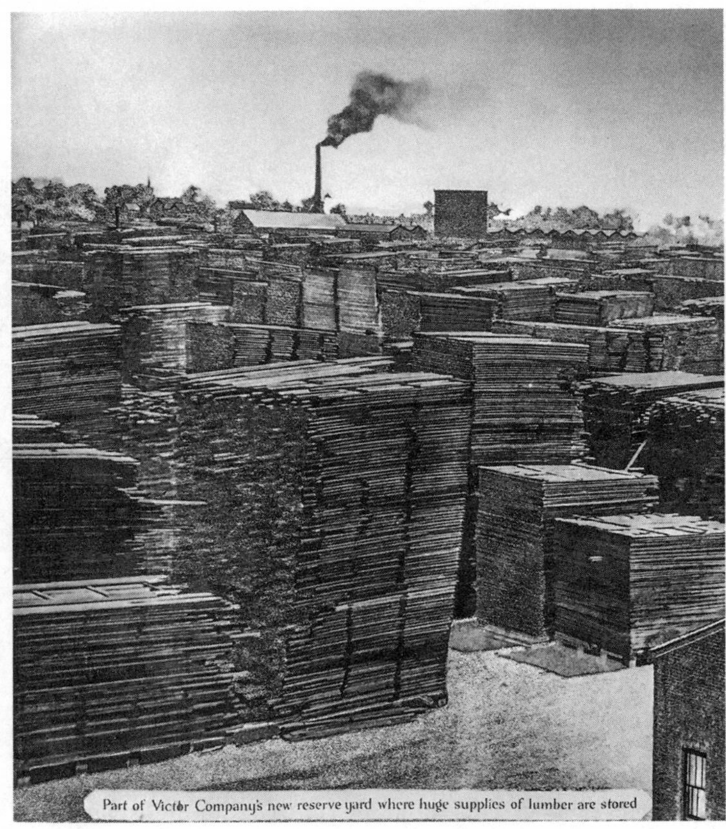

Part of Victor Company's new reserve yard where huge supplies of lumber are stored

Figure 1.3
Victor's hardwood lumberyard, ca. 1920. (Courtesy of Hagley Museum and Library)

included a picture of the operation, which Victor encouraged dealers to frame and display in their shop windows.[82]

Inside the plant's pressing department, records were mixed and mashed into existence. In describing a 1910 tour of the Victor Talking Machine Company, a *Talking Machine World* author was fascinated by the size and scale of the undertaking, calling Victor "the largest buyer of shellac in the world"—a point that was driven home upon seeing "yards and yards" of the "doughy stuff." After being kneaded in cauldrons and flattened by rolling mills, the "thick and pliant" shellac was left to stand, "smoking and cooling… like a singularly uninviting kind of cake." From there it was taken to a room upstairs, where a little time and a lot of hydraulic pressure transformed the "black cake" into a record.[83] A later, in-house RCA document patted itself on the back for the impressive intricacies and industrial strengths of the pressing process:

> With infinite care the workmen carefully mix and blend the dozen ingredients. After a precise screening operation, the blended materials are drawn off in a powdered form and dumped into one of the most amazing machines in the record industry—the Banbury mixer. This machine, which towers through two complete floors of the RCA Victor plant, was originally developed for the rubber industry for the manufacture of plastic and rubber compounds.…
>
> In the Banbury mixer, the record ingredients are thoroughly blended and fused into a black, plastic mass resembling asphalt. Steaming hot, this material is dropped on a rolling machine which kneads it back and forth like a monster rolling pin, finally sheeting it on a long conveyor belt on which it moves through a set of revolving knives that cut it into sections known as "biscuits," each biscuit containing sufficient material to make a record.
>
> The operation now moves into the pressing department.… The record press resembles a huge waffle iron, with one stamper at the

> bottom, the other at the top.... The "biscuits," which have been allowed to harden in storage banks, are reheated on a steam table adjacent to the presses. As soon as they become soft and pliable they are folded and placed in the press. The press, which has been heating meanwhile, is closed and hydraulic pressure of many tons is applied causing the plastic record material to flow over the surface of the stampers. Live steam circulates through the press, then in a few seconds the steam is turned off automatically and cold water circulates, cooling the press and hardening the record. The press is opened and the completed record is exposed.
>
> When it leaves the press, or is lifted out as a waffle from an iron, the record has a rim of excess material known as "flash." This excess material is shorn off by nimble fingered operators and then the record goes to the finishing department where it is placed on a lathe, the edge is ground down to perfection, first with fine emery paper, and then plain white waxed cloth which leaves it smooth and polished.[84]

From there, records were sent to the shipping department, where they were loaded onto trains and sent out in 10,000-kilogram batches.[85]

The EMI campus near London was equally impressive, according to a group that toured the facilities in 1919. This had something to do with hospitality: visitors were treated to a "fine luncheon" in "the company's famous oak-paneled boardroom." But the real awe was inspired by the "forest of belting" and "wonderful human-like machines" that were "busily stamping, punching or pressing" records and playback equipment "in musically pleasant contrast to the war-time production of shell cases, fuses, primers, ammunition cases, aeroplane parts, etc." The record factory itself was found near "the huge power house, past the voracious furnaces, where fuel was simply gobbled without a thought on the stokers' part of the threatened six-shillings-a-ton coal increase." Inside the pressing plant, the tour reached its high point:

> The sifting of the foreign elements from shellac by the magnetic process, the machines devoted to the mixing of the various ingredients in the composition of Zonophone records, the rolling mills which "blanket" and cut the material ready for the pressers—five rollers were on the job day and night—the pressing and finishing touches to the completed articles, caused the visitors to exclaim enthusiastically as the process was revealed to them.[86]

You can almost hear the oohs and ahhs, over and above the hydraulic hisses and fuming furnaces.

The coupling of music and industrialization conjured not only boastful mailers and gawking articles. It was also a target of cultural critique. Theodor Adorno, for example, derided the resemblance of phonograph production to the progressive assembly of the Ford Model T, worrying about the parallels between the standardized goods industries and the standardized culture industries. The filmmaker René Claire offered a similarly concerned cinematic comparison between the "prison regime and the production line in a gramophone factory."[87] George Orwell, for his part, wrote a poem "On a Ruined Farm Near the His Master's Voice Gramophone Factory":

> As I stand at the lichened gate
> With warring worlds on either hand—
> To left the black and budless trees,
> The empty sties, the barns that stand
>
> Like tumbling skeletons—and to right
> The factory-towers, white and clear
> Like distant, glittering cities seen
> From a ship's rail—as I stand here,
>
> I feel, and with a sharper pang,
> My mortal sickness; how I give
> My heart to weak and stuffless ghosts,
> And with the living cannot live.

The acid smoke has soured the fields,
And browned the few and windworn flowers;
But there, where steel and concrete soar
In dizzy, geometric towers—

There, where the tapering cranes sweep round,
And great wheels turn, and trains roar by
Like strong, low-headed brutes of steel—
There is my world, my home; yet why

So alien still? For I can neither
Dwell in that world, nor turn again
To scythe and spade, but only loiter
Among the trees the smoke has slain.

Yet when the trees were young, men still
Could choose their path—the winged soul,
Not cursed with double doubts, could fly,
Arrow-like to a foreseen goal;

And they who planned those soaring towers,
They too have set their spirit free;
To them their glittering world can bring
Faith, and accepted destiny;

But none to me as I stand here
Between two countries, both-ways torn,
And moveless still, like Buridan's donkey
Between the water and the corn.[88]

Orwell's 1934 poem is about the same record pressing facility near London that so impressed its 1919 visitors. But Orwell's observer is anxious and ambivalent, not awestruck. For him, the gramophone factory encapsulates his alienation from both a sacred, agricultural, environmentally pristine past that he believes is gone, on the one hand, and a profane, industrial, environmentally spoiled future that he knows is inevitable, on the other. Like Buridan's donkey, which finds itself equidistant from ample water and ample food yet, because it is equally thirsty and hungry, cannot choose between the two and so withers and dies, Orwell's protagonist confronts the undecidability of progress and nostalgia, development and decay.

Another piece of cultural commentary warrants mention. *Duffy's Tavern*, released in 1945, is a musical comedy set in New York City during World War II. The film is about a group of nondrafted and veteran workers who have lost their jobs at the National Phonograph Record Company, because the pressing plant has shuttered as a result of wartime shellac shortages. In between musical numbers, the plot revolves around a search for shellac in order to get the plant going again. The protagonists do so partly in the interest of getting themselves back on the job. And they do so partly in the interest of financially redeeming Archie, the manager of Duffy's Tavern, who has been taking on debt because his compassion and patriotism compel him to keep the out-of-work record pressers in food and drink.

The film was not a runaway at the box office. And it was largely dismissed by critics for its "blowzy characteristics" and a "story that pretends to do no more than usher some comedy."[89] Indeed the plot is in many ways an excuse for broad jokes, silly antics, and musical cameos by Bing Crosby and the like. Yet it is hard not to take the film at least a little seriously. For in this comedy we encounter yet another way that the staple commodities and supporting casts of recorded music can be seen as central to its history—and yet another way that music as such is not central to its historical effects. As with Adorno, Clair, and Orwell (albeit in a different register), *Duffy's Tavern* provides a sensitive and insightful commentary on the sites where and conditions under which 78 rpm records and phonographs were made—as well as the wider cultural significance of modernization, industrialization, and mobilization.

The inextricability of the recording business from its wider political ecology says something about how we should view this line of work: not only as part of the consumer electronics industry, but as part of a much larger story about political ecology—the intersections and trajectories of resources, supply chains, industrialization, and labor around the world.[90] This inextricability makes it methodologically difficult to research the recording industry on this level, because it is always hard and sometimes impossible to find exact figures on which materials the recording has used, where those materials originated, and which labor forces were exploited. But the inextricability also says something about what we can trace in the grooves of a shellac disc. We can hear musical forms and features, if we want. We can listen through the 78's distinctive thin sizzle that results from the contact between the needle and the disc, straining to hear the voice of that old blues singer or the instrumentation on that old blues record. But we can also address the surface noise itself, which is a remainder that serves as a reminder of the ways that this format enfolds and indexes broader global frictions such as exploited resources and workers, the traumas of war and waste.

Conclusion: A More Convivial Phonography?

The political ecology of the 78 rpm disc highlights seemingly unlikely connections between the industries of music, insect farming, forestry, mining, and chemical engineering. Such relationships were not incidental. They were integral to the everyday operations of making and selling recorded music. This is clear, for example, in the Mangers Committee meeting minutes of Victor during this period. Yes, the minutes contain plenty of sales figures on Victrolas (Victor's highly popular talking machines) and their prestigious classical Red Seal records. And yes, these reports keep track of recording contracts (John McCormick apparently earned $75,000 a year around 1928, or about $1 million in today's money). But they also portray other integral aspects of this industry that are not normally considered musical. These meetings were also about where to put new washrooms for the growing numbers of women employees, shortages of coal and parking spots, raises and redundancies for factory workers. And the minutes contain detailed, weekly reports on the company's existing stocks and ongoing purchases of shellac as well as running tabs on the always fluctuating shellac market in Calcutta.[91]

The history of sound recording is about more than hit records and A&R representatives looking to sign the next Bessie Smith or Bing Crosby. It is also about office workers on the phone to India, wondering about the status of the next shellac crop. It is about the people who risked their health to harvest and process raw shellac, about those who mixed batches of shellac and operated record presses, and it is about the chemists and materials scientists who developed and refined the formulas in the first place. This story is about quarrymen and beetles as much as the Quarrymen and the Beatles. To understand how the price and availability of raw materials influenced business decisions is to appreciate more fully how the record industry functions *as an industry*. What's more, to observe the import–export patterns of feedstocks such as shellac and limestone is to extend back the timeline of musical globalization, past the debates about "world music" that emerged in the 1980s.

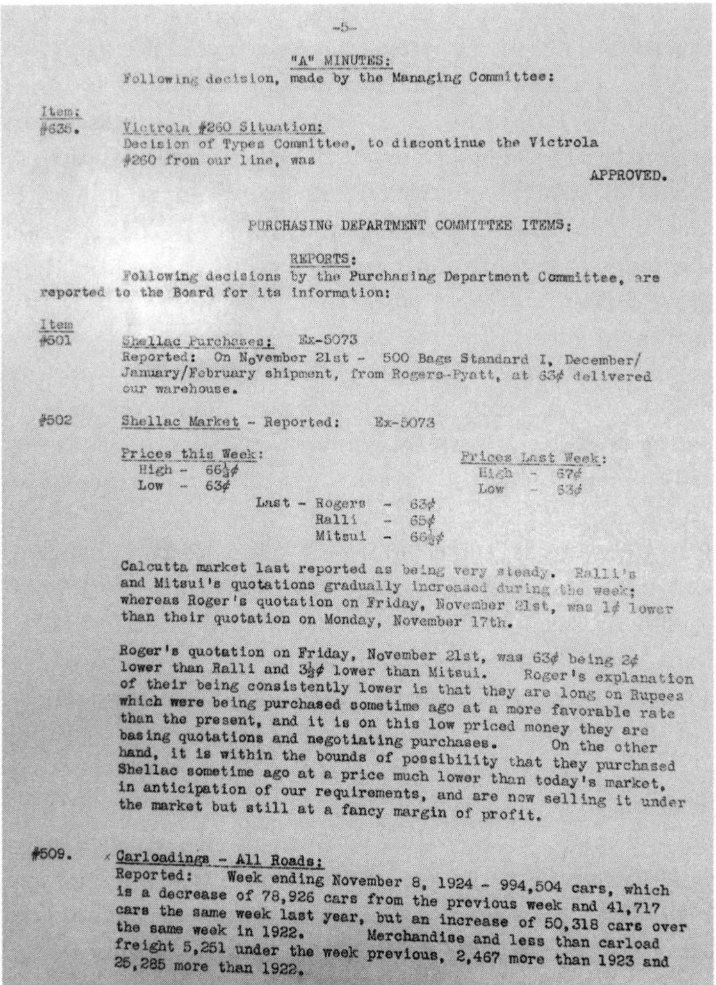

-5-

"A" MINUTES:

Following decision, made by the Managing Committee:

Item:
#635. Victrola #260 Situation:
Decision of Types Committee, to discontinue the Victrola #260 from our line, was

APPROVED.

PURCHASING DEPARTMENT COMMITTEE ITEMS:

REPORTS:

Following decisions by the Purchasing Department Committee, are reported to the Board for its information:

Item
#501 Shellac Purchases: Ex-5073
Reported: On November 21st - 500 Bags Standard I, December/January/February shipment, from Rogers-Pyatt, at 63¢ delivered our warehouse.

#502 Shellac Market - Reported: Ex-5073

Prices this Week:
High - 66½¢
Low - 63¢

Prices Last Week:
High - 67¢
Low - 63¢

Last - Rogers - 63¢
Ralli - 65¢
Mitsui - 66½¢

Calcutta market last reported as being very steady. Ralli's and Mitsui's quotations gradually increased during the week; whereas Roger's quotation on Friday, November 21st, was 1¢ lower than their quotation on Monday, November 17th.

Roger's quotation on Friday, November 21st, was 63¢ being 2¢ lower than Ralli and 3½¢ lower than Mitsui. Roger's explanation of their being consistently lower is that they are long on Rupees which were being purchased sometime ago at a more favorable rate than the present, and it is on this low priced money they are basing quotations and negotiating purchases. On the other hand, it is within the bounds of possibility that they purchased Shellac sometime ago at a price much lower than today's market, in anticipation of our requirements, and are now selling it under the market but still at a fancy margin of profit.

#509. Carloadings - All Roads:
Reported: Week ending November 8, 1924 - 994,504 cars, which is a decrease of 78,926 cars from the previous week and 41,717 cars the same week last year, but an increase of 50,318 cars over the same week in 1922. Merchandise and less than carload freight 5,251 under the week previous, 2,467 more than 1923 and 25,285 more than 1922.

Figure 1.4

Victor Managers Committee weekly meeting minutes, late 1924. (Courtesy Hagley Museum and Library)

Similar points about this longer history of musical globalization have been made by others, albeit in relation to hybrid aesthetic and identity formations and, implicitly, transnational movements of musical commodities as finished products.[92] Together, these emphases have defined the study of musical globalization largely as a study of "song networks."[93] But there are other factors at play. To paraphrase Arjun Appadurai, although the social lives of some things (such as 78s) may be more noticeable (because they garner more symbolic investment) than that of some others (such as shellac and limestone), these other staple commodities and their supporting casts are no less important.[94] The industrial–aesthetic textures of song networks take shape only in relation to the industrial–material circulations of resource networks. A critique of music's political ecology thus shifts not only the timeline of musical globalization but also the character of the questions that can be asked about that phenomenon. In this way, the shellac era is part of a longer and broader history of musical globalization—a history that is not only about the movement of recordings around the earth, but also the movement of earth to make recordings.

Common sense might suggest that we should look to the shellac era as a model for "a more convivial phonography."[95] Indeed, it is true that shellac 78 rpm records are in a sense "green discs." For example, shellac itself is a renewable resource and biodegradable material, while the formats that followed in the recording industry's fifty-year plastics era made use of nonrenewable resources (oil) and produced nonbiodegradable commodities (LPs, 45s, cassettes, CDs)—not to mention the energy-intensive server farms that store today's digital audio files or the wasteful devices required to access those files. It is equally true that the recording industry's demand for insect resin offered livelihoods to millions of Indian harvesters and tens of thousands of Indian processors, while the shift to plastic threw the shellac industry into crisis and left many of those workers without jobs and in financial difficulties. But to romanticize the shellac era's conviviality is to dismiss the actual working conditions of those who cultivated, harvested, and processed shellac in India. It is to ignore the pollutions and problems of factory work in which those records were formed. And it is to forget that one of the shellac disc's most crucial resources by volume, limestone, is neither renewable nor environmentally friendly to excavate.

To call for a return to shellac, even in the face of the very real problems of music on plastic and the very real downsides of music as data, would also be unsound. The fact that lac insects breed effectively only on trees that grow well only in regions such as India raises questions about trade relations between the Global North and the Global South, which would require a sensitivity to postcolonialism and neocolonialism that seems beyond the conscience of the capitalist recording industry. Even if these conditions were justly met, and even if the processes of making shellac records were made more efficient and enduring, the Jevons effect expects that greater resource efficiency leads to greater resource consumption. What then would it mean for the recording industry, not only to return more centrally to forms of insect farming and mining, but to extract and use far more of those resources? To confront the wider political ecology of recorded music is to stand with Orwell at the lichened gate, stuck between the water and the corn.

2 Plastic (1950–2000)

The vinyl revival, the cassette renaissance—maybe even the CD resurrection. It is not difficult to find these themes in music journalism, these patterns in music consumption, these interests in music scholarship. Many people are keen to put a finger on why retro-romantic revivalism is so prevalent. This book is about the political ecology that it perpetuates. Regardless of the reasons people love vinyl, it is possible to ask different questions and tell different stories. Why did the recording industry turn to vinyl in the first place? And to what effects?

The conditions of the contemporary vinyl revival were established in the middle of the previous century, when the recording industry abandoned shellac and adopted plastic. Although this moment is understood as a material shift, it is most commonly viewed as a transition through which the recording industry remained a consistent entity (signing bands, selling records) except for its introduction of two new-and-improved formats: the LP and the 45. Musically and economically, the motivations for and implications of developing these formats are well known. In the case of the LP, Columbia Records envisioned a market for a format that could fit entire symphony movements on one side of a disc. With the 45, RCA Victor foresaw a market for a format that was cheaper to produce and that worked well in jukeboxes, thereby enabling them to better keep pace with the hit charts and shifting youth tastes. In these ways, the two new formats were articulated to different musics and markets—lasting and "serious" musical statements for adults on LPs, ephemeral and "cheap" pop singles for youth on 45s—and they accrued different kinds of cultural symbolism.

Of course, pop and rock bands did eventually appear on LPs. When they did, it was seen as a kind of honor, a valorization by which they were "elevated" onto the more respectable format. Certain folk and rock musicians were therefore attracted to LPs, partly because these genres imported the ideals of artistry found in classical music and jazz. As a result, LPs produced in the popular music world, while originally no more than collections of various songs, became seen as something more. Indeed, through the latter half of the 1960s, folk and rock musicians began to write songs that were meant to be heard together, and in a particular order. The LP became thought of as an ideal medium through which musicians could present a unified (or at least thematically coherent) artistic statement. In this way, the term "album" made its journey from an allusion to a nineteenth-century book of photographs to a term that denotes a musical–technological unit. Even today, when musicians approach the craft of songwriting, they often work with albums in mind. The album thus became a technological format can be thought of as a type of compositional form that defines many genres. Recording industry activities in those genres accordingly revolve around the album, both then and now (even though there is no longer any strict technological reason that they should).

These well-known affordances of the LP—its mutual mediation of technological and aesthetic possibilities—have been described in terms of phonograph effects, which are the audible incarnations of recording's influences on music.[1] Similar stories could be told about magnetic tape and cassettes (the development of splicing techniques, the significance of the rewind function, the shifts in listening practices made possible by portable devices) as well as CDs (the "perfection" of sound, the introduction of shuffle functions, the consecration of incoherence).[2] Again, it is tempting here to view the recording industry as an entity that remains basically the same between 1950 and 2000, save for its promotion of several changing formats. Yet while the labels themselves may not have changed, beneath their surfaces there emerged entirely new supply chains and waste streams among various new industrial subsectors. In other words, while the public face of the recording industry may have remained recognizable, its underlying political ecology became almost unrecognizable. This fundamental shift from shellac to plastic underwrites all recorded music during this period, and the political ecology that was established generates phonograph effects that are much farther reaching (and much less audible) than the usual attention to the musical affordances of formats suggests.

The organization of the recording industry shifted around 1950 from bug harvesting and rock quarrying to oil extraction and petroleum refinement, to petrochemical and plastics corporations, to automotive interests, and more. It moved from 78 rpm concoctions of primarily natural and biodegradable ingredients to a series of plastic formats that consist of toxic carcinogens and nonbiodegradable substances. It transitioned from factory processes that readily connote industrialization to those that more resemble futuristic sci-fi laboratories. Opening up the relationship between the histories of plastic and recording is to become aware that, despite a nominative continuity in what we call the "recording industry" before and after 1950, the industries to which that term has been attached underwent deep transformations. The recording industry may have been consistently in the business of selling records, but almost everything about how those records were made and unmade was reorganized during this period. These transformations relate not only to different formats and musical possibilities but shifts in staple commodities, supporting casts, and political ecologies.

Shackled by Shellac

The dominance of the shellac 78 rpm format was doubly challenged in the late 1940s. It was at this time that Columbia introduced its 33⅓ rpm long-playing (LP) album, and RCA Victor introduced its 45 rpm single. Following a drawn-out format war, the LP was crowned the "core commodity" of the Western recorded music industry, steadily increasing its market share through the 1950s and representing 80 percent of record sales by 1960.[3] The core materiality of that core commodity—and of recorded music commodities for the rest of the century—was plastic.

In accounting for the recording industry's shift from shellac to plastic, in particular the polyvinyl chloride from which LPs are made, most writers point to technological advances. That is certainly one kind of explanation. As a writer for the trade journal *Modern Plastics* noted in 1947: "The vinyl record … is practically impervious to cracking, breaking or chipping. The playing life, of the vinyl record … is as great or greater than that of the shellac.

And with all this, the vinyl product gives infinitely better quality reproduction than has ever been obtained from a shellac recording."[4] Indeed, LPs were more durable than 78s: "We all know the fate of the shellac record that is dropped on the floor." They were said to have "very quickly assumed a position of general superiority as to quieter playing surface, frequency range, and clarity." And their "hair-width" microgrooves were celebrated for their increased playback time.[5] It is possible to suggest, however, that the "downfall" of shellac was not strictly a matter of sound quality. "Despite the 'frying-bacon' sizzle of its surface noise," says Richard Osborne, "shellac was a format capable of withstanding continued audio improvement."[6] Accounting for the downfall of shellac and its succession by vinyl therefore requires a more complicated explanation than straightforward technological progress. Political ecology is an important part of that story.

The Second World War looms large here. Shellac rationing was part of a broader initiative whereby many of the products needed to manufacture records, including barite, rottenstone, limestone, and carbon black, as well as many materials required to make record players, were "sharply curtailed" by the US War Production Board (WPB) and funneled instead into the making of "weapons, planes and ships."[7] Even playback needles were affected. From the early 1940s, for example, record companies such as Columbia were sending out mailers to various suppliers, inquiring about unfilled orders and hoping to source new materials (needles were in short supply largely due to restrictions on osmium). One metalworking company, Goldsmith Bros. Smelting and Refining, responded positively: "We think we will be able to show you a very desirable new war-born phonograph needle" made of "a substitute alloy … on which there should be no WPB manufacturing restrictions."[8] The General

Phonograph Manufacturing Company, by contrast, was "disturbed" by Columbia's pushiness regarding an undelivered order for millions of needles: "We want you to know that our lack of shipments is occasioned only the war. … In any occasion war orders and priorities come first and this is the way it should be, as otherwise our side would lose the final victory."[9] Still, shellac was the biggest problem, and for two main reasons.

First, through 1940 and 1941 the Japanese army began occupying key shellac-producing regions. This meant that supplies in the West were reduced, because "normal ocean routes from Calcutta, main export port for shellac, were cut."[10] Second, and related, in the spring of 1942 the War Production Board introduced a "shellac conservation order."[11] The WPB's shellac restrictions did not technically limit the number of recordings that the industry could press. Rather, the order froze 50 percent of all shellac stocks over 4,500 kilograms, limited the "consumption of shellac to 30 per cent of the past rate of consumption," and required the industry "to make [a] formal application for each allotment of shellac."[12] As long as they played by those rules, record companies were free to manufacture as many records as they could. By the summer of 1942, though, speculation was mounting that existing shellac supplies would be entirely frozen and that future supplies would be completely cutoff.[13] The "industry's fears were realized" in early November, "when [the] War Production Board sent word that, under present conditions, there would be no further amounts of shellac available after this month."[14] Nevertheless, "none of the firms [were] squawking."[15] Rather, they did their best to remain upbeat and optimistically turned their attention to solutions such as stretching supplies, salvaging scrap, and synthesizing substitutes.

Salvage campaigns were especially "heartening."[16] In 1942, the recording industry launched "a concerted effort to impress upon juke box operators, dealers and the public the urgent need for salvage."[17] Writing for *Billboard*, Gladys Chasins described the variety of such efforts. Strategies included "scrap barrels outside stores, scrap appeals over p.-a. systems, scrap reminders enclosed with bills ... and radio broadcasting of scrap drives." Victor offered a free phonograph needle for every ten records returned. Decca "worked out campaigns with theater operations, where theater patrons pay admission in scrap records," while Columbia "enlisted the aid of janitors, air raid wardens and superintendents in combing houses for old records." A New York teachers' organization paired with the recording industry to send "prominent recording artists to entertain school children, urging them to dig up old records"—a drive that "collected close to 400 tons of scrap records."[18] Canadian and UK industry arms and government bodies also instituted salvage campaigns, which brought in tens of millions of used 78s.[19] It wasn't enough. The industry needed a substitute.

In a letter to W.A. Donner, the managing director of Columbia Graphophone in Australia, Columbia Recording Corporation vice president James Hunter described the gravity of the situation during the summer of 1942. He noted "tremendous production problems ... as a result of restrictions in the use of certain raw materials, such as shellac ... that heretofore have represented the main portion of our resin binder. ... We would be interested in knowing if there are any natural resins available in Australia or nearby islands that you have found to be good enough to take the place of shellac."[20] No such luck. Hunter repeated his request in September of 1942:

> As you doubtlessly know, severe shellac restrictions have been imposed on record manufacturers in the United States and we are all searching frantically for a substitute. We have done considerable work with other natural resins and have had varying degrees of success. In the event that you come across a substitute material we would be very much interested in hearing from you concerning this material.[21]

Donner's answer from Australia came in December, and it was curt: "I do not know of any substitute for shellac."[22] Around the same time, the shortage of shellac and other materials was such that Hunter wrote a memo to his boss, Columbia president Edward Wallerstein, proposing to "offer cash rewards or prizes to any of our [employees] who develop the substitutes for any of these items."[23] A year later, the lack of shellac led the US government to establish a Standards Division within the Office of Price Administration and Civilian Supply (OPA), which addressed, among other shellac-related issues, the "serious deterioration in quality" of "domestic phonograph records."[24] The OPA even planned a conference for "several representatives of manufacturers of phonograph records," which was also attended "by representatives of the Chemicals Divisions, the Office of Civilian Requirements, and other interested Government agencies."[25]

Although no natural resin was able to replicate or replace shellac, a synthetic substitute had been known and used, in fits and starts, since the 1930s: vinyl. Like shellac, vinyl during the Second World War was subject to shortages and inflation as a result of military rationing and restrictions, which meant that it was too expensive and too scarce to offer a viable alternative to shellac at this time. Only in the aftermath of World War II did vinyl become a fully commercially viable material in the record industry.[26] Indeed, unlike the shellac situation around World War I, where postwar demand offset wartime inflation, the embargoes and restrictions of World War II created a conjuncture in which the recording industry considered other materials with added urgency. The recording industry was thus an early adopter and innovator in the world of synthetic plastics—which is to say petrocapitalism.[27] Even though this shift alleviated various production problems stemming from the instabilities and irregularities of the shellac market, the political ecology of plastic posed its own challenges and raised its own questions.

The Plastic Age

Cultural studies of plastic typically begin with a second-person thought experiment: "Look around you!"; "Try to imagine a world without plastic."[28] It's impossible. From credit cards to playing cards, toilet brushes to toothbrushes, cigarette boxes to Corvette bodies, water pipes to water pistols, shower curtains to shoes, toys to Teflon—plastic is everywhere.[29] It is a way of life (and death). The plastics industry grew rapidly during the twentieth century and continues to expand in the twenty-first. Whereas the industry produced a few hundred thousand kilograms of materials per year around 1944, that amount grew to millions of kilograms per year by 1950. By 1979, the United States was producing a higher volume of plastic than steel. The annual amount of plastics produced today is in the hundreds of billions of kilograms.[30] Although the excitement surrounding the development of this industry is hard to ignore in its trade papers, plastic garnered a bad reputation through the second half of the twentieth century.

Whereas it had once represented a seemingly limitless and futuristic world of opportunity, plastic was increasingly viewed with doubt and suspicion. It came to represent the worst of environmental wrongdoing and to symbolize all that was wrong with a materialist, meaningless, throwaway society. The tension between the promises and the perils of plastic is well expressed in that famous advice offered to Dustin Hoffman's character in 1967's *The Graduate*: "I just want to say one word to you. Just one word ... Are you listening? ... Plastics ... There's a great future in plastics." The humorous incongruity of this advice, given by a straight-laced adult to a disaffected twenty-one-year-old and thereby representing wider tensions between the establishment and the counterculture, was not lost on audiences. Other commentators, from Roland Barthes to Norman Mailer to Tom Wolfe, either struggled with what to make of plastic or cursed it outright, while synthetic polymers became a lightning rod for the rising environmentalist consciousness as well as various health-and-safety organizations.[31] The history of recording is part of these larger triumphs and tribulations of plastic in the twentieth century.

Scholarly and fan discourses surrounding music have paid most attention to plastic's technological triumphs. They have had less to say about the material and symbolic ambiguities that accrued to plastic in the wider cultural imagination. Despite the socially conscious discourses and oppositional politics that are common in many popular music genres, musicians rarely question the wider political ecologies of their favorite plastic formats. Although this may seem like a strange contradiction, it makes sense as an effect of the particular forms of mystification and fetishism that were established in music's plastic age (and which continue in today's vinyl revival).

Synthetic plastics actually took hold in other parts of the musical world before they did so in commercial recording—especially in the musical instrument and audio electronics industries. For example, plastic had supplemented wood in radio housings and replaced ivory in piano keys by the 1930s, while instruments such as harmonicas, accordions, bugles, and electric guitars were widely available in plastic, or with plastic parts, from the 1940s.[32] Although the exacting standards of the recording industry meant that plastic's full commercial arrival there happened later than in instruments, several firms had been experimenting with nonnatural plastics in record-making since the moment such products had been commercially synthesized. They did so in connection with companies such as Shawinigan Chemicals in Canada, and the Carbide and Carbon Chemicals Corporation in the United States.[33]

Shawinigan Chemicals accidentally concocted a polyvinyl acetate resin in 1928, which served as an early shellac substitute. Their resins were "mixed in two large pots outside the plant" and by 1938 the company was selling significant quantities of polyvinyl acetate to Compo Records of Lachine, Quebec—Canada's first independent pressing plant and one of the industry's earliest adopters of synthetic plastic. By the 1940s, the company was among "the world's foremost producers of vinyl resins."[34] Shawinigan president H.S. Sutherland recalled that their "big market" for vinyl in the early 1930s "was gramophone records."[35]

Similarly, when the US Carbide and Carbon Chemicals Corporation succeeded in copolymerizing vinyl chloride and vinyl acetate around 1930, resulting in a substance known by the trade name Vinylite, one of their first calls was to the recording industry. RCA Victor employee Frederick Barton worked with Carbide for over a year to test and develop the new material's suitability for records. According to a report summarizing the experiments, these recordings seemed "to have somewhat lower noise

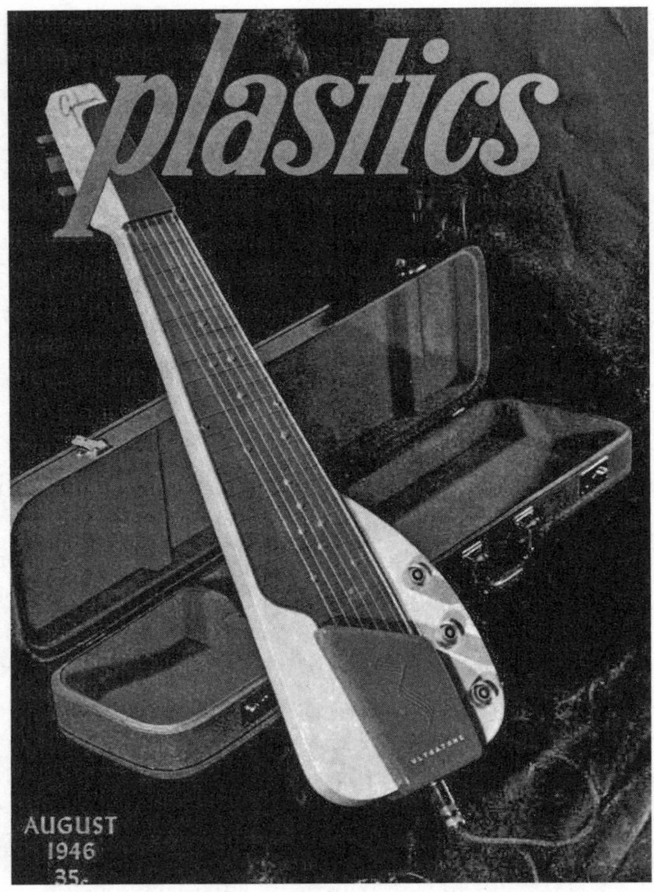

Figure 2.1
Music was a significant herald of the plastic age, though plastic made inroads into musical instrument manufacturing before it fully took hold in recording. (*Plastics* trade journal cover, August 1946)

level than shellac and seemed to be quite tough and difficult to break."[36] Thus, in 1931, RCA began receiving the first commercial shipments (over 2,000 kilograms) of vinyl in the recording industry. This Vinylite resin was similar to that which became widely used in the recording industry following the introduction of the LP after World War II. In these ways, the predawn of plastic in recording begins to show that, like most technological developments, the rise of plastic in the musical world was not an overnight success but, rather, a slow and uneven process involving changes in science, industry, and culture—a gradual realignment of recorded music's political ecology.

Before the end of the Second World War, these early vinyl records were neither widely available to the public nor widely commercially successful. Their principal uses were as transcription discs at radio stations, for broadcasting background Muzak, and in synchronized sound films.[37] Such uses represented relatively small amounts of plastic in relatively small commercial ventures. The more substantial (and the most written about) use of synthetic plastics by the record industry in the days before LPs and 45s was a nonprofit venture in Vinylite. During the war itself, Vinylite was restricted to military applications—except, at first, in V-Discs. The V-Disc program, which ran from 1943 until 1949, was an effort to musically boost the morale of US troops stationed far from home.[38] It resulted from cooperation between the Pentagon, the American Federation of Musicians, and the recording industry. Ideologically, the program "represented a fundamental change in the government's official understanding of the role of music in making war.... Let the U.S. Armed Forces motivate the young men to fight; V-Discs would remind them of home and what they were fighting for."[39] Materially, it was up to the record industry to find a substitute for shellac and to adapt existing pressing processes for a new material. Vinylite was the obvious solution, as it was already in limited use among record manufacturers. Yet, like shellac, Vinylite soon also found itself on the United States's critical materials list, meaning that another form of vinyl was required. The answer, even though it cost three times that of Vinylite, was Formvar—a polyvinyl acetate resin that had been produced by Shawinigan Chemicals since 1934 (and which was a descendent of the resin produced by the company in 1928).[40] More than enhanced sound quality, it was the availability and durability of Formvar that led to its use in V-Discs. Formvar was not on the restricted materials list, and these vinyl records could be shipped—sometimes even parachuted—into battle zones with less breakage than shellac.[41]

The gun barrels had barely cooled when, following the Second World War, record companies again began pushing to commercialize vinyl. "With a loud roll on the drums" in October 1945, a month after the conflict had ended, RCA Victor released a series of records in "ruby-red, translucent vinyl resin plastic."[42] Other labels such as Decca, Cosmopolitan, and Vogue were ready and waiting for the right time to market vinyl records of their own. These recordings did generate some interest among audiophiles. But they were too expensive to achieve widespread commercial appeal and were generally treated as novelties by the public. The market potential of vinyl during these pre-LP years was most apparent, not with audiophiles, but mothers and fathers: "Parents of very young children…were willing to pay a premium for plastic, not for its obvious sonic superiority but for its safety and durability in the nursery."[43] Indeed, these Vinylite "kidisks" represented up to 20 percent of the recording industry's sales by 1947—a market deemed so successful that other businesses such as the Synthetic Plastics Company diversified their interests and entered the recording industry.[44] "It was with children's records," writes David Bonner, "that vinyl recordings found their first mass market."[45]

Yet it was not until after 1948, when Columbia Records introduced the long-playing record, which contained nearly half a kilometer of "phenomenally narrow" microgrooves that increased a disc's playing time to over 20 minutes per side, that the recording industry began to fully embrace—and propel—the plastic age.[46] One of Columbia's stated aims was to remedy the mismatch between the symphonic repertoire and the 78 rpm format, which played a maximum of about four minutes of music per side. This was plenty of time for popular songs but not enough for concert music. According to Columbia president Edward Wallerstein: "We knew that when great symphonies were played on the phonograph there was a distinct drop in listening pleasure when the recorded ended in the middle of a movement and had to be changed."[47] Wallerstein figured that about seventeen minutes per side was necessary, because that was the approximate length of the first movement of Beethoven's *Eroica*—which, according to Wallerstein's calculations, meant that most of the symphonic repertoire would fit on the two sides of a long-playing record.[48] Peter Goldmark, a recording engineer who was also involved in shaping the LP, was apparently motivated to create a longer-playing record when one of his favorite pieces, Brahms's Second Piano Concerto, had to be flipped in the middle of a shellac-bound cello solo.[49] Although Wallerstein and Goldmark disagreed on who did what in the lead-up to the LP, and while these origin stories should be taken with salt, the marketing rhetoric of Columbia's original press release registers a bit of both their accounts. "The new record," said the initial press release, "is capable of producing entire symphonies and concertos ... on a single record."[50] LPs were thus imagined as a format for "serious" music and initially marketed to adults. Nevertheless, it is a pleasing irony that vinyl sales first caught on with Bozo the Clown, not Beethoven or Brahms—that the mass market for vinyl was established among pragmatic parents and their careless kids, not audiophilic adults and their serious symphonies.[51]

Another youth market was equally crucial in this industry-wide shift to plastic: that for the seven-inch 45 rpm disc. Introduced in 1949 and made initially of Vinylite and then polystyrene, RCA's disc was smaller than the LP, used less material than the LP (making it cheaper to produce), and held only one song per side. It was therefore more suited to popular music, youth (who had less disposable income), and the jukebox market. Indeed, the 45 was designed explicitly to work more effectively with automated jukebox disc-changing mechanisms, given that this market that had grown tremendously since the 1930s. These discs have generally been of less interest to scholars than the LP—but this reflects the biases of historians more than the innovativeness, importance, or political-ecological effects of the format as such.[52]

"The stories we tell about formats matter," says Jonathan Sterne.[53] He's right. Tales of overnight technological revolution and higher fidelity misrepresent the timelines, the reasons, and the consequences of the recording industry's entry into the plastic age. Political ecology—the uncertainty of lac crops, the unjust conditions of lac harvesters and processors, the material sciences and unstoppable expansions of petrochemical corporations, the shortages of war—helps provide a more effective explanation for the transition to plastic and offers a broader view of the stakes and effects of this transition. With political ecology, it becomes possible to show that the rise of music on plastic marks the moment when the recording industry's geopolitical and environmental center of gravity shifts from the forests of the Southeast to the oil fields of the Middle East. This is also the moment when the recording industry embraced the plastic age—sharing in and contributing to its triumphs of science and engineering as much as its excesses of consumption and waste, not to mention continued hazardous working conditions and international conflicts.

Plastic Makes Perfect

Polyvinyl chloride (PVC) is a synthetic polymer derived from a petrochemical called ethylene. Although the recording industry's transition to plastic was a more drawn out and uneven affair than is suggested in popular discourses of sound reproduction, its adoption of plastic following the war was relatively rapid, with record companies quickly using increasingly spectacular amounts of the material. When the LP had firmly taken hold of the market in 1960, UK record companies annually consumed 5 million kilograms of PVC.[54] With the LP's peak in Britain during the late 1970s, at nearly 130 million units, the amount of vinyl jumped to 22 million kilograms—which was 5 percent of the country's total yearly PVC output. In the United States, the amount was closer to 80 million kilograms.[55] Extending this to the height of worldwide sales—nearly a billion units worldwide in 1978 alone—the amount of PVC used to manufacture LPs weighed in at about 160 million kilograms. The success of the relationship between plastics and recorded music looked so promising during this period that the Union Carbide Corporation's *Bakelite Review* celebrated "The Record-Setting Business of Records" as an industry "enjoying an upward spiral with no letup in sight."[56] In fact, the road was a lot bumpier than Union Carbide—or anyone else—predicted.

In sourcing all that PVC, and in refining its suitability for sound reproduction, the record industry cut its ties to the shellac and limestone industries, forging instead new partnerships with petrochemical and plastics corporations.[57] The largest single PVC producer in the UK was British Petroleum. Major US suppliers included the Union Carbide, Dow Chemical, and Keysor-Century corporations as well as diversified automotive interests such as Goodrich, Goodyear, and Tenneco.[58] Indeed, the LP was seen as "a monument to the cooperation of the record industry with the plastic industry."[59] As in the shellac era, industry requirements and listener expectations meant that recording was an especially fussy customer for chemical and plastics industries and sciences. Although recording was not, by volume, a primary downstream market for plastic compounds, it was seen as a symbolically important early market and the standard of materials required for records pushed basic science in the plastic field.

When he reviewed the still-new LP format in 1954, *High Fidelity* critic Emory Cook noted: "Breakfast foods may snap, crackle and pop. Records shouldn't, but a few do." If a record did sound like Rice Krispies, it was a "discophile's nightmare": "The needle in the groove sounds like a hoe in a gravel pit.... your favourite concerto ... spews more grit than Grieg. Strawberry shortcake and sand make about as pleasant a combination." Nevertheless, Cook was quick to put things in perspective:

> True, perhaps the next record you acquire ... *may* contain two pops half way through the second side. In a 12-in. record ... there are approximately 2,250 grooves or revolutions. Pops in two of these grooves would represent a flaw of 1/10th of 1%—in other words, a record which was 99.9% perfect. No other publisher is confronted with such a criterion of perfection as exists in records today.[60]

The situation over twenty years later was not so different. Record companies strove for continued improvement in the compositional formulas and manufacturing processes of their discs. And they continued to demand more of these scientific and technological fields than did other industries.

One result of this, according to Sarwan Khanna, a materials scientist in RCA's Record Division, was that "only a small portion of [vinyl] goes to the record industry. The remainder is used in floor coverings, special type films and in the coating industry. Many of these other users are less critical of the resin quality than the record business."[61] Indeed, according to a representative of the Allied Chemical Corporation, "LP pressing PVC requirements were so much more exacting for pure vinyl than those of competitive users like toy and industrial pipe manufacture."[62] This meant that making records "in some cases demanded some basic development work in material science. The molding of a disk is the most critical application of plastic this writer has known.... We are attempting to understand these molding problems and the relationships of plastic structure, compounding technology and molding conditions. Rheological studies, a $10 word for our work, are tedious and time consuming. Expensive laboratory tools and qualified technical personnel are required to investigate these variables."[63] Even if the recording industry had shifted from a chemical supplier, as it had briefly been in Edison's time, to a chemical buyer, it was evidently no less demanding of the chemical and material sciences.

It has been productive in music research to describe how technological developments in one industry can ricochet throughout others. This is known as transectorial innovation, a "phenomenon in which innovations developed to meet the needs of a specific industrial sector come to play an important role in the creation of new innovations and commodities in a formerly unrelated industry."[64] Paul Théberge was the first to describe transectorial innovation in relation to music, noting in particular how achievements in the computer industry came to influence musical instrument manufacturing and musical practice in the 1980s. Although it has been most common to notice how the direction of innovation runs from other industries into music, the case of the LP highlights that innovations may also begin with music and lead elsewhere. Aesthetic expectations of precision and demands for inscriptive density in recording have called for advancements in the plastics industries. Music is not simply a passive observer of the plastic age. It is an active contributor to petrocapitalism, an agent of petroculture. Although the two other main formats of recorded music during the plastic age—cassettes and CDs—offer alternate takes on themes established with the LP, an excursion through a failed and forgotten format drives these points home.

The RCA VideoDisc was designed as an audiovisual media system that would play music videos, concerts, and films when connected to home televisions. RCA's commitment to the VideoDisc was substantial. It represented more than fifteen years of research and development (from the conception of the VideoDisc in the mid-1960s to its eventual release in 1981), involving thousands of employees (from metallurgists to mathematicians, chemists to physicists) and an investment of $200 million.[65] RCA pinned its hopes for the future on the VideoDisc, forecasting that the format would generate $7.5 billion in sales—which implied that, by 1990, "as much as 30 to 50 percent of RCA's entire sales revenue could come from the VideoDisc business."[66] Although the investment was huge, sales were small. With the benefit of hindsight, the format seems to have been doomed to fail. Owing to several problems in what Margaret Graham describes as "the business of research," the system was much delayed and effectively obsolete by the time it was released. VideoDiscs did not seriously compete with rival audiovisual formats such as laserdiscs, Betamax, or VHS. The format was such a flop that it contributed significantly to the downfall of RCA in 1986. RCA's VideoDisc is a fascinating story of missed opportunity and spectacular failure. But it equally illustrates the everyday research-and-development work and petrochemical partnerships that were central to the recording industry during its plastic era.

VideoDiscs look like 12-inch vinyl records—which, in many ways, they are. Indeed, the "starting point" of the VideoDisc was "the long and firm foundation of the audio disc mass production techniques."[67] Unlike audio recordings, though, a VideoDisc is housed in a plastic cartridge (or caddy). When a VideoDisc is inserted into its dedicated playback device, a mechanism extracts the disc from its caddy and spins it at 450 revolutions per minute. The grooves themselves are much finer than on a standard audio recording. In the same space that a vinyl record contains 300 grooves, a VideoDisc contains 4,000. This required some "big changes" in established disc materials and manufacturing.[68] In the words of Leonard Fox, one of the key developers of the format, "the audio wavelength recorded [on an LP] is 400 microinches vs. 20 microinches for the VideoDisc. From the latter dimension, it is reasonable to assume [that] a 20 microinch high bump, caused by a dimple in a stamper, will obliterate a video signal. The same size bump on an audio disc causes no problem whatsoever."[69] Moreover, the grooves in a VideoDisc are not soundwave analogs but encoded audiovisual signals that, in the contact between a microscopic playback needle and the disc surface, create an electrical current that is decoded inside the

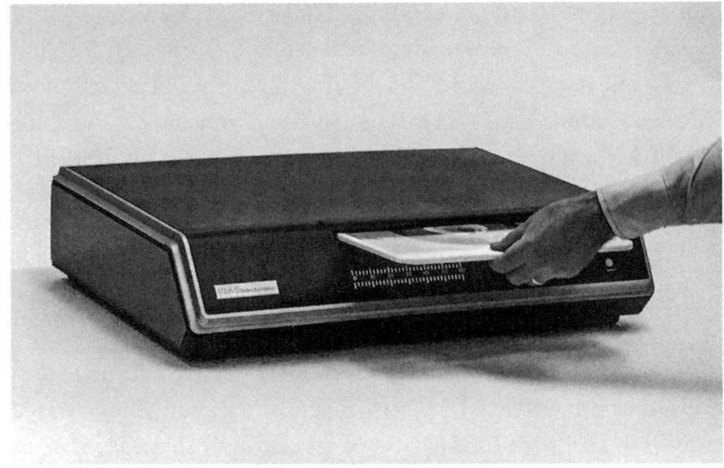

Figure 2.2
RCA's VideoDisc system, showing a VideoDisc caddy being inserted into the playback device. (Courtesy of Hagley Museum and Library)

playback device. This meant that VideoDiscs themselves had to be conductive, which created "some unusual molding and compound requirements" and which placed "extreme demands ... on both the materials and processes used for disc replication."[70]

While early efforts to produce an electrically conductive disc revolved around coating a typical vinyl record with silicon, RCA found it better to mix a special additive into the PVC compound itself: Ketjenblack. RCA purchased this conductive carbon powder from Akzo Engineering of the Netherlands. At the time, Akzo was a $6 billion chemical company with 85,000 employees around the world.[71] Akzo produced Ketjenblack using leftover resins that they purchased (and using techniques that they licensed) from another Dutch company: Shell. In a series of meetings between 1979 and 1980, RCA personnel visited

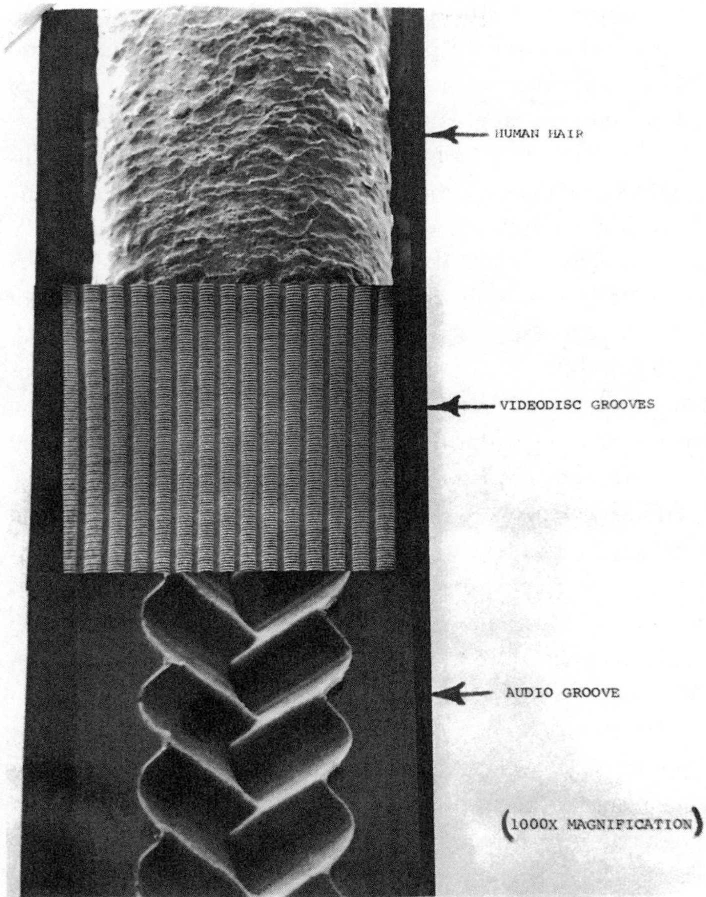

Figure 2.3
Magnification comparing VideoDisc grooves with a vinyl record and human hair. (Courtesy Hagley Museum and Library)

Akzo's Amsterdam offices, toured their production facilities in Ireland, and compiled reports on similar facilities in Japan and Finland. The in-house memos and reports include details of hydrocarbon cracking. They contain confidentiality agreements (which threatened a $5 million penalty if RCA released details of Akzo's proprietary Ketjenblack process). And they cover the "difficult environmental questions" associated with the carbon slurry needed to make the conductive carbon.[72] These reports also indicate that RCA used between 3,000 and 6,000 tons of Ketjenblack in the two years that the company produced VideoDiscs.[73] Although RCA's VideoDisc represents a conspicuous format failure, the scientific developments and petrochemical partnerships forged during its development were utterly typical of the recording industry in the plastic age.

The development of new plastic bases for cassettes and CDs posed similar challenges to the recording industry and continued to deepen its connections with material sciences and petrochemical industries. These challenges and relationships were widely recognized and reported. In the words of one label owner, "Whereas one can get away with an awful lot of loose practice in a record factory … one certainly can't with the CD manufacturing process. The procedures are very important. … Making CDs is many, many times more difficult than making black records."[74] Indeed, the reject rate of early CD factories was as high as 30 percent.[75] Part of the reason for this was that, although polycarbonate "is a very strong, dimensionally stable, engineering polymer … it was never originally developed for optical use, so there's been a considerable amount of activity amongst the major polymer suppliers."[76] As with the adaptation of vinyl for musical uses, refining polycarbonate for CDs required hard work and involved big business.

In the mid-1980s, in response to the beanstalking CD market (and in anticipation of its further growth), Bayer established a subsidiary optical media research laboratory in Pittsburgh. The lab's "extensive corporate analytical and polymer physics facilities" were some of the most advanced of their time: "Almost any thinkable analytical method is available in the facilities, including scanning electron microscopy (SEM) with energy dispersive X-ray capability…Fourier transform infrared and NMA techniques, as well as automated particle analysis, all of which can be called upon at short notice."[77] The Bayer lab exemplifies the "high premium [that] has been placed on polymer development and processing innovation" for use in the recording industry.[78]

As with the significance of figures such as Thomas Edison and Jonas Ayslworth, as well as Emile Berliner and Joseph Sanders, in developing the chemistry of wax cylinders and shellac discs, the purpose of highlighting the roles of science, engineering, and big business in the history of plastic recording formats is neither to geek-out on technical details nor to celebrate genius minds. It is, rather, to underline the extent to which such forms of labor and industrial–scientific structures were inseparable from the everyday act of buying a recording and listening to it. Indeed, these are the preconditions of music on plastic. And, again similar to the shellac era, the story of music on plastic opens out onto other aspects of political ecology: labor and exploitation, corporate recklessness and environmental degradation, war and waste.

Pressing Issues

About halfway between Toronto and Montreal, on the Canadian Pacific Railway, sits Smiths Falls, Ontario. This small town has

Figure 2.4
Aerial view of the RCA Victor plant at Smiths Falls, Ontario. (Fred Gorman / Joel Gorman Collection)

lately received a bit of fanfare, for it was here where North America's first Beatles records were pressed.[79] Observers north of the forty-ninth parallel are proud to point out that this is where the British Invasion *really* began, months before the Beatles became widely known in the United States. But the pressing plant at Smiths Falls is less interesting as an origin story than as a window onto the typical operations of vinyl pressing plants during the plastic age.[80]

Capitol Records of Canada released *Beatlemania! With the Beatles* in 1963. The actual pressing of the record was subcontracted to RCA Victor, which had opened a pressing plant in Smiths

Falls a decade earlier, in 1954, because its Montreal facility had reached capacity. The plant was designed to house thirty pressing machines (soon expanding to over forty), with a manufacturing target of 20,000 records per day, or about 8 million per year. For every two steam-powered hydraulic presses there was one operator—many of whom, as with RCA Victor's earlier factories in Camden and Bloomington, were women. Indeed, women comprised about two-thirds of the workforce at the Smiths Falls plant. Women vinyl workers were subject to the same inequalities and stereotypes as their shellac predecessors. They were paid less than men. They were typecast as being better suited for certain types of work than others (photos of plants from this era suggest that many women also worked in quality-control, presumably because of the same assumptions about attention to detail and suitability for delicate tasks that animated their work at RCA). They had a different dress code (only women who operated presses were allowed to wear trousers; the rest were required to wear dresses). And they were expected to give up their jobs once they married.

Working conditions inside the plant were often uncomfortable and dangerous. One employee, Vera "Hawkeye" Burt, of the quality-control department, remembered the cold winters: "Windows would be thick with ice, caused by the steam from the presses." Joan Youngcliss, who managed the factory chemistry lab, recalled that summer weather made the plant so hot that plant managers provided salt pills and glasses of water to prevent workers from fainting. Both women remember the risks of factory work. Burt witnessed fingers mangled by the presses and hands sliced by the blades used to trim excess vinyl after pressing. Youngcliss herself was badly burned when a vat of plating liquid (made of copper, nickel, or silver) exploded in her face.

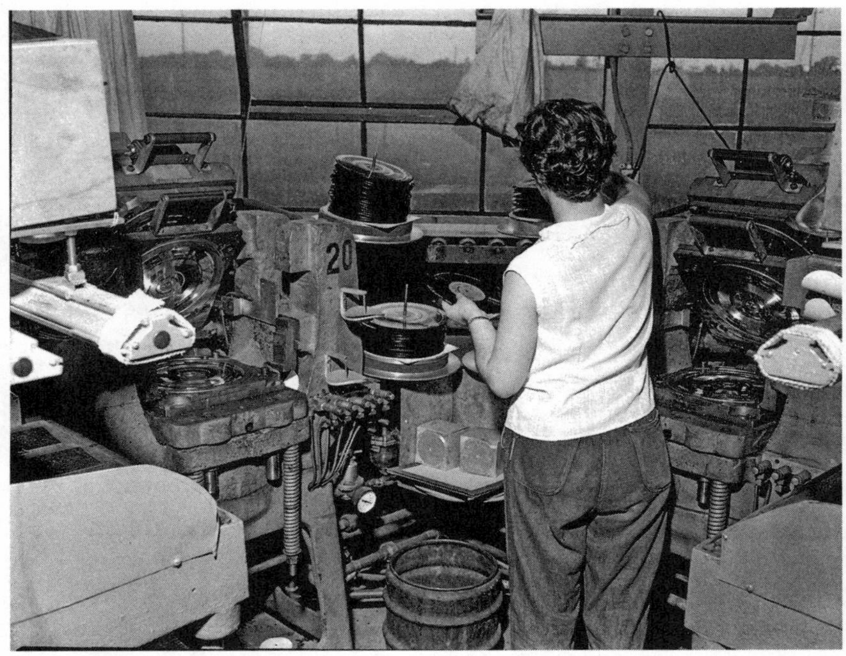

Figure 2.5
Pressing records for RCA Victor at Smiths Falls, Ontario. (Fred Gorman / Joel Gorman Collection)

Injuries and sex-typed labor notwithstanding, these women also found value and meaning in their work. For example, several women were chosen for key roles at the plant. Youngcliss was sent to Montreal on a six-month course so that she could run the chemistry department, while Mary Gallipeau was put in charge of the recording studio upon her return from a similar course. And there were lasting friendships forged on the pressing floor, at the cafeteria, and through the women's bowling league. As with the workers at RCA's earlier plants in Camden and Bloomington, while social inequalities certainly found expression in the work of record pressing, these other aspects of working life serve to complicate any straightforward narrative of exploitation. Additionally, if the history of the recording industry has often been told as a story of men and machines, then attending to staple commodities and supporting casts furnishes a more accurate picture of the indispensable but inaudible role of women's labor in that history.[81]

Smiths Falls's vinyl compound arrived in rail tankers from Indianapolis. By the late 1970s, during the heyday of vinyl, the plant had installed its own railway sidetracks so that train cars could pull up and park beside the building, allowing vinyl compound to be offloaded straight into the pressing plant. Such was the scale of these operations. Although memories have faded regarding the exact company that supplied the vinyl compound to Smiths Falls ("probably" the Superior Oil Company), evidence from another firm fills in the blanks regarding the conditions in which this vinyl compound was produced—conditions that resemble those of the Thai corporation that supplies much of the compound for today's vinyl revival.

The Keysor-Century Corporation not only pressed its own records but was for many years "a major supplier of basic vinyls to pressing plants."[82] Located just north of Los Angeles, Keysor-Century was also a felonious pollutant. For about a decade (ca. 1963–1974), employees illegally discharged the waste generated by PVC production and record pressing into a pond on its property, which risked poisoning the local supply of drinking water.[83] The Corporation was under investigation as early as 1977, when it was visited by the Environmental Protection Agency (EPA), which was concerned about the high levels of carcinogenic vinyl

Figure 2.6
A record ready to be pressed at RCA Victor in Smiths Falls, Ontario. (Hy Fund Studio, Smiths Falls, Ontario)

chloride particles found in the air—both in the plant itself and in the elementary school across the road.[84]

The EPA returned to Keysor-Century at the turn of the millennium, this time with the FBI, noting that the corporation "had been the subject of intense investigations since 2000. The EPA's Criminal Investigation Division discovered that the company knowingly released toxic wastewater into the Santa Clara River and emitted cancer-causing air pollutants at high levels, while falsifying emission reports to state and federal agencies."[85] As the *Los Angeles Times* put it, "Keysor employees cited 'frequent unreported spills' of contaminated waste water from the plastic-making process. The waste water gushed out of manholes in Keysor's parking lot.... In November, the Los Angeles County Fire Department cited Keysor for an 'intentional or suspicious act' that caused the release of 3,000 gallons of waste water into storm drains."[86] The result of the investigation was that Keysor-Century "agreed to plead guilty to a series of federal felony charges and to pay more than $4 million in civil and criminal penalties and restitution for polluting from its Saugus manufacturing facility, as well as lying about its employee's over-exposure to toxic chemicals."[87] This single corporation provided the US record industry with about 20 million kilograms of vinyl per year in the early 1970s, which amounts to nearly a third of the total supply used in the United States at the time. It is safe to assume that much of the other two thirds of the vinyl compound used in those years was produced under similar conditions—and that, as the sales of LPs increased through the 1970s, the transgressions would have been even greater.

Exposing workers to hazardous fumes, releasing toxic chemicals into the air, and dumping wastewater down the drain were not the only questionable practices of vinyl suppliers and pressing plants. Although employees at Smiths Falls followed the usual industry procedure of regrinding and re-pressing factory rejects and dealer returns, it was just as common to bury faulty and unsold discs in the plant's backyard. Those records must be there still, slowly decomposing and leaching hazardous chemicals into the groundwater. The practice of media corporations cutting losses, hastily and irresponsibly disposing of their unsellable commodities, is particular neither to the Smiths Falls plant nor to sound reproduction more generally. In the best-known example, Atari sent truckloads of worthless videogame cartridges to a New Mexico dump in the early 1980s.[88] Only a literal media archaeology, digging up the long-abandoned graveyards of defective discs at RCA Smiths Falls and elsewhere, could begin to unearth the extent of this aspect of pollution in the plastic era.

Cassettes, CDs, and Oil Crises

The political ecologies of cassette tapes and compact discs are in many ways variations on themes established in the LP era. In the late 1940s, magnetic tape recording seemed as poised as vinyl to become a dominant format.[89] Owing partly to technological hiccups and partly to the momentum of the disc format, however, the industry put more of its weight behind vinyl.[90] The reel-to-reel home tape machine never caught up. Following the introduction of the cassette tape in 1963, though, and especially through the 1970s and 1980s, the cassette market's "rate of increase" was actually higher than the LP's.[91] Eventually, so were its worldwide sales, estimated at 1.4 billion units in 1988, compared to 500 million LPs. Indeed, the cassette was integral to establishing mass music markets in Africa and Asia.[92]

From this perspective, despite the symbolic importance that has been ascribed to vinyl in the historiography of sound reproduction, the cassette arguably had greater musical and economic significance as well as greater longevity—and a similar political ecology.

Although various types of base film have been used in the history of magnetic recording, since 1973 the standard substrate of cassette tape has been polyester terephthalate (PET). In terms of PET, at the height of the cassette format in 1988 the industry was producing an astronomical amount of tape per year: at least 150 million kilometers of it—enough to stretch from the earth to the sun. This does not even take into account the massive parallel sales of books on tape (including the Bible), cassettes for the medical, legal, and real estate professions, or educational cassettes for students and libraries—all of which sold millions and millions of units.[93] Nor does it take into account the equally significant sales of blank cassettes or the untold hours of reel-to-reel tape used in radio and studio work.[94] What is more, like LPs and CDs, PET tape is hydrocarbon based (ethylene), which again highlights connections between the record industry and chemical companies such as DuPont and conglomerates such as 3M. Although the "media logics" of magnetic cassette tape differ in significant ways from LPs and CDs, the conditions of its political ecology are the same.[95]

Manufacturing CDs, even though they are digital media, is not categorically different from manufacturing LPs. Essentially, both processes involve squishing a molten glob of plastic so that it contains playback information. But there are some key differences. For example, whereas LPs are typically compression-molded, CDs are injection-molded (then metallized, lacquered, and silkscreened). And whereas the acoustic information on an

LP is inscribed in analogous grooves that are ridden by needles, CDs use digital optical pits that are read by lasers. Additionally, CDs are made from polycarbonate, not polyvinyl chloride. Nevertheless, polycarbonate plastic, like PVC, is hydrocarbon based. This means that CDs still require petroleum in their manufacture (propylene, though, instead of ethylene). But polycarbonate is less toxic than PVC and CDs also use less plastic per unit than LPs: a CD itself weighs 15 grams, while an LP is typically about 100 grams. As CD mass production stabilized through the 1980s, the smaller amount of raw material had lowered the per-disc manufacturing cost by as much as 75 percent compared to LPs—economic savings that, controversially, were not passed on to consumers.[96]

In 1996, when CD sales peaked at 2 billion units worldwide, the record industry devoured 170 million kilograms of polycarbonate and polystyrene plastics.[97] The "production impact" of this activity was such that 2 billion kilograms of carbon dioxide equivalents were released into the atmosphere—more than the total emissions of some small countries.[98] Other factors add to the overall bulk. Although overproduction is the norm in CD duplication, one of the most egregious examples is Robbie Williams's failed 2006 album *Rudebox*, the unsold copies of which were sent to China to be crushed and used as road surfacing.[99] And then there is illegitimate CD recording and pressing. To take just one example of this practice, during one bootlegging raid in Manila, authorities confiscated 50,000 kilograms of polycarbonate.[100] Still, these figures represent small fractions of the approximately 30 billion tons of global greenhouse gases released and 250 billion kilograms of plastics consumed per year in the mid 1990s.[101] Nevertheless, this is a stark confirmation of how the rise of the CD further solidified the relationship between the recording industry and petrocapitalism. And it highlights some distinctly musical markers of what some scholars call the Anthropocene.[102]

If record pressing plants in the shellac and vinyl eras were sites of heavy industry, CD production more closely resembled the ultraclean and airtight laboratories of science fiction.[103] The temperature is kept steady at comfortable 22 degrees Celsius, and the relative humidity a constant 55 percent. A breeze rolls along at 0.75 meters per second, ensuring that dust and dry skin and hair are kept away from the discs. The air may be clean, containing particles no larger than 0.3 microns, but it is filled with sound: hazmat-suited feet shuffle on polished floors; HEPA filtration systems purr; hardworking robots hiss and clank in almost musical time.[104] In a 1987 publicity stunt, the Virgin Megastore in London "pulled back some screening from the bottom end of the CD shop basement to reveal a fully-fledged CD factory." Long-time audio journalist Barry Fox described the scene:

> Though a glass wall into the clean room area, CD shoppers can watch what was claimed to be the first "monoline" in the world. A Nestal press produces discs from Bayer polycarbonate, at a rate of around one every 10 seconds. A robot arm picks the discs from the press mould and loads them on to a carousel.
>
> From there they are pulled up through a bulkhead into a Denton Vacuum vacuum chamber. Inside the chamber the clear discs are sputtered with aluminium; a high voltage strips metal atoms from a block of aluminium and deposits it on the discs.
>
> The metallised discs—now looking silver—fall gently back down onto the carousel. This transfers them to a short conveyor belt moving past a lacquering nozzle. The disc then spins to spread the lacquer evenly while the conveyor moves the wet disc under an ultraviolet curing lamp.
>
> At the last stage of the monoline an inked silicone rubber pad prints a two colour label.[105]

The idea here, Fox explains, was to "put raw polycarbonate plastic in one end and lift spiked piles of finished discs from the other." But the process was neither simple nor reliable, as Fox discovered on follow-up visits to the Megastore: "On two occasions the line was stationary, with worried-looking Virgin staff poking it with screwdrivers. Other times the line was running, but like something out of a Jacques Tati movie, the robot handling arm was flinging them out of the press and onto the floor. There they piled up as a sea of unusable rejects."[106]

By volume, CD packaging is more of an environmental concern than the discs themselves. Compact disc packaging has long been an issue. In fact, one of music's earliest concerted environmentalist efforts revolved around a form of holdover packaging called the longbox. The longbox was a 12-inch tall paperboard package that was used through the 1980s. It enabled CDs to fit into existing sales racks, which were made to house LPs. The anti-longbox campaign was taken up by musicians ranging from Raffi to Peter Gabriel, who called the longbox "a ridiculous waste of resources," and the longbox was abandoned by the industry in the early 1990s.[107] Whereas the longbox controversy revolved around paper, enduring questions surround plastic.

Unlike the polycarbonate disc, the CD case is made from polystyrene. Polystyrene is another petrochemical product, derived not from ethylene or propylene but benzene. The polystyrene case makes up about half the weight of the total CD package and, along with the polycarbonate disc, necessitated a close relationship between recording interests such as the International Federation of the Phonographic Industry and corporations such as Bayer, Dow Plastics, GE, and various other international polymer suppliers.[108] Cassette cases are also made of polystyrene. Even early on in the commercial history of music on tape, in 1969 the

US industry used nearly 30 million kilograms of plastic to produce only the casings of audio recordings and music cassettes.[109] In the case of all these formats, shortages of petroleum led to price hikes, the dynamics of which were closely monitored in the trade press.[110]

The oil crisis of 1973 brings these issues into focus. When the Organization of Arab Petroleum Exporting Countries (OAPEC) blocked its exports as a response to US action in the Yom Kippur War, global petroleum prices increased dramatically. The plastic-dependent (and therefore petroleum-dependent) recording industry felt the pinch almost immediately, prompting *Billboard* to run headlines such as "Industry Tackles Plastics Shortage" and leading *Melody Maker* to declare a state of emergency on its cover: "Rock Crisis! Plastic, Paper, and Petrol Famine Shakes the Whole Music Scene"—"No records, no vinyl, no petrol, no nuthin'."[111] The problem was double-headed: booming sales compounded by shortages of raw materials induced by the OAPEC embargoes. As one spokesperson for Imperial Chemical Industries, one of the largest PVC suppliers in the UK at the time (along with British Petroleum), told *Melody Maker*:

> The situation has been building up for a year or so. The trouble is that there's not enough plant [sic] to ease the pressure of demand. It's a world crisis—plastics as a whole have gone through the roof as far as sales are concerned. But coupled with that, of course, there's the increasing shortage of raw materials. This has come to a head with the Arab–Israeli war and the oil cut-back, but I'm afraid it looks as though it's going to be with us for another year or two—at the very least.[112]

In fact, questions and problems associated with raw materials never truly subsided. They reverberated through the decade and beyond, continuing to affect LP production as well as cassettes and CDs.

Mirroring the wartime destabilizations of shellac, the oil crisis caused fluctuations in the price and composition of vinyl records that lasted into the 1980s.[113] Indeed, while worldwide vinyl sales grew consistently through the 1970s, UK figures show "the amount of raw PVC delivered to record companies has remained fairly steady since 1973."[114] Whereas the British Phonographic Industry took this as "an indication that companies are now able to produce lighter discs due to refinements and improvements in production techniques," US industry insiders admitted certain difficulties: "In an age where the price of petro-chemicals is a political football that changes with the whims of the various OPEC nations, it has grown tougher and tougher to produce vinyl at a reasonable price and quality."[115] *Billboard* and *Modern Plastics* reported often at this time about oil prices rising this or that percent, and PVC pellets rising so many cents per kilogram. Under these conditions, many manufacturers were forced to use greater amounts of a product called extender, "a substance that stretches the quantity of PVC, just as those new soya substances increase the quantity of your hamburger."[116] Richard Osborne notes that the resultant records met with "consistent outcries from consumers and an increase in returned faulty goods."[117]

Around 1980, when the discussion of poor quality LPs was reaching a boiling point, various tape products were also "Rocked by Higher Oil Costs."[118] Similar problems continued into the 1990s, affecting the cost and availability of magnetic tape, cartridges, and packaging materials.[119] CDs were also affected. In the words of one *Billboard* title, "Polycarbonate Supply Barely Meets Demand as Manufacturers Explore Options."[120] As with earlier LP production difficulties, CD manufacturers were faced with an increase in demand for finished products (based partly on the unexpected success of Elton John's "Candle in the Wind" in 1997) combined with a lack of Bisphenol-A, a chemical essential to the production of polycarbonate. Changes in the feedstock and raw material industries necessitated close connections between the recording industry and corporations such as Bayer, Dow, GE, and Teijin Chemicals. Fluctuations in the oil market, and the production capabilities of plastics suppliers, as well as their experiments with potential replacement materials (e.g. polycyclohexylethylene), thus directly affected the recording industry, and as such were tracked with interest in both the music and plastics trade papers.[121] Whatever else it may have been between 1950 and 2000, and whatever changing formats it may have introduced, the recording industry was fundamentally and consistently a petrochemical industry.

Disposability and Dispossession

Plastics perish. In addition to the challenges and hazards of producing polymer compounds, and in addition to the social inequalities and environmental infractions of record pressing facilities, plastic recordings that reach consumers eventually wear out, or they become individually unwanted, culturally unfashionable, or technologically obsolete. Disposal and dispossession are the versos of newness and desire, which are the driving forces of record production and possession. The ends of plastic lead to additional questions about the political ecology of recording.

Nowhere is the recording industry's passage to the plastic age better illustrated than in a story told by the comedian Barry Humphries, also known as Dame Edna Everage. In the mid-1950s, Humphries took a job at EMI in Melbourne. After apprenticeships in "push[ing] boxes of records around the warehouse" and "wandering amongst the aisles of steel shelving," Humphries got his first big break:

> I got a job working for a very famous gramophone company, and this was at the time when 78 records were becoming obsolete, and LPs and microgroove records were coming into fashion, and I had the job of sitting in a small room smashing 78s.... I was given piles of 78s: Sibelius, Mahler, Arnold Bax, Conrad Veidt.... Everything I had to smash and throw away.[122]

There Humphries sat, in the basement of EMI, taking a hammer to the company's stock of discontinued shellac 78s—shattering it, disc by disc, making way for microgrooves. What a waste. Surely these recordings should have been sold off to collectors, donated to museums and archives or, as Humphries himself protested, given "to hospitals, to old people's homes." But they weren't. Part of this has to do with copyright legislation: catalog deletions cannot legally be sold or given away. But it also says something about the temporal logic of the recorded music commodity.

This actually takes us back to the beginning of sound reproduction, where the new technological possibility offered remarkably strange temporal possibilities. "If there was a defining figure in early accounts of sound recording," says Jonathan Sterne, "it was the possibility of preserving the voice beyond the death of the speaker."[123] But the possibility of preservation actually gave rise to a tension between permanence and ephemerality—a "preservation paradox" that has "been a fundamental condition of recording throughout its history."[124] In the words of Daniel LeMahieu, writing about the rise of the gramophone in Britain, "Recorded sound transcended time, and yet in another sense, this modern, technological form of permanence contributed to the transience of music."[125] He explains:

> Until Edison made his discovery in 1877, no sound survived the moment of its passing. The gramophone allowed music to transcend the boundaries of time, thereby offering the performer a new promise of immortality.... This hope for immortality on shellac often became lost, however, in the continual and often extraordinarily rapid turnover of records.... Popular records became almost as transitory in the market-place as the ephemeral sound which they preserved.... Within a few generations, records produced by the thousands and millions became rare items. Many were lost altogether. The promise of immortality ... was often broken by the realities of commerce.[126]

These temporal dialectics gave rise to a "collecting impulse" that has defined sound recording from the beginning.[127] Interestingly, as LeMahieu notes, this impulse became especially pronounced with the rise of electrical recording and the standardization of the 78:

> The eclipse of acoustical recording ... accelerated the trend whereby old records were traded in, destroyed, or forgotten in favor of more current performances. By the late 1920s, the much-heralded claim that the gramophone immortalized the talents of long-dead singers and musicians fell into doubt; the records of many opera singers from the earliest days of the gramophone became distressingly rare.[128]

One response to that distress came in the form of a new column in *The Gramophone*: "Collector's Corner," which "during the 1930s defined the art of collecting historic recordings." What's more, this *Gramophone* column emerged alongside related commentary in venues such as *Melody Maker* and *Down Beat*, as well as a new literature in collector guides and discographies. It was also around this time that US libraries started seriously collecting sound recordings.[129] Such commentaries and practices existed in relation to classical and popular repertoires (especially jazz) and the practice of collecting was guided not only by the rationale of cultural preservation but also completism, discrimination, and distinction.[130]

Shellac records were thus collectible from early on. People felt attached to them, in terms of both the anxieties of heritage and the pleasures of fandom.[131] Yet most of the artifacts of the 78 era have disappeared.[132] Part of this has to do with the infamous fragility of shellac discs: the durability of their aggregation as a symbolic format paralleled the durability of their aggregation as a material form. But delicacy alone cannot explain why, apart from a minority population of antiquarians, 78s have been so readily trashed, so easily lost, and so quickly forgotten.[133]

An important aspect of that explanation stems from changing forms of care for the self that had been emerging since the 1920s. This was a conjuncture in which new ideologies of cleanliness and new expectations of convenience shaped a new "ethos of disposability: chewing gum, cigarette butts, razor blades, and paper products."[134] As cultural commodities, recordings are of course subject to different cultural logics than throwaway packaging and disposable razors (even if certain types of popular music have been scoffed at for their resemblance to bubblegum). Still, the apparent appetite for the supersession of shellac by plastic must be seen, not only as part of the preservation paradox that marks all recording, but as part of the particular culture of disposability and dispossession that developed in the twentieth century.[135]

Vinyl is also part of this moment, although the two formats have different afterlives. They do not meet the same ends, physically or symbolically. Whereas the cultural and economic value of obsolete shellac bottomed out and met with destruction, Will Straw shows that undesirable vinyl records tend to circulate almost endlessly in secondary economies where, even though their value is exhausted, they accumulate in "museums of failure" in which "their bulk nevertheless functions almost monumentally."[136] In other words, shellac 78s seem predisposed to be disposed of, while vinyl LPs seem prone to pile up.

One reason for this difference has to do with the way LPs that were articulated to the seriousness of adult culture and the contradictory anticommercialism of rock music. As Keir Keightley argues, "long play" refers not just to "the extended duration of musical playback" but also "the album's ongoing cultural and economic presence."[137] Indeed, in contrast to the ephemerality that characterized both its predecessor (the 78) and its contemporary (the 45), the LP possessed "heightened symbolic capital" and was "more and more perceived to occupy a cultural space similar to that of books."[138] This is what Keightley refers to as "the slower temporal logic of the LP." While shellac and vinyl were subject to broadly similar forms of attachment, the slower temporal logic and particular accumulative tendency of the LP stem not only from its physical durability or its individual attachments but from the meanings that accrued to it as a format. These micro- and macrorhythms shed light on the LP's recent revival, as well as and its longer-term (if belittled) survival.

The valorization of the LP represents a curious irony, given the wider cultural history of plastic, throughout which the material has been derided as a symbol of a cheap, artificial, throwaway society.[139] Yet it is not surprising when we consider the firmly entrenched and properly ideological anticommercialism of many musical worlds, especially rock music: "One of the great ironies of the second half of the twentieth century is that while rock has involved millions of people buying a mass-marketed, standardised commodity (CD, cassette, LP) … these purchases have produced intense feelings of freedom, rebellion, marginality, oppositionality, uniqueness and authenticity."[140] The fact that such intense feelings are produced by an industry that is not only defined by record contracts and the mass distribution of LPs as finished products, but also by infrastructures and political ecologies that are inseparable from petrocapitalism and by a commodity form (plastic) that has otherwise been subject to widespread material scrutiny—this only adds to the irony.[141]

Of course, some LPs do not survive. While the PVC in LPs is technically recyclable, it is generally not economically worthwhile to do so.[142] As such, when truly exhausted LPs finally die, they are either buried (where their decomposing bodies leach poisons in landfills) or cremated (where incineration frees their spirits in the form of greenhouse gases).[143] Given their temporal and accumulative logics, however, for the moment it seems that the social death of the LP will weigh more heavily on our shelves than the environment.[144]

Uniquely, compared to commercially released 78s and LPs and CDs, the cassette is re-recordable. While this characteristic has most often been thought of in terms of the political economy of piracy, or the romance and nostalgia of the mixtape, it is also possible to see re-recordability as a kind of inbuilt recyclability.[145] This invites consideration of the ongoing political ecology of tape.

While "tape lives on, infesting houses and cars," the decline of the cassette is also measurable and widely reported.[146] In this way, despite the current renaissance of cassette culture, and despite any continued relevance of magnetic tape that may come as corporations such as IBM search for ways to increase the density and durability of tape storage as an alternative to hard drives, the artifacts of the cassette era are deteriorating. In Paul Hegerty's words, "their primary exoskeleton preserv[es] slowly rotting insides."[147] Indeed: "Decay is a fundamental part of tape's existence, due to the presence of oxides that initially fixed the recording. But crucially," Hegerty continues, "the inside and outside do not necessarily die at the same pace."[148] Cassettes thus instantiate the topology of durability and transience that defines all cultural artifacts.[149] At the same time, their temporal logic instances a kind of reversal compared to 78s and LPs. Whereas the packaging of those earlier recordings was less durable than the materials they contained, the cassette's silent shell outlasts its sonic substance. The dynamics of remembering and forgetting that define the cassette—its preservation paradox—is a kind of material amnesia.

As CD sales plummet and CD collections are disowned, here too the question shifts from manufacturing to afterlife. Of the billions of compact discs produced since the 1980s, the CD Recycling Center of America estimates that thousands of kilograms of CDs become obsolete each month. One online marketplace guesses that over a million tons of CDs are "collecting dust in people's homes."[150] Indeed, according to a 2003 report on *The Environmental and Social Impacts of Digital Music*: "Most of the CDs sold to date have not as yet entered the waste stream."[151] But they will; they are. As this happens, despite the fact that CDs are technically recyclable, most will end up in incinerators and landfills—scenarios in which various toxins, including carcinogenic dioxins, will be released into the atmosphere and groundwater.

In the present moment, though, we witness an anomaly in the CD's logics of temporality and accumulation. The decline of shellac was marked by disappearance. The decline of vinyl was marked by particular modes of attachment and monumentality that lent it longevity—and which contribute to its so-called revival. By contrast, the decline of the CD is paradoxically "signaled in its very ubiquitousnes."[152] The CD seems to have reached a critical mass where its ubiquity threatens its implosion. In other words, if the 78 disappeared quickly across a kind of cultural-material event horizon, and if the LP has been subject to a kind of gravitational time dilation, it is possible to argue that the CD has gone supernova. The impending economic decay of all this plastic thus underlines the impossibility of its physical decay. And political ecology confronts the particular topologies of durability and transience that define all recordings formats as cultural artifacts, at the point where "the future meets the past in the dying body of the commodity."[153]

Conclusion

Such are the conditions and consequences of plastic music formats. As for the reasons that many fans are rediscovering or newly discovering what they perceive to be the specialness of LPs, cassettes, and CDs, I have said that the causes of revivalism are less important than the effects. The recording industry feels the same—albeit for different reasons.

While some smaller record companies may be recommitting to plastic formats for ideological reasons, the major labels are not pressing vinyl and duplicating cassettes because it makes them feel good. In returning to plastic, the recording industry is doing as it has always done: bending supply to the winds of demand. This way of thinking about industrialized musical culture can clash with the social criticism of Theodor Adorno—or at least the version of Adorno's account of mass culture that exists as a kind of dinner-table discourse or common sense. Adorno, and critics like him, thought that the mass media (or the culture industry) exerted a kind of social control over mass audiences. These critics worried that the capitalist culture industry force-fed its worldviews to the masses though standardized cultural products such as popular songs, simultaneously creating and satisfying the needs of these audiences (needs that, anyway, were fake).[154] Music thereby became a fetishized and standardized commodity, and the critical potential of listening was inherently corrupted and deliberately impeded as a result. Adorno's main concern was for the symbolic products of the culture industry, and the attendant ways that musical forms might contain within themselves the jumper cables to boost the masses into critical awareness and resistance to the powers that be. There are numerous existing criticisms of Adorno's philosophy of music. From the perspective of music's political ecology, though, the important thing to note is that Adorno's theses on the culture industry, musical commodity fetishism, and the supposed regression of listening paid little attention to how the recording industry actually works.[155]

Forty years ago, it was possible to see that the mass culture critics had things at least partly backward. The recording industry does not lead with supply; it follows demand.[156] Antoine Hennion makes a similarly pragmatic point about record producers, one that equally applies to record pressers: "They do not manipulate the public so much as feel its pulse.... [They] do not control the public's desires but rather fulfill them."[157] Although the raw materials of Hennion's anti-musicology are songs and singers, rather than the shellac and plastic and data that drive this book's musicology without music, the implications for the politics of the industry–consumer alliance are similar: "Power lies not in imposing a particular view... but in proposing one." In this sense, "social domination gives way to complicity": the complicity of the musical public that craves and consumes the commodities that the industry offers and produces; the complicity of the musician who releases an album on plastic because it suits her or his taste; the complicity of the band that endorses plastic formats because a recording company believes it fits their image.[158] Particular songs and singers and styles, no matter their meaning to a listener or audience, no matter their intrinsic features or influential statuses or political messages, are not very important from this perspective. As long as we prefer music on plastic, the record industry will continue to give it to us. And as long as the record industry keeps pressing vinyl and duplicating cassettes and manufacturing CDs, the political ecology of music is inseparable from the wider political ecology of petrocapitalism.

To return to LPs, cassettes, or CDs is to renew our vows to factories, to toxic waste, to the oil market, to wars, to human and environmental suffering. It is to reaffirm music's complicity in the politics that surround the production and perishing of plastic. If the solution to the problem of recorded music's political ecology is not found in shellac, it certainly is not located in plastic. It might seem like digitalization is the answer. With the shift to music downloading around the year 2000, and to music streaming after 2010, it might seem that recording companies, musicians, and fans were finally freed from their reliance on unpredictable materials markets, environmentally taxing production processes, exploitative labor practices, and wasteful consumption habits. They weren't.

3 Data (2000–Now)

Online culture seems so completely virtual. Reading the news in the form of bytes and lights, for example, appears self-evidently less material than reading something made of ink and paper. Gaming online seems obviously more efficient than using specialized consoles and individual cartridges or discs. Likewise, common sense suggests that downloading or streaming a digital audio file represents a definite reduction in the material magnitude and energy intensity of music listening, compared to the more obviously physical recording formats that have been made and destroyed by the billion since 1900.[1] Booting up Spotify feels so easy and insubstantial. In order to hear music on shellac or plastic, by contrast, workers from all over the world first have to harvest various raw materials including bugs, rocks, oil, and other substances. Such materials must then converge in a factory of some sort, where large amounts of energy are channeled into heat and pressure to transform lumps of goop into listenable goods. These goods must then be packaged and distributed by trucks, trains, ships, and planes. Only then can recordings arrive on the shelves at local shops—or, in the case of mail order, at your doorstep. This seems a far cry from clicking a mouse. On the surface, then, the digitalization of music looks very much like the dematerialization of music.

Many journalists buy into this equation of digitalization with dematerialization. Take, for example, the writer and broadcaster Michael Smith. For Smith, the 2012 release of Beck's conspicuously old-fashioned *Song Reader*, a book of sheet music, prompted a spirited reflection on the fate of music in the digital age. Smith appreciates the *Song Reader* because he sees it as a statement against the "digital deluge" that "fundamentally questions how we experience and consume music" and which calls for a return to "the old ways."[2] He gets these ideas partly from Beck himself, whose motivations for releasing the *Song Reader* stemmed from a feeling that making music "with your own hands" is an art that has been lost to recording.[3] Actually, though, Smith is less interested in returning to sheet music than waxing nostalgic about the waning of vinyl. "I used to love me records," he says: "the cover art, the way they crackled from overplaying, their weight—the sheer physicality. But I have to admit: I haven't bought an album, let alone an actual record, in years. Now I listen to all my music on the internet." He sees his own experience as part of a broader historical trajectory:

> The story of music in my lifetime has been a trajectory wherefrom the precious totemic object [the LP] to a dematerialized data stream—an online cul-de-sac where the vast body of recorded music is a lukewarm corpse to be picked over at the click of a mouse, rented from somewhere up there in the cloud for a tenner a month.[4]

Smith argues lovingly that LPs "condensed and stored [music's] spirit," whereas "online consumption has dissolved and devalued everything." He believes digital listeners are "negligent, abusive listeners" and that "the art of the album is wilting as a result."

There are numerous aspects of Smith's nostalgic plea that warrant criticism. For example, he implies that digital music is music stripped of its aura and somehow, therefore, colder and deader than earlier recording formats. This is a familiar stance, and a problematic one. It is problematic because Smith misses the fact that similar critiques go back to the dawn of mechanical sound reproduction: historically speaking, the LP is less precious than he realizes.[5] He also misses the subtlety and ambiguity with which such questions have been treated elsewhere: conceptually speaking, the loss of aura and the politics of distraction are more multifaceted than he allows.[6] Indeed, this whole chapter could be devoted to unpicking the "dubious metaphysics" of Smith's grievance.[7] But such critiques are established. In terms of political ecology, Smith makes one slip that is particularly noteworthy.

In revering "the precious totemic object," Smith picks up an LP. In mourning music's transition to "a dematerialized data stream," he picks up a smartphone and points to the sky—to "somewhere up there in the cloud." But Smith is misinformed. Smartphones are nothing if not material devices. Ditto the global telecommunications network that is necessary to stream data from "the cloud." The so-called cloud is a definitely material and mainly hardwired network of fiber-optic cables, servers, routers, and the like. Even the aspects of digital music streaming that seem most immaterial—including digital files themselves as well as the electromagnetic waves that travel to personal listening devices from local wireless routers, cell phone towers, or satellite dishes—are in fact only invisible.[8] Digital music streaming is undeniably material, and it requires both a lot of energy and a lot of labor. To think otherwise is to be fooled by the commercial rhetoric of streaming and cloud computing, to underestimate the material infrastructure and energy usage of data processing, and to misunderstand their consequences.[9]

Scholars, too, can slide into uncritical assumptions about digital dematerialization. Here is Timothy Taylor:

> Most people today acquire or rent their music via various digital delivery systems, whether iTunes or Spotify or Pandora or others, removing music as a tactile object from their lives. Physicality and tactility—the sound of the cellophane, the smell of the cardboard liner, the feel of the disc, whether digital or analog—are gone.[10]

Although Taylor's point here is in the service of a larger and more sophisticated argument about how musicians earn a living in an age of digitalization and information capitalism, and while it is true that certain aspects of recorded music have become less tangible with the rise of digital files and online listening, physicality and tactility are not "gone."[11] This is not just the case with regard to the resolute materiality of digital listening's accessory technologies and delivery infrastructures. And it is not only a matter of a nostalgic uptick in the sales of supposedly more physical formats in the digital age, as in the so-called vinyl revival or cassette renaissance. What about the gratifying click-click-click of a spinning iPod wheel, or the satisfying swipe of a smartphone screen? What about the anticipation of tapping a new band name into a search engine, or the strangely appealing scent of new electronics products?[12] The phenomenology of listening in the digital age has always been tactile, material, objectified. Notwithstanding Taylor's broader argument, then, his equation of digitalization and dematerialization echoes that of Smith. Together, these examples show just how easy it is to fall into the rhetorical traps of thinking about the digital in terms of the immaterial, in both journalistic and scholarly discourse.

Emerging research, in cultural studies as much as industrial ecology, confirms that online consumption is not only resolutely material but also significantly dependent on various forms of energy, resources, and laborers. Indeed, in highlighting parallel instances of these factors in relation to other forms of online consumption—reading, gaming, viewing—it becomes apparent that no form of digital consumption can be thought of as immaterial. Large data-processing centers, for example, can use tremendous amounts of electricity, raising what Sean Cubitt and his coauthors refer to as an "emerging energy crisis of information."[13] The massive throughput of consumer electronics and worldwide fiber-optic cable networks, which necessarily undergird online cultural consumption, raise their own environmental questions in the forms of resources, labor, electricity, and e-waste. An emerging movement in environmental media studies is beginning to address such issues, including materials extraction and processing, energy usage, data storage and transmission, device assembly, and obsolescence and waste, especially in digitally mediated commodity culture. This work has sparked a research program that complements traditional notions of critical media literacy, content analysis, and the political economy of labor, by placing an equal emphasis on the material substrates, resource networks, and forms of energy—which is to say the staple commodities and supporting casts—that undergird those cultural realms. Music is complicit in all these issues. But the details and the extent of its complicity are largely unknown.

Despite the fact that the entire history of recorded music has been defined by material limitations, resource scarcity, and energy consumption, these issues have not figured prominently in everyday fandom and listening. Nor do they figure into the consciousness of streaming companies, which in their very name connote a naturalized and effortless fluidity that submerges the real work of the digital. These lacks of attention, awareness, and accountability seem set to continue at a time when the idea of storing a few thousand songs on an iPod has become quaint, in an era when streaming services offer seemingly effortless access to multimillion-song libraries and listeners expect, without a second thought, "all the memory in the world, all the music in the world."[14] Actually, though, and as the Jevons effect predicts, the miniaturization of music formats and their increased energy efficiency are offset by massifications of devices and listening. By using greenhouse gas equivalents as a baseline to compare the energy intensity of music streaming today with that of earlier formats, it becomes apparent that the environmental cost of music is now greater than at any time during recorded music's previous eras. And then there is the human cost of digital labor—which, although subject to the same myths of immateriality that circulate around digital artifacts, is material every step of the way.

In examining the human and environmental conditions of the contemporary digital world, we can also set our sights toward the future with a view that is anchored in lessons from the past. One key past lesson emerges from an epochal shift in the mediatic conditions of music that occurred around 1900. Given the move from musical notation to recording technology as the predominant means of storing and circulating compositional ideas and playback information, it is possible to suggest that this new recording-oriented media morphology paralleled a new social morphology of listening: listeners became consumers; they became attached to music in new ways. Later, with the mass acceptance of digital means of production, musicians also became consumers. And with the rise of online networks, the lines between musical production and musical consumption have become even blurrier—perhaps meaningless.[15] While observers like Smith and Beck may think of these changes in terms of nostalgia and loss, such developments are better understood as having furnished additional ways of making music, of loving music, and of defining ourselves through music.

In the twenty-first century, a new social morphology of listening has arguably emerged alongside a new digital media morphology.[16] Yet these morphologies are defined less by absolute ruptures than by overlaps and intersections. They are marked less by logics of subtraction and erasure than by logics of addition and recursion. The digitalization of music does not remove all traces of previous musical practices or media systems. It absorbs them, reconfigures them, magnifies them, and is dependent upon them. And if media morphologies provide not only "distinctive protocol[s] of listening" but also "the contours in which cultural expression is contained and shaped," then perhaps part of the promise of our contemporary situation is that these developments will signal the emergence of another new form of self-conscious attachment to music—a form of attachment in which an awareness of material intensity, energy consumption, human labor, and political ecology may become an integral part of what it means to be a music fan.[17]

Digital Media and Contemporary Music Formats

Looking broadly at other digital media serves to underline the political ecology of online consumption, challenging any simplistic correlation of digitalization and dematerialization. The material dimensions and pollution factors of the online world—what industrial ecologists call the energy intensity of the internet—are controversial and almost incalculable metrics.[18]

Nevertheless, researchers and environmental agencies are doing their best. In terms of reading publics, for example, studies have shown that printed magazines are not automatically more materially intensive than electronic editions. The actual amounts of resources used and pollution generated depend on the size of the readership and the status of the publication (whether it is emerging or established), on image resolution and file sizes, on tablet use habits, and other factors.[19] From an environmental perspective, then, reading a magazine online can be better than print in some cases, and worse in others. The question of purchasing physical DVDs versus streaming movies online raises similar questions. Certain studies even estimate "that a smartphone streaming an hour of video on a weekly basis uses more power annually than a new refrigerator."[20]

With regard to video games, industrial ecologists have similarly questioned whether the carbon footprint of online gaming is actually lower than console systems. Contrary to what the rhetoric of digital dematerialization tells us, some researchers find that downloading games can be more materially intensive than producing and distributing Blu-ray discs.[21] They also register the difficulty of obtaining accurate information on internet energy usage, however, and they note that the most significant factor is often consumer behavior: how much users play, whether they download games directly or use a background download feature, how they travel to stores to purchase discs. The energy intensity and pollution quotients of online culture thus depend significantly on user practices. Yet the authors of the video game study end with a shrug: "The results of this study are unlikely to change or influence consumer behaviors; the carbon emissions of production and distribution are not known to be factors consumers consider when buying electronic goods or electronic media."[22] The challenge, then, is to change this perception.

When it comes to recorded music, there is some truth to the equation of digitalization and dematerialization. While digital audio files are not immaterial (the scale of their materiality is invisible), such files do have less "physical presence" than earlier formats.[23] As Jeremy Morris puts it: "Album art, jewel cases, and other packaging remnants have morphed into metadata, tags, software interfaces, and other less tactile forms."[24] For this reason, some environmental reports claim that downloading can reduce the material intensity of recorded music by as much as 80 percent, compared to CD-oriented physical retail and e-commerce scenarios.[25] But this research brackets two central material components of listening to music as data: delivery infrastructure and accessory hardware.

In terms of delivery infrastructure, downloading digital files may indeed use fewer resources (no shellac or plastics) and generate less pollution (no physical shipping or driving to the shop) than other formats—but only in specific circumstances. Most studies advancing arguments about the reduction of material intensity in online scenarios assume that listening to music as a digital file is a matter of downloading an album or song once (from iTunes, say) and accessing it forevermore on a local hard drive. This form of listening, however, exists alongside (and increasingly in the shadow of) streaming and subscription services as well as the extremely high traffic in musical audio tracks and video clips on YouTube.[26] While such media channels place even more power in the hands of major labels and technology companies, allowing them greater control over how music is presented and commodifying "every instance of music playback" not only through subscriptions but also surveillance and data mining, the political economy of this model of unending cultural consumption is also a political ecology of unending energy consumption.[27] Although the material intensity of this delivery infrastructure is distant and distributed, it is nevertheless substantial.[28] It is necessary here to call attention to the "aggregate material effects of discrete acts"—such as music downloading and streaming—"that seem, to the online user, utterly virtual."[29] In looking at those aggregate material effects, a different picture emerges. A single server farm, for example, can consume thousands of megawatts of electricity (enough to power millions of homes). It is for these reasons crucial to counter the "big white fluffy" connotations of cloud computing by stressing "the cold hard physicality of warehouses, servers, generators and climate control devices."[30] Such an understanding not only provides grounds for a critique of the commodity status of digital music. It also asserts the material intensity of digital music's political ecology.

The question of how to access this network, this infrastructure, opens up another corrective to notions of digital dematerialization. Hard drives, routers, laptops, data sticks, personal listening devices, smartphones, headphones—these devices are resolutely material and, in various configurations, absolutely essential to digital music listening. The amount of such accessory technologies is not only massive—it is growing.[31] Other researchers therefore suggest that any dematerialization wrought by digital music delivery systems is offset by a larger overall throughput of digital devices.[32] What is more, these accessory technologies point to a world in which digital labor is not only postindustrial and problematically "immaterial" (e.g., the "social factory" that produces content for web 2.0) but also still firmly industrial and brutally material (e.g., the industrial sites where the components of digital hardware are extracted from the earth and assembled). As Trebor Scholz notes: "Conversations about digital labor should start with conversations about the all but 'immaterial' practices all along its global supply chains."[33] Yet it is more common, as in Smith's discussion of Beck, to tune out the hardware and speculate on the supposedly supernatural qualities of the data.

Anxieties about the material status of music have "wound their way through the long history of philosophical aesthetics."[34] But such anxieties take on a distinctive shape in relation to sound reproduction, and they possess a distinctive urgency in relation to the popularization of digital audio files. The ostensibly disembodied character of file formats such as MP3 gives rise to some particular ways of thinking about digital permanence and ephemerality. Here, for example, is André Millard:

> Recordings once had a permanence that price, rarity, and beauty gave them, but nowadays they are invisible digital files winging their way through cyberspace—easily duplicated and just as easily thrown away. Digital recordings ... are disposable in a way that expensive discs of vinyl or shellac could never be. Once consumed they do not even have to be thrown away: a press of a button and they are erased or dumped into the computer's invisible wastebasket.[35]

Journalist Llewellyn Hinkes provides a snappier summary of this discourse in his article "The Transient, Digital Fetish": "Old formats ooze historical significance," he says; "new ones are deleted with a tap."[36]

With downloading and data streaming, there is indeed a sense in which digital audio files sever the connection between economic and physical decay that defines earlier formats. For, regardless of the value of a song or album, its conditions of possibility pull in two directions at once. Availability seems assured in the cloud network, on the one hand, and deletion is always threatened by the fussiness and impermanence of digital storage, on the other. In Elodie Roy's words, digitalization is at once "a way of prolonging the life of the tangible music object…a total, continuous archive" *as well as* "a space of loss, degradation and ultimate erasure."[37] Jonathan Sterne puts this in historical perspective: "If early recordings were destined to become lost recordings," he says, "digital recordings move in the same direction, but they do so more quickly and more fitfully."[38] Ultimately, then, the future of digital music will be governed by a logic of the trace. It will be "a future where most digital recordings will be lost, damaged, unplayable, or separated from their metadata, hopelessly swimming in a potentially infinite universe of meaning."[39]

Devices

Apart from any potentially unique aspects of the relations of disposability and durability that animate the social lives and social deaths of digital audio files themselves, and aside from the work of remembering and forgetting that defines digital music as a politics of the archive, the question of the digital music commodity's temporal logic is also in a sense transposed onto accessory hardware.[40] Of course, the recording industry has always been aligned with makers of accessory hardware, which is to say the consumer electronics industry.[41] Indeed, a comprehensive political ecology of recorded music would have to account for a broader history of playback technologies such as phonographs, radios, home stereos, and portable devices, as well as all their woods and wires, papers and plastics, tubes and transistors—technologies that have been largely bracketed in this book's history of the materialities of recording formats themselves. Of most concern here, though, is the sense in which digitalization intensifies the relationship between the recording and consumer electronics industries.

The circumstances of digital listening devices in contemporary musical culture can be seen as extensions of patterns described by Paul Théberge in relation to the arrival of digital instruments. Théberge notes both "the degree to which technological innovation in the [musical] field has become dependent upon ... technologies originating within the computer industry" and "a new temporal dimension" in purchasing habits: "the increasing pace of technical innovations within the microprocessor-based musical instrument industry since the 1980s suggests that an investment in high technology will likely become obsolete within one or two brief product cycles."[42] This is a form of industrial and hardware convergence that accompanies the content convergence discussed by analysts of contemporary media consumption.[43] And it goes beyond standalone and dedicated listening devices such as iPods, given the extent to which the global proliferation of gadgets such as smartphones and laptops has been bolstered by the ways that these devices function as partly (but significantly) musical devices.[44]

Music has been here before. In the early days of radio broadcasting, "manufacturers liked vacuum tubes because they ... burned out like flashlight bulbs and had to be replaced," which "encouraged repetitive consumption." As transistors replaced tubes in the 1950s, radios themselves became "disposable products because their circuit boards were too small to be repaired by hand." What is more, "the actual durability of the parts used in the radio could also be controlled with frightening accuracy by scientific product and materials testing." In these ways, music (via radio) was a key player in establishing the ideas of planned obsolescence and death-dating in the consumer electronics industry.[45]

Digital devices instance an even higher turnover rate than earlier ones. The accelerated temporal logic of contemporary electronics devices is rooted in an industrial–cultural conjuncture that demands constant software updates and insists on newness.[46] Repetitive consumption in relation to components and devices has thus given way to a pathology of unending consumption. Jack Linchuan Qiu emphasizes that these are "not ordinary goods. Rather, they are addictive substances … which the Old World craves in huge supply, to be shipped to the other side of the planet for consumption by people with lighter skin … without ever needing to know about the harsh reality of the factories, oceans away." Qiu focuses on the 1.4 million laborers that assemble these electronics in China's Foxconn factories:

> These millions of bodies—with massive labor power—gather in factories to produce coveted commodities. They face punishment if they disobey. If they cannot take it anymore and attempt "to go away"—a euphemism for suicide—they have to penetrate the physical barrier of a tall fence or "anti-jumping net" in order to free themselves from this hopeless world.[47]

Although Foxconn happens to be the manufacturing arm for some of today's most iconic digital brands (Apple, Google, Intel), it is only the most infamous example of a much larger problem. Qiu does not mince words in describing the global conditions of the contemporary information technology and consumer electronics sectors. He sees them as continuations of slavery and he calls for digital abolition. If the factory floors of record pressing facilities in the shellac and plastic eras were sites of social inequality and exploitative labor, digital electronics assembly in places such as China is truly chilling.

The trouble only increases in considering the sites where the materials assembled in electronics factories are first mined and processed. Again, the similarities here to the supply chains and human conditions of shellac and plastic are telling. Take an iPhone, for example. These stylish little streamers contain aluminum, arsenic, cobalt, copper, glass, gold, neodymium, nickel, silicon, silver, tin, and many other metals and minerals. Often, these materials come from areas stricken by conflict and are mined or processed in conditions that are unjust and unethical. Child labor is common, life expectancies are low, and pollution and waste are rampant. To make aluminum, for example, which is the majority metal in the iPhone because it constitutes the device's chassis, a rock called bauxite is strip-mined and then smelted at a ratio of four tons per ton of aluminum. The process consumes 3.5 percent of the world's power and releases greenhouse gases that are over 9,000 times more harmful than carbon dioxide. Cobalt, which is used mainly in the battery of the iPhone, is mined primarily in the Democratic Republic of the Congo by laborers (including children) who toil "around the clock with hand tools in small-scale pits" and who "rarely [wear] protective gear."[48] Brian Merchant puts this in perspective:

> To obtain the 100 or so grams of minerals found in a single iPhone, miners around the world have to dig, dynamite, chip and process their way through about 75 pounds of rock. On just about every continent, many of those miners are risking their lives to provide you with a device that lets you read this while you're waiting in line for the bathroom.[49]

For all this resource extraction and backbreaking work, even though digital commodities are not quite "made to be wasted" in the way that plastic water bottles are, in terms of both technology and fashion they are built to obsolesce—born to die.[50] Digital music thus contributes to another problem: electronic waste.

The Environmental Protection Agency estimates that hundreds of millions of new electronics products are sold in the United States every year, with tons and tons of similar devices either in storage or "ready for end-of-life management."[51] About 75 percent of those devices are disposed of, rather than recycled in some way. Quantitatively, music is only a small part of this much bigger problem.[52] But the very fact of its contribution emphasizes that digitalization does not dematerialize the production or consumption of music. Rather, it changes the scale and character of music's materiality. Analogously, digitalization neither extinguishes the emissions profile nor sublimates the scrap signature of the recording industry. It changes them in complex ways. Like earlier predictions about the paperless office, claims about the possibility of a weightless musical culture assume an untenable lightness of being.

Digital music's material intensity is additionally consequential in the postcolonial world. This is partly because the so-called Global South is seen "a reservoir of First World hand-me-downs and sleepy-eyed memories of its earlier consumer items," thus serving as a dumping ground for a substantial amount of the North's e-waste.[53] But it is also because the centrality of mobile listening technologies is equally and perhaps even more pronounced than it is in the North. This is partly due to the fact that, in infrastructure-challenged parts of the world, internet penetration via underground and submarine networking cables lagged behind the availability of personal, mobile, wireless digital devices. In places such as Europe and the United

States, by contrast, hardwired and PC-based internet access was more quickly established as a norm. As such, many areas in the Global South are developing their own logics of possession and dispossession—and, thus, generating their own debris fields.

Consider for instance the ubiquity and significance of data sticks, memory cards, music download vendors, and mobile phone listening in India.[54] Such developments, which represent a marked change from the earlier cassette culture described by Peter Manuel, are attributed to the "increasing affordability of multimedia-enabled phones and voice/data plans and wider penetration of mobile coverage," and they mean that "the mobile phone has quickly become the most prevalent digital music device."[55] The rise of the mobile phone and digital music, which may be considered part of India's "media urbanism" and its "pirate modernity," is linked to an alarming rise in local e-waste generation.[56] Nevertheless, the influx of e-waste from other countries still represents a significant challenge. The memory of one northeastern Indian recycler highlights the role of music in a longer history of electronic waste and media culture: "At first, we dealt with record players, radios, VCRs and black-and-white TVs. Later on, CD and DVD players followed. Finally, computers arrived, and we started business with e-waste."[57] In these ways, the political ecology of music in India has transitioned, over the course of a century, from tree branches to data sticks. Shifting musical formats and listening practices are thus tied to shifting practices of dispossession and disposal. This is the often-hidden topology of making and unmaking, at simultaneously local and global levels, that a political ecology of recorded music seeks to understand.

Similar issues arise in other places. In Kenya, for example, where the local record industry "has been largely informal and undercapitalized since the multinational record companies pulled out of the country in the 1980s," the surge of a music-based subsector of the telecommunications industry has marked a new beginning.[58] Kenya's digital music listening practices and economies—as with those of India and increasingly numerous other African nations—take place primarily through mobile and handheld devices.[59] In addition to streaming and downloading, there have been significant markets in ringtones and ring-back tones, a service by which subscribers can customize the sound heard by callers as they wait for someone to answer. Regardless of the questionable long-term financial viability of such developments (due to licensing and piracy among other issues), the increasing centrality of personal electronics in the contemporary global listening formation makes it necessary to face the ways that m-commerce means e-waste.[60] To uncover such ties, to account for their mutual influences and consequences, even when they are obscured by the rhetoric of digital dematerialization, is a key challenge for any critique of music's political ecology at the outset of the twenty-first century.

Infrastructures

Although the recording industry continues to rely on the production and obsolescence cycles of the consumer electronics sector (thus sharing in their horrors), David Hesmondhalgh and Leslie Meier outline the ways that, since 1999, a new alliance between the recording industry and information technology (IT) companies has emerged. Conglomerates such as Amazon, Apple, and Google are now taking on central roles that resemble earlier corporations such as RCA. In their words: "There has been a move from a situation in which prevailing forms of consumption have been largely determined by interactions between companies in two sectors—the music industries and CE [consumer electronics]—to a more complex set of relations between companies in four sectors: music, IT, CE and telecoms, but with IT as now dominant."[61] Hesmondhalgh and Meier are mainly concerned with describing the "new ecology of musical consumption" afforded by the entry of these new players into the music market. Yet this new ecology of consumption is rooted in the political ecology of energy.

The amount of energy that it takes to stream a song is difficult to measure. One starting point is offered by Greenpeace's Click Clean Scorecard extension for the Google Chrome Web Browser. Click Clean is a basic but interesting tool that identifies the forms of energy that power a given website. It shows that Spotify and Pandora, to take two prominent examples of streaming services, have failed Greenpeace's tests of commitment to and use of renewable energy.[62] The energy required to store and process Spotify's data came primarily from nuclear, coal, and gas facilities (respectively: 29, 22, and 20 percent). Just 29 percent of the website's energy usage was what Greenpeace calls "clean." Pandora, meanwhile, was only 11 percent clean or renewable. The rest of its energy, like Spotify, came principally from dirty and nonrenewable sources (31 percent nuclear, 27 percent coal, 23 percent gas). The reason for these failing grades is due to the fact that Spotify and Pandora used the same database provider: Equinix.[63] To stream music is to burn uranium and other fuels.

But these are percentages and not absolute amounts. We can know that a cloud server requires "deadly 4,000V DC submarine cables, 96 tonnes of batteries, thousands of litres of diesel fuel, millions of miles of last-mile cabling" and an electricity bill that "comfortably reaches five figures" every month.[64] Yet database providers and streaming services are not forthcoming about their actual energy consumption, making it difficult to compare streaming with earlier formats. How does streaming compare, for example, to the fact that in a single year, 1946, one Columbia Records plant used nearly 12,000 tons of coal, over 8 million kilowatt-hours of electricity, and over 840 million liters of freshwater—enough to fill more than 330 Olympic swimming pools—to operate its presses?[65] How does the proliferation of digital listening devices today compare to the fact that manufacturing 13 million radio-phonographs in 1941 required 280 tons of nickel, 2,100 tons of aluminum, 10,500 tons of copper, and 70,000 tons of steel?[66] Is it possible to find concrete grounds of comparison?

Streaming services would prefer that we don't ask and that they don't tell. Spotify, for example, variously ignored and turned down my requests for interviews and tours of their facilities. Surely this had something to do with the usual corporate secrecy of the information technology sector—though it probably also had something to do with the fact that Spotify had recently been infiltrated and embarrassed by a team of Swedish researchers.[67] Other services were similarly cagey. One company, though, was willing to speak with me: Tidal.

Much has been written about Tidal—about its origins in another Norwegian streaming service, WiMP; about its high-profile sale to Jay Z and its star-studded but lackluster launch in the US market; about its higher sound quality and higher prices and higher artist royalties; about its legal troubles and, most recently, the allegations that the company has reported falsely inflated streaming figures (and therefore royalty payments) for Beyoncé's *Lemonade* and Kanye West's *Life of Pablo*.[68] None of that matters here. For the purposes of this story, Tidal offers a

Figure 3.1

Here is a six-ton lump of coal, which is displayed at the Lackawanna Coal Mine in Scranton, Pennsylvania. Although I have no reason to believe that Lackawanna produced coal for the recording industry, I include the photo here to give readers a sense of just how much coal the industry used. It is hard to even imagine the 2,000 similar sized pieces of coal that Columbia used in just one year—let alone the amount used by record presses around the world over the entirety of the shellac era.

case study of the technological and discursive infrastructures that are more or less representative of the streaming industry as a whole.

Tidal's headquarters in downtown Oslo is nothing special. It consists of a relatively large open-plan office with rows of desks and computers, walls covered in festival posters, and meeting rooms adorned with signed pictures of obscure Scandinavian musicians. The employees dress casually and many wear headphones. After a quick walk-through, I ended up in the canteen for mediocre machine-made coffee (I said no thanks to the foot-long sausages bathing in lukewarm water). My contact was most eager to discuss the ways that Tidal is distinct from its competitors. Spotify, he tells me, was built on "pirate DNA," meaning that Spotify grew out of the peer-to-peer (P2P) file-sharing model of earlier downloading sites such as Kazaa and Napster. Tidal, by contrast, began with a centralized server model and two basic ideas. First and foremost, the thinking in the pre-Tidal days of WiMP was that the company could reach a specific demographic and charge a bit more money if it offered a superior product—a higher-definition musical experience. Second, the technological time was right to offer such a service. Lossy file formats, such as the MP3s on which many sharing and downloading sites were built, were created for an earlier configuration of telecommunications infrastructure and internet bandwidth. These formats offered a listening experience that my contact compared to "chewing on white sugar." With the increased bandwidth, storage possibilities, and processing power of the internet and digital devices since the days of MP3, streaming providers were no longer beholden to lossy file formats.[69] With the basic ideas and infrastructures in place, WiMP needed content.

The story of how WiMP got its music is less cloak-and-dagger than the criminal entourage that smuggled prerelease CDs out of a Universal pressing plant and leaked millions of tracks to P2P networks. It is less controversial than the story of how Spotify, during its beta phase, allegedly accumulated its content by plundering MP3s from the Pirate Bay. And it is less mysterious than the members-only worlds of certain file-sharing communities.[70] Unadventurously, WiMP resourced its entire startup catalogue of about 20 million songs through official channels and in partnership with various record companies. Once terms were agreed, a company such as Universal would ship a pallet-load of hard drives to Oslo. The files were then transferred to servers at a more or less local data center. The process took between six and nine months—but it ensured that the Norwegian company had the file resolutions it needed to support its business model.

By the time WiMP had spawned Tidal, the infrastructure of streaming was changing. Many streaming services began closing their own data centers and relying on cloud servers for their data storage and processing needs. Netflix, for example, moved to the Amazon Web Services (AWS) cloud network in 2011. Spotify made a similar move in 2016, switching to Google's Cloud Platform. According to Nicholas Harteau, Spotify's vice president of engineering and infrastructure:

> Historically, [Spotify has] taken a traditional approach to [data]: buying or leasing data center space, server hardware and networking gear as close to our customers as possible.... This approach has allowed us to give you music instantly, wherever you are in the world. But in a business growing quickly in users, markets and features, keeping pace with scaling demands requires ever increasing amounts of focus and effort. Like good, lazy engineers, we occasionally asked ourselves: do we really need to do all this stuff?[71]

Like Netflix, Tidal also uses AWS. When a subscriber clicks "play" on a track by, say, one of those obscure Scandinavian musicians on the walls at Tidal, the file is transferred from an AWS server (wherever in the world that might be) to a local content delivery network (CDN)—which, if the listener is in Oslo, could be just outside the capital at a place such as Fornebu. The file will remain cached at the CDN for a set time, as transmitting files on more localized networks decreases the potential for lags and errors. Indeed, local caches tend to keep those tracks and albums most likely to be streamed in given regions. This lends a degree of cultural and geographic specificity to the apparently placeless internet.

If the story about Tidal's pallets of hard drives is a good reminder that all streaming media are on some level recorded media (and that even streamed recordings take up space), the realities of CDNs are a good reminder that all transmission media are on some level wired media (and that even light-speed transmissions take time). There are established questions here concerning the conceptual conundrums and cultural conditions that arise from the fact that media of transmission overcome space but cost time, while media of recording overcome time but cost space. From the perspective of political ecology, the point is that all media cost energy.[72]

The speed, efficiency, and reliability of Tidal's infrastructure are all impressive. My contact was obviously pleased to talk about its technological ins and outs. Yet he neither knew nor was concerned about the energy required to stream music. I jokingly asked him if he had ever seen an electricity bill from AWS, and of course he hadn't. When I asked him what he thought about the energy intensity of music streaming, his "gut response" was that "we got rid of plastic and a load of external hard drives" and that, therefore, from a material and energy perspective, we are better off in an online musical atmosphere. The rhetoric of dematerialization that influences how consumers think about digital culture is apparently also influential among those who work in music's IT sectors. One likely reason for this seems to be that when streaming companies subcontract their server and processing needs to companies like AWS, they also in a way subcontract their consciousness of the energy intensity of digital music's infrastructure. As my Tidal contact told me: "We live in the cloud—as long as we have an ozone layer, we live in the cloud." A recording engineer sarcastically told me that the *psychological* effect of millions of people streaming Rihanna was a graver concern than any possible environmental effect.

It is precisely this lack of awareness—and lack of foresight—that needs to change. For a long time, fishers did not consider the limits of the ocean. And around 1900, automobile manufacturers would have laughed at suggestions to consider oil reserves or smog. But here we are. Music is not the same kind of problem as ocean reserves or peak oil. We do not need to worry about it as much as food and biodiversity, cars, or energy writ large. But this is not a good argument for ignoring music's contribution to global environmental concerns or its relation to capitalism in the web of life. It is a difference in degree, not kind. Moreover, material and energy issues have always effected musical manufacturing and listening—albeit not usually in the minds of music consumers themselves. As one *High Fidelity* journalist noted in relation to the oil crisis of the 1970s:

> What man raised on western movies, with their vast herds of longhorns, could consider a beef shortage? What hot-rod enthusiast could imagine his amusement curtailed by a gasoline shortage? And what record collector, even as little as a year ago, knew that his latest

> treasured album ultimately had come from a hole in some wasteland of Arabian sand? We know now.[73]

Although this writer's insensitive language is regrettable, his point should nevertheless give us pause in the present moment.

A similar shock of awareness was expressed in the future tense in one recording engineer's summary remarks offered after the 1979 Audio Engineering Society meeting in Los Angeles, in the midst of another oil shortage:

> As expected, some pretty "far out" ideas were in the scenario for home entertainment in the year 2000, with the consensus being that the home will have a central "media room," where at the punch-up of a program in a personal computer you command an incredible diversity of audio-visual sources, all presented in wall-sized three-dimensional holographs and 360-degree "live" sound. It was sort of ironic that this vision of the "brave new world" was being proposed in the midst of a gasoline crisis, since the energy requirements for this kind of installation and, indeed, many of the materials of the media complex itself are dependent on petroleum. It is obvious that, 21 years from now, we had better be operating on fusion power and have developed alternative materials for our "media rooms" or they will forever remain a fantasy.[74]

This writer's predictions for home entertainment were not far off. Today, we can watch endless YouTube videos on enormous 3D flat-screen televisions in enveloping surround-sound systems. Except we are not running on fusion power and we are still largely unware of the material and energy intensity of listening to music as data. Even sound engineer Richie Moore's optimistic view of digitalization from 1979 is confounded by today's material realities. Writing about a "fiber optic boom," Moore described the digitalization of the recording studio as "a great asset to those of us who want to hear what pure sound is really like. From one of the earth's most abundant materials, sand, will come a system that will shed new light on the aural dimension.

In the near future the interfacing of the recording studio will resemble a web of glass."[75] Moore's vision of the recording studio has come to pass. As with oil, though, the world is also running out of sand.[76] These past predictions, whether pessimistic or optimistic, lead to contemporary questions. What if the emerging energy crisis of information associated with increasing online cultural consumption—which is the biggest factor behind the growth of online traffic and which amounts to at least 5 percent of global electricity consumption—adversely affects our access to online music collections?[77] It has happened before. It could happen again.

The Costs of Music

In order to make informed decisions and recommendations about the future of online modes of cultural consumption such as music, Greenpeace recommends, first of all, that customers and consumers need "energy transparency" on behalf of the industries. Sean Cubitt and his colleagues agree: "Sustainability will only be achieved once the larger population realizes that the internet is not weightless and information is not immaterial."[78] It is apparent that understanding and influencing consumer behavior—listening practices—is a significant part of the equation. But it is equally important to understand and critique the conduct of producers all the way through music's supply chains and waste streams, in ways that will lead them to act in genuinely responsible ways.[79] In these senses, music researchers have the opportunity to generate transformative knowledge about the cultural underpinnings of the changing global climate, to shed new light on the inseparable relationships between the media industries and environmental sustainability, as well as cultural research and environmental policy. First, though, we need something other than relative percentages of the types of energy used by streaming services. We need more absolute grounds of comparison.

People used to say that a single split-second Google search used the same amount of electricity needed to boil a kettle.[80] That's not right (Google claims the amount is ten times lower). But it does offer a concrete image that most internet users can relate to. In terms of streaming, current estimates indicate that downloading a gigabyte of data uses the same amount of energy that it takes to shine a domestic 60-watt lightbulb for an hour (i.e., 0.06 kilowatt-hours of electricity). That amount used to be higher and it will get lower in the future, given that "the electricity intensity of data transmission ... has decreased by half approximately every two years since 2000 (in developed countries)."[81] Still, the 0.06 kilowatt-hours figure is useful as an average. Although streaming an album uses only about one-tenth of a gigabyte of data, meaning that the energy required is negligible, what we require is a basis to understand the aggregate energy effects of billions of listeners streaming billions of albums—and to compare this with earlier formats.

One such basis would be the amounts of plastics used by the recording industry at different moments in its history. When we think about the industry in terms of the plastics that make up those recordings in the United States alone, an interesting picture emerges.[82] Looking at the years 1977, 1988, and 2000—the US sales peaks of the LP, cassette, and CD—we can see that despite various formats rising and falling in terms of total sales (and record sales generally increasing), when totaling the amounts of its main formats the amount of plastics used by the US record industry remains relatively constant over this period: 58 million kilograms at height of the LP, 56 million kilograms at

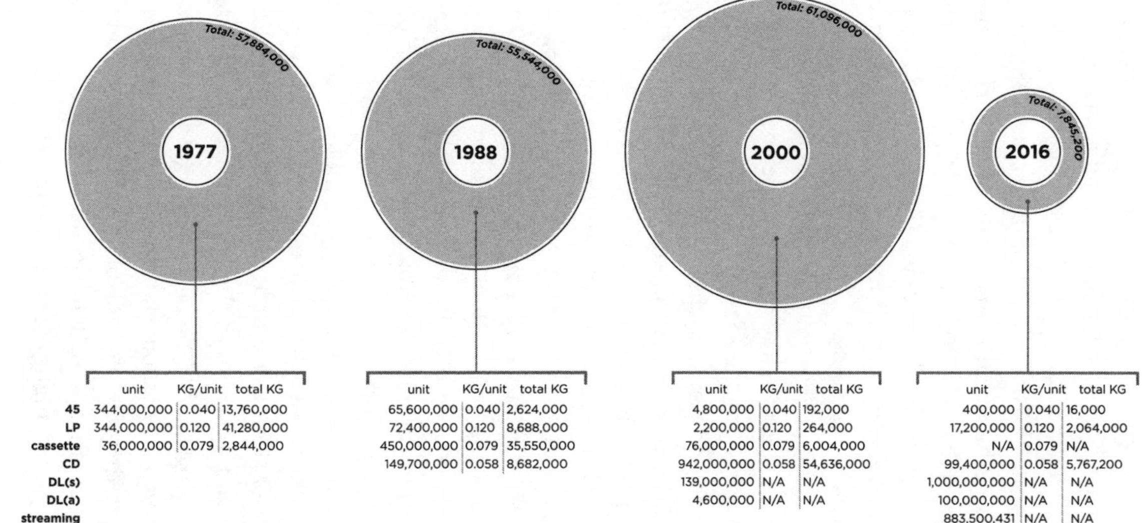

	1977 unit	1977 KG/unit	1977 total KG	1988 unit	1988 KG/unit	1988 total KG	2000 unit	2000 KG/unit	2000 total KG	2016 unit	2016 KG/unit	2016 total KG
45	344,000,000	0.040	13,760,000	65,600,000	0.040	2,624,000	4,800,000	0.040	192,000	400,000	0.040	16,000
LP	344,000,000	0.120	41,280,000	72,400,000	0.120	8,688,000	2,200,000	0.120	264,000	17,200,000	0.120	2,064,000
cassette	36,000,000	0.079	2,844,000	450,000,000	0.079	35,550,000	76,000,000	0.079	6,004,000	N/A	0.079	N/A
CD				149,700,000	0.058	8,682,000	942,000,000	0.058	54,636,000	99,400,000	0.058	5,767,200
DL(s)							139,000,000	N/A	N/A	1,000,000,000	N/A	N/A
DL(a)							4,600,000	N/A	N/A	100,000,000	N/A	N/A
streaming										883,500,431	N/A	N/A

Figure 3.2

Total kilograms of plastics across all major recording formats, 1977–2016. (Graphics designed by Martin Elden; graphics produced by Graeme O'Hara). Note that DL(s) refers to downloaded songs, while DL(a) refers to downloaded albums.

the height of the cassette, 61 million kilograms at the height of the CD. Then, when downloading and streaming take over, the amount of plastics used around 2016 drops dramatically—down to 8 million kilograms.[83] This seems to undo my main argument. It seems to confirm the equation of digitalization and dematerialization, to suggest that the rises of downloading and streaming are making music more environmentally friendly. But a very different picture takes shape when we think about the energy used to power online music listening.

Another way of comparing the amount of plastics used to make recordings like LPs, cassettes, and CDs with the energy intensity of storing and transmitting music as digital files is to convert both plastics production and electricity intensity into greenhouse gas emissions, also known as carbon dioxide equivalents—CO_2(e). From this perspective, and in a way that parallels the consumption of plastic by the recording industry, the greenhouse gas emissions of recorded music remain relatively constant over our core samples: 140 million kilograms of CO_2(e) in 1977, 136 million kilograms of CO_2(e) in 1988, 157 million kilograms of CO_2(e) in 2000.[84] Knowing that the amount of plastic decreases as downloading and streaming increase, and given the amount of dematerialization rhetoric that surrounds digitalization, common sense suggests that the amount of greenhouse gases would also drop around the year 2016. It doesn't. In considering the energy intensity of storing and transmitting digital files alongside other residual formats, even the most current and conservative estimates suggest that the amount of greenhouse gases increases—to over 200 million kilograms. A more pessimistic estimate suggests that the amount of carbon dioxide equivalents could be more than double in the age of streaming when compared to even the highest output during the plastic era.

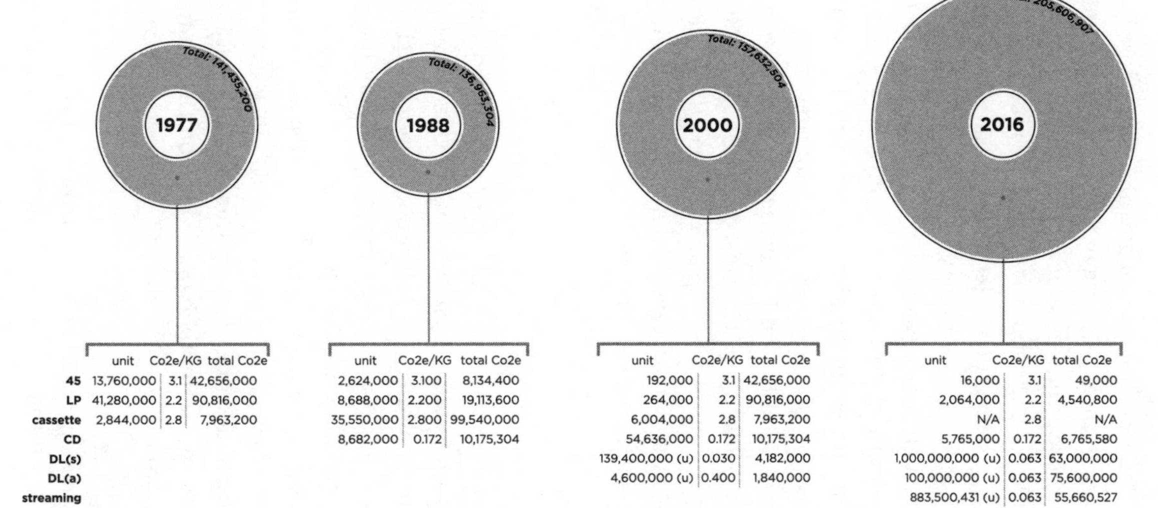

1977

	unit	Co2e/KG	total Co2e
45	13,760,000	3.1	42,656,000
LP	41,280,000	2.2	90,816,000
cassette	2,844,000	2.8	7,963,200
CD			
DL(s)			
DL(a)			
streaming			

1988

	unit	Co2e/KG	total Co2e
45	2,624,000	3.100	8,134,400
LP	8,688,000	2.200	19,113,600
cassette	35,550,000	2.800	99,540,000
CD	8,682,000	0.172	10,175,304
DL(s)			
DL(a)			
streaming			

2000

	unit	Co2e/KG	total Co2e
45	192,000	3.1	42,656,000
LP	264,000	2.2	90,816,000
cassette	6,004,000	2.8	7,963,200
CD	54,636,000	0.172	10,175,304
DL(s)	139,400,000 (u)	0.030	4,182,000
DL(a)	4,600,000 (u)	0.400	1,840,000
streaming			

2016

	unit	Co2e/KG	total Co2e
45	16,000	3.1	49,000
LP	2,064,000	2.2	4,540,800
cassette	N/A	2.8	N/A
CD	5,765,000	0.172	6,765,580
DL(s)	1,000,000,000 (u)	0.063	63,000,000
DL(a)	100,000,000 (u)	0.063	75,600,000
streaming	883,500,431 (u)	0.063	55,660,527

Figure 3.3

Estimated total greenhouse gas emissions across all major recording formats, 1977–2016. (Graphics designed by Martin Elden; graphics produced by Graeme O'Hara). Note that DL(s) refers to downloaded songs, while DL(a) refers to downloaded albums.

That's over 350 million kilograms of greenhouse gases released each year through musical listening in the United States alone.

These are of course estimates. In reality it is almost impossible to calculate, with accuracy and certainty, how much energy is used by the internet in general—let alone music streaming in particular. There are simply too many variables.[85] We know one thing for sure, though: storing and processing music online uses a tremendous amount of resources and energy.

Every so often, stories emerge that use inflation-adjusted figures to show that listeners today spend less of their disposable income on recorded music, and less money per record, than in the days of LPs and 78s.[86] This raises real questions about the cultural value of music. But if we are in an era where the economic cost of music is lower than in previous times, the environmental cost of music is higher than ever before.

Conclusion

What about the future of listening? It is now well known, thanks to a generation of research, that listening devices and listening practices—technologies and techniques—are coefficients.[87] Changes in one domain affect the other so integrally that it is meaningless to speak of one without the other. In fact, they are one domain—albeit a complex and recursive domain in which chickens are forever laying the eggs from which they hatch.[88]

Certain scholars describe this relationship—the idea that shifts in music's media morphology correspond to shifts in music's social morphology—in terms of "the modern discomorphosis of listening":

> The record, by making of it something to *listen to*, has created a new music. Before its existence, whether at home or at a concert, music

> was first something to *do* (including for its audiences), and most often to do together. From the availability of a repertoire to its facility of immediate acquisition and selection, from the importance of the physical position to that of the hi-fi system that goes from the body to the sound enveloping it, from free listening to unlimited repetition, there is now actually a "listening" function.[89]

Discomorphosis thus names the rise of the "listener-turned-consumer"—a "child born of the marriage of music and market"—that occurred as the proliferation of commercial sound recording supplemented the score-based musical culture that preceded it.[90] Recent scholars suggest that the rise of the internet, file sharing, digital audio formats, digital storage and playback devices, streaming services, and recommendation algorithms constitute a significant revision of media morphology that has precipitated a new social morphology of listening in the twenty-first century: digitamorphosis.[91]

This term, introduced by Fabien Granjon and Clément Combes, suggests that the present moment can be distinguished from the earlier morphologies in terms of "the dematerialization of contents as well as new conditions of ownership surrounding the networks of information and communication technologies," and by virtue of the fact that such conditions "are contributing to a more general access to cultural works, as well as to the wider diffusion and circulation of cultural content." Together, these shifts are "triggering a reorganization of the practices of music lovers."[92] Granjon and Combes argue that such a reorganization represents neither a straightforward technological shift nor an absolute rupture:

> Obviously, it is not possible to summarize the transformations engendered by digitalization in terms of a simple change of formats (e.g. the passage from disc to MP3). The observed changes come, not only from the explosion of the stabilized frameworks of discomorphosis, but also from an important multiplication of the modes of

> consumption related to the multiplicity of technological prostheses that are now mobilized.[93]

In this way, digitamorphosis is not necessarily marked by the senses of mourning, nostalgia, and rupture found in commentators such as Beck and Smith. Rather, digitamorphosis speaks to the proliferations and intersections and mutual dependencies of dominant, emergent, and residual media that we see in the contemporary format revivals (and indeed across all of recorded music's history).

Yet as an idea digitamorphosis should be approached with caution, and not just because it is an inelegant term. Many of the keywords used by Granjon and Combes—dematerialized content, new networks, easier access, wider diffusion—are caught in wider webs of rhetoric and metaphor that, though they are commonly used to describe musical culture in the age of online data, are problematic. These figures of speech are surface effects of the underlying media morphology more than a critical and epistemologically differentiated engagement with it. In contrast to their notion of dematerialization, for example, I have been most concerned to uncover the unavoidably material dimensions of online music's political ecology. But Granjon's and Combes's other figures of speech also conceal more than they reveal.

Gavin Steingo notes a general tendency in scholarship on music and digitalization to describe "music's increasing ubiquity, availability and fluidity. Music, it seems, is more accessible than ever, moving at an ever-faster pace in an unimpeded flow." Yet, he continues, "several key assumptions about music and mobility run aground when confronted with sonic practices" in situations "where musical equipment and storage devices constantly break down and where people are largely immobile."[94] This is an important insight. At the same time, the notion of flow, as a metaphor of movement, is just as problematic in contexts where music does indeed appear to travel through our world with newfound fluidity. In describing the movement of digital information in terms of flow, commentators unwittingly participate in a longer history of mystification and commodity fetishism. According to Augustine Sedgewick: "The modern usage of the flows metaphor took shape within linked nineteenth-century transformations in capitalism and social thought. It vanquished a rival concept of motion and change, 'work'—meaning both labor, and, in a technical sense, the energy required to move or transform matter in space, force times distance."[95] To engage critically with the political ecology of online music requires swimming against the currents of streaming and flow that typify discourses of the digital.

Notions of fluidity also call to mind the flow of information in what has been called the network society.[96] As a metaphor for connection, the everyday language of networks tends to favor a sense of abstraction in which data are purely virtual and, simply, out there.[97] Of course, the online world is certainly networked in both material and social terms. But digital networks function like any of the other networks that have been traced by researchers in science and technology studies. If there is a global telecommunications network that offers music to some people at unprecedented degrees of ubiquity and access, like any network this one requires continuous and performative labor to draw together its heterogeneous elements.[98] Without the work underlying the net, it would disappear or cease to matter.

It is easiest to see what is concealed by these metaphors of connection and movement in moments of malfunction. For example, Steingo has shown how that most fundamental precondition of electronic music—electricity—can be taken for granted only so long as the power "network" keeps the electricity "flowing." When the power goes out and the electricity stops, which happened often in the South African township where

Steingo did his fieldwork, the infrastructural dependencies of music are "rendered sensorial and aesthetic"—as glitches and dropouts.[99] Yet even in cases where infrastructures are operating smoothly, when they readily fade into invisibility and inaudibility, this is when they are doing some of their most powerful work to mystify all the people and things needed to build them and keep them running—as well as all the influence they hold over us. If data may be streamed, if digital commodities may circulate, and if such processes are ubiquitous, nothing about this is automatic, abstract, or given in the ways implied by the cloud as a metaphor for storage, by flow as a metaphor of motion, or by network as a metaphor for connection. Jonathan Sterne notes that the stories we tell about formats matter. So do the figures of speech we use to talk about them.

Although the exact character of the relationship between music's digitalized social and media morphologies is constantly unfolding and only beginning to be understood, and while sweeping generalizations such as discomorphosis and digitamorphosis should be approached with caution, maybe we should hold out some hope for them. If discomorphosis names those processes by which a new form of reflexive attachment to music emerged in the twentieth century, then perhaps the promise of digitamorphosis is that it could name the rise of an equally significant form of reflexive attachment to music in the twenty-first century. Maybe listeners can become accountable consumers, not only monitoring their own purchasing habits and disposal practices but demanding that producers throughout music's supply chains and waste streams conduct themselves responsibly. This is not as far-fetched as it might seem. Similar transformations have already occurred in relation to food, coffee, and clothing, while many live music festivals have embraced an environmental conscience. Why not everyday listening, too?

Afterword: What about Vinyl? What about the Music? What Next?

They're good questions. I asked them of myself. And they came up in almost every conversation I had about this book while I was writing it. Even though my answers to these questions are peppered throughout the previous pages, I want to gather and review them here by way of closing. So, what about the vinyl revival? What about the music? What next?

When the inevitability of these questions became apparent, it bugged me. My initial reactions to them were just that—reactions. At first, I thought of these three questions as everyday reflexes that were problematic in various ways and that misunderstood my project to varying degrees. They represented grains of common sense that my research required me to cut against. I began to tell people that this book was not about the vinyl revival, not about music, not about next steps.

Gradually, though, I saw that the persistence of these three questions said something about their importance—personally, intellectually, politically. I came to realize that this book *is* about the vinyl revival, albeit obliquely and not in the way it is presented in the media or discussed by scholars. It *is* about music, just not in the way most music researchers are accustomed to thinking about their object of study. And it *is* about what comes next, though not in the way that issue is normally framed. The point of ending in this way is to reflect carefully on matters that concern us all.

What about Vinyl?

A lot of people jumped to the conclusion that the point of writing a book about the material history of recorded music would be to clarify why vinyl sales have been escalating since about 2005. This group thought that my goal was to explain the so-called vinyl revival—maybe even to celebrate it. What they meant was something like this: Isn't it clear that LP sales are rising because vinyl sounds so much better, looks so much better, and feels so much better than listening to music as a digital file? Isn't it obvious that we are renewing our vows to vinyl because we long for the material aspects of music that digitalization has robbed from us? In a sense, the answers to those questions are yes and yes. But not in terms of absolute sound quality or absolute materiality.

Situations that people define as real are real in their effects, and the discourses and practices of vinyl lovers are no exception. In other words, to the extent that arguments about the specialness of vinyl's sounds and experiences are made and believed, they are not just make-believe. They construct a reality that can be measured by increasing LP sales. However, I have chosen not to write a book about the social construction of "fidelity."[1] I am not interested in defending or deriding the aesthetics or phenomenology of vinyl. Whatever the reasons people are releasing and buying vinyl again, the so-called revival of this format entrenches the political ecologies of plastic and petroleum that emerged during the second half of music's twentieth century. To reproduce sound in particular ways is to reproduce particular sets of social relationships. While many musicians and listeners may be invested in reviving particular formats because they believe such media provide aspects of the listening experience that are lost when music is encountered as a digital file, it is simply not true that music downloading and streaming are less materially hefty, less laborious, or less experiential than those formats that we are accustomed to thinking of as having more physical presence.

One problem with those ideas is that they ignore music's digital infrastructures and accessory technologies, which are energy hungry, labor intensive, wasteful, and inseparable from the seemingly virtual act of clicking a mouse. Another problem is the Jevons effect. Even though the development of digital audio files could hypothetically mean that Spotify and YouTube are all we need to enjoy recorded music and to build senses of identity and community through it, the reality is that the number of available music formats and the weight of our music consumption are increasing in the twenty-first century. This is not just the case with regard to recording formats, either. The recent success of the live music industries (concerts, tours, festivals) is often explained in terms that mirror the format revivalists. In the age of recording, and especially digital recording, people pay top dollar and travel great distances to attend live concerts. They do so with the expectation of encountering assembled communities (not just imagined ones) and of experiencing immediate connections to their favorite musicians (not just mediated ones).[2] Matt Brennan puts this in historical and environmental perspective:

> It has not been typical for the music industries (let alone fans) to focus on the un-glamorous and even downright ugly aspects of live music's infrastructural conditions.... This is not a popular line of inquiry for those who advocate for music in the face of cuts to

> arts funding and education that routinely threaten access to musical opportunities.…Against this backdrop, research into the environmental effects of music can be at best unwelcome—and at worst met with open hostility. Such issues can become especially acute in contexts where music events marketed as sites where alternative ideas of utopian communities are performed. From the 1960s onward, for instance, music festivals became represented not just as events where fans gathered together through their shared musical tastes, but also through a shared political ideology aligned in theory (though not always in practice) with hippie counterculture, escaping routines of mundane life, experimenting with alternative ways of living, and "getting back to nature."[3]

Of course, the live music sector is just as commercial and commodified, mediated and material, as any other. Indeed, live music is not only one of music's largest revenue sources but also one of its biggest polluters, owing to masses of fans driving to festivals as well as musicians shipping their equipment around the world.

The parallels between live and recorded music are apparent. Both intensely believe in their disruptive potential in ways that are rooted in 1960s ideology. Both give only particular types of attention to their actual material constitution. Both are undergoing degrees of renewed cultural participation, media attention, economic buoyancy. And both, regardless of the reasons that they are so alluring and profitable in our digital age, have troubling political ecologies.

What about the Music?

The second frequently asked question came from musicologists. They wanted to know where the music was. They questioned whether my research belonged in musicology. Some even confidently asserted that this book would be illegible as a work of musicology. Of course, I hope this book is relevant to musicologists (not to mention scholars in other fields). But if musicology is defined only by studying so-called texts in relation to their so-called contexts, or only by engaging with those domains of ordered audiovisual practice that readily offer themselves to established and institutionally recognized tools of analysis, then these musicologists are right: *Decomposed* is not about music and it is not musicology.

Political ecology does offer a framework for aesthetic attention. But it is a framework that does not assume its object of study from the outset. It is a framework that neither begins with the poetics of obviously musical texts or the circulations of evidently musical commodities, nor proceeds at the level of recognizably musical forms of labor and leisure. The most apparent avenue for aesthetic attention in political ecology is that of generalized musical textures in relation to their media morphologies. If textual significations in music reflect and inflect broader social realities, the textures of music formats index broader social frictions. Such an approach requires a deflationary understanding of music. It insists that ordinary staple commodities and supporting casts are just as important as extraordinary songs and star musicians.

We do not normally notice the roles played by such humble things and people in the history of music. Exceptions seem to come mainly when accidents and failures draw attention to music's mediality, allowing its political ecology to break the surface. An especially noisy 78 indexes a bad lac crop; a warped LP indexes an oil crisis; a sloshy MP3 indexes an earlier configuration of the internet; a glitched track indexes a power outage. Although political ecology may be most noticeable when formats and infrastructures malfunction, it is always present in them—apparently or not. Political ecology is not dependent on phenomenological revelation, conscious attention, or meaningful interpretation. Jonathan Sterne illustrates a related point about the mediality of culture when he notes that people who lift their hats when greeting others unknowingly embody a historical gesture whereby those bearing arms would raise their helmets in order to signal that they came in peace. Will Straw, meanwhile, describes how bagels retain the ring-around-the-pole shape of their original retail method even though it is rare today to see bagels sold on sticks. Similar issues are always quietly at work in music's matrices of generation and degeneration.[4] Although they influence how music is made and heard, such conditions are not accessible to close reading or textual analysis. These conditions therefore invite us to think differently about musical culture and music research.

It is a disheartening feature of the history of musicology that departures from established theoretical premises, methodological frameworks, and definitions of music invoke backlashes from certain corners of the profession. Susan McClary, for example, along with other critically minded and politically invested scholars associated with various alternative, feminist, and queer musicologies, have been subject "not only to negative reviews but outraged, vitriolic reactions—a more than few death threats."[5] William Cheng's thoughtful plea for a restorative, care-oriented ethics of musical culture (including the profession of musicology) has been met with similar resistance and even categorically dismissed: "This is not musicology."[6] In the cases of McClary and Cheng, the dissent condenses around the idea that musicology has no business engaging in projects of socially transformative criticism, which supposedly come at the expense of *real* research and education in the *real* figures and facts of *real* music.

Likewise, in Suzanne Cusick's investigations of music and torture, she not only fielded the usual disciplinary questions—"Yes, but is this musicology?"—but also doubt (including self-doubt) about whether she was studying music at all. Indeed, she found that that "among the most horrifying aspects" of the use of music as an instrument of torture was "the degradation of this thing we call 'music.'" Here, the myth of musical exceptionalism wears thin:

> We in the so-called West have long since come to mean by the word "music" an acoustical medium that expresses the human creativity, intelligence and emotional depth that, we think, almost lifts our animal selves to equality with the gods. When we contemplate how "music" has been used in the detention camps of contemporary wars, we find this meaning stripped away. We are forced, instead, to contemplate "music" as an acoustical medium for evil. The thing we have revered for an ineffability to which we attribute moral and ethical value is revealed as morally and ethically neutral—as just another tool in human beings' blood-stained hands. This feels like the stripping away of a soul from a body, and therefore like some kind of violent, violating death. It is, therefore, as horrifying *for us* as it is for its obviously intended victims (though not as painful), tearing away parts of the collective subjectivity—the culture—we have for so long taken for granted, and subsumed under the heading of "Western values."[7]

Cusick says degradation; I say deflation. Our points are similar. Although music can be a source of delight and wonder (both aesthetically and socially), the reasons many people revere and exalt it (often above other cultural forms) are historically conditioned and ideologically indefensible in many situations. This is true not only in cases where music is used as a means to repulsive ends, but also in terms of the everyday realities of political ecology.

If Cusick's work on torture alerted her to the fact that music functions as a sensational and abrupt means of violence, the political ecology of recorded music since 1900 calls our attention to a variety of long-term and distributed cruelties that resonate with what Rob Nixon calls slow violence. This is "a violence that occurs gradually and out of sight, a violence of delayed destruction that is dispersed across time and space, an attritional violence that is typically not viewed as violence at all ... a violence that is neither spectacular nor instantaneous, but rather incremental and accretive."[8]

The slow violence of music comes in the form of Britain's colonial control over the shellac trade and, with the relatively abrupt shift to plastic formats around 1950, the unemployment of workers in India and the United States. It comes in the form of major corporations migrating from one economically depressed community to another, taking advantage of cheap labor, leaving human and environmental wreckage in their wake. It comes in the form of recklessly extracting resources such as oil and cobalt in conflict-ridden geopolitical regions. It comes in the form of greenhouse gasses emitted in the synthesis of plastic and the storage of data. And it comes in form of mismanaged waste of various sorts. Music's slow forms of violence, as much as its sudden ones, challenge assumptions about the goodness and beauty of music as both an experience and a means of connection. Like the capitalist world of which it is part and parcel, though, music's political ecology is also shot through with tensions. The slow violence of music's political ecology hinges on many remarkable achievements: the ingenuity of scientists and industrialists who have developed the forms of recorded music, the (partly) gratifying labor of record pressers, the meaningful music contained in those formats that have brought so much enjoyment and so many forms of connection to so many—and that may themselves carry critical messages about capitalism or the environment.

Of course, many of the musicologists I spoke to about this book saw the importance of critiquing music's political ecology. But they still felt this project was incomplete as a work of musicology because it does not attempt to explain how seemingly nonmusical political ecologies are made manifest in textually and experientially meaningful ways in apparently musical practices. Some musicians of course weave environmental themes into their music, and there are studies of such practices. Yet focusing on compositional imaginations and their semiotics of landscape, or examining musical practices that style themselves as vehicles of environmental communication or critique—important though these issues are—actually serves to ratify existing textual methods and participates in a form of music-centered exceptionalism that a critique of political ecology requires us to work against.

Discomfort and disquiet about decentering "the music" in music research and music education are widespread.[9] Take, for example, the well-known debate between Gary Tomlinson and Lawrence Kramer, which occurred during the early 1990s. As the cultural turn of the so-called new musicology was reaching a peak of excitement and redefining the political potentials of music research (which, since Joseph Kerman and Rose Rosengard Subotnik, had been suspect for its apolitical positivisms, formalisms, autonomies, and transcendences), Tomlinson noticed that the invigorations offered by close reading were beset by problems of ahistoricism, subjectivism, and aestheticism. Close reading tended to smuggle aesthetic advocacy through the back door of critique. This meant that critical analysts actually valorized the music that they happened to like best, even as they revealed its ideological underpinnings. And they did so in ways that did not fully interrogate the principles of music, of the aesthetic, or indeed of musicology that conditioned their investigations in the first place—notions that are "darkly tinted" by the preoccupations of Western modernity.[10] For Tomlinson, a fundamental task of music research should instead be to "interrogate our love for the music we study" and to "dredge up our usual impassioned musical involvements from the hidden realm of untouchable premise they tend to inhabit." From here, "the primary stimulus for musicology, instead of our love for this or that music, might more luminously be our love of, concern for, commitment to, belief in, alienating distance from ... the others who have made this or that music in the process of making their worlds."[11]

Kramer answered that Tomlinson went too far. In his defense of close reading as a critical project that traces "the interrelations of musical pleasure, musical form and ideology," Kramer argued that Tomlinson's position was "tantamount to denying ... the two cardinal, historically grounded truths that music (or art) is meaningful and that music (or art) gives pleasure." This led Kramer to wonder: "What would happen if we gave up listening with the kind of deep engagement, the heightened perception and sense of identification, that both grounds and impels criticism?" He offered some thoughts on where this would lead:

> Tomlinson in effect asks for ... the dispersal into context of what we usually grasp as the immediacy of music. What he wants, if we take him at his word, is music under erasure: a music so decentered ... that we can no longer claim to know it, or claim it as ours to know. In this dispensation there would be no criticism because there would be nothing to criticize; the death of criticism would follow on the death

> of what we currently think of as music. For some of us that might seem a steep price to pay.[12]

In moving precisely in those directions, Kramer suggested that if Tomlinson's position "can develop only as a musicology without music, then our situation is pretty grim."[13]

Similar lines of thought are playing out again today in musicology's "material turn." The takeaway from the approaches that underwrite this turn should be, in Benjamin Piekut's words, that we cannot "pre-restrict our investigations to the musical domain, but rather throw out the idea of the musical altogether."[14] Indeed, in the same way that various materialist encounters have led to sociologies without the social, ecologies without nature, and media studies without content, so do we need a musicology without music.[15] Yet certain scholars use the ideas of the so-called material turn to suggest that musicologists should get back to square one, that they should organize their research and teaching around the music they know best and most love, around those aesthetic experiences that most move them and which drew them to the profession in the first place. These scholars perform a tricky operation where they simultaneously take apart and take for granted the musical domain that critiques stemming from intellectual histories, anthropologies, and renewed materialisms say they should detonate or dissipate. They not only trade in emic musical discourses that have been forged in Western modernity but also on some level welcome and double-down on them. The force of the preconstructed weighs heavily here.[16]

Nicholas Mathew and Mary Ann Smart have offered an insightful and awake overview of the disciplinary trajectory of musicology. They note that as the paradigm of close reading became methodologically suspect through the 1990s, it gave way to a paradigm of quirk historicism—a paradigm they exemplify with reference to some widely described musical oddities: enamored elephants, defecating duck-bots, mechanical music boxes.[17] Mathew and Smart find these examples in the writing of numerous music scholars, all of whom use their preferred object to illustrate something different. It is precisely the adaptable and intrinsically interesting character of such quirks that makes them potentially less suited to sustained critique than superficial chatter: "the quirky historical detail, in all its titillating strangeness and open-endedness, is almost endlessly productive of discourse."[18] Indeed, they "lament that the ethical and political impulses" of musicology have "been lost in a manic collecting of historical curiosities that … could underwrite an almost infinite array of arguments. The collateral damage from that proliferation of details included the dispersal of our discourse into a sea of scattered and isolated quirks, leaving no basis for dialogue and disagreement about shared information and methods."[19] As such, if close reading is politically effective but epistemologically fishy, then even though quirk historicism possesses "subversive power," commands "formidable energy and appeal," and is therefore "worth saving," the paradigm is ethically iffy.[20]

Accordingly, Mathew and Smart consider what should come next for musicology. Their answer, like Kramer's a quarter-century ago, is that we should "return to explicating and openly loving the artworks and musical practices that lured most musicologists into their line of work to begin with."[21] Indeed, Mathew and Smart argue that "the first step in any course correction after quirk historicism should be to write openly about what moves us musically, rather than displacing our musical attractions onto nearby objects"; that "musicologists might pursue not only the fact of social relations but the precise nature of the musical transactions and human investments that help to secure them."[22] These are crucial goals for music research. In fact, similar projects have been carried out for decades by researchers such as Georgina Born, Tia DeNora, and Antoine Hennion (none of whom receives any substantial attention in Mathew's and Smart's analysis).[23] However, two seemingly innocent phrases in Mathew's and Smart's sentences—*nearby* objects, *only* relations—actually underscore a major difference between what they propose and what the broadly post-Bourdieu and post-Latour sociology of music (not to mention the mediatic perspective of political ecology) set out to achieve. These two phrases reveal not only an uneasiness about decentering music in musicology but also an assumption that there is something called "music" that can then be articulated to material objects and social relations. Yet objects are not nearby; they *are* music. As for social relations: "There are only relations, and this 'there are only' is not understood in a critical and sociological mode (in fact these are *only* social relations), but in a full and ontological mode."[24]

If Mathew and Smart call for a return to music that is on some level out of sync with the perspectives that they are drawing on, Emily Dolan advocates something similar in relation to the protection and cultivation of musical culture. She finds this imperative at the roots of musicology as a profession, noting that in 1885 Guido Adler already thought of the role of the musicologist, not just as a systematic analyst of musical works, but "as a kind of hybrid gardener and historical preservationist."[25] Such forms of loving guardianship cannot today be uncritical, as Dolan recognizes, for we have learned the lessons of musicology's cultural turn. As a result, music researchers are often "in the business of historicizing music, unmasking its ideological underpinnings, pushing it back into a thickly textured context, examining its material and technological enabling conditions, and recovering musical practices that have been overshadowed or marginalized. Rather than adoring music in its verdant temple, we frequently ... cut art down to size." She continues by noting a recent and prominent "trend" along these lines, which "seeks to achieve this by collapsing 'music' back into the bodies, instruments, and machines that produce it."[26] This, for her, is a key part of what defines musicology's material turn.

Dolan (as well as Mathew and Smart) rightly see that too much of the scholarship in musicology's material turn has been satisfied to discover, with both decreasing surprise and decreasing returns, that musical cultures are material cultures, that people and things make music together. In this way, contemporary materialist music research often stops where it actually should start, and it begins to look like the collections of technological curiosities, amusing anecdotes, and interesting details that mark the lack of an overarching critical or ethical agenda in quirk historicism writ large.[27]

This is indeed a dissatisfying state of affairs. Yet Dolan's next step also leaves me wanting more. She suggests that the work of the material turn actually grants musicologists "permission to carry on doing the kind of cultural histories we have been doing all along," that this turn offers "a path back to Adler's garden, whereby we can recast the loving adoration of musical culture as a new kind of worthy intellectual engagement."[28] Back to basics, back to the music, back to the garden. Even though Dolan's versions of musical love and adoration are neither uncritical nor unreconstructed, her general sentiment is related to that of Mathew and Smart, and it resembles Kramer's earlier reservations about departing from those definitions of music and those forms of musical experience that he holds dear. A critique of political ecology grants no such permission to return to personal phenomenologies or humanistic hermeneutics—even reconstructed ones—and it offers no invitation to simply compile and catalogue stories about interesting artifacts and their object lessons. Admittedly, the scales of dispersion and analysis encouraged by political ecology may not get us very far in terms of pursuing "the precise nature of the musical transactions and human investments" that draw people to particular musical forms and experiences (which is still of course a crucial task).[29] But that is only if we subscribe to limited definitions of musical transactions and human investments. The equally important question here is why we should embrace, valorize, and call for returns to particular definitions of music and particular forms of aesthetic experience. What are the circumstances that allow something like "music" to be true and precious for us in the first place?[30]

For all the discerning thoughts on the state of musicology offered by Mathew and Smart and Dolan, their starting points and final conclusions are that there exists a bounded domain of cultural practice called music and that the experiences and artifacts of this domain are valuable and possess power. By contrast, the lesson of actor-network-influenced music sociologists such as DeNora and Hennion is that music does not exist and that its value and power must not be assumed but observed. Hennion puts this clearly:

> We will have a much better understanding of what [music] can do and cause to be done, what it transmits, why it is or is not important for the public or for specialists, if we do not start from the hypothesis that music has a power of its own, that it is "already there." In other words, the point is not to reduce musical reality to its social determinants (or, inversely, in opposition to sociological reductionism, to argue in favor of the existence of musical autonomy per se), but to show how unprecedented pleasure, the love of music, and the object of this love gradually shaped one another. If music is music, it only remains to endow it with autonomous capabilities (internal

> analyses) or to relate its use and its effects to social, cultural, or psychological determinations (external analyses). But if, on the contrary, we advance the hypothesis that we do not know what music is, and if we adopt as objects of study the variable mechanisms through which it appears at different times, giving rise both to the increasingly emphatic reality of an autonomous domain and to an increasingly self-confident individual and collective competence on the part of the music-loving public, it becomes clear that the previous position is an anachronism, for it evaluates musical reality retrospectively using the very criteria that music history has created.... Music and taste should not be the *resources* of our analysis, but its *topics*. They have written the history which is our source for claiming to write theirs.[31]

From this perspective, even though scholars such as Mathew and Smart and Dolan have rebuilt the cart, they nevertheless keep it in front of the horse. They still want to value music in particular ways and to lean on "the hard-won techniques and expertise of [musicology] to illuminate beloved musical objects, rather than to critique them into thin air."[32] They still want, on some level, to use music and musicology as resources for analysis and as ends that justify their own means—rather than treating them as discursive effects and topics of investigation.

Hennion's stance, by contrast, leads not only away from music as such but toward a different kind of recursive maneuver. If music's history is working on our thoughts and feelings about music, then those thoughts and feelings about music are also working on our music histories.[33] This epistemological bind requires not only a critique of music but also a reflexive critique of musicology itself, which was formed in the same modern and Western mediatic moment that has shaped our understanding of music. Political ecology attempts to escape the gravitational pull of these ideas, choosing not exactly to abandon music and music-specific research altogether but to understand them as contingent phenomena and, while not denying their potential importance, instead wishes to see them dispersed into their mediatic conditions. The goal is to describe their constitution and their effects from the outside—without a pre-given concern for experience or meaning. Such a perspective assumes a different starting point regarding music and moves in a different musicological direction. Music is not special. It is ordinary. This is where we must begin.[34]

I write from a privileged position. I have a permanent job in a secure department, based in a country where the threat of neoliberalism in relation to culture and research is not as bad as it is elsewhere. For now, anyway. Others are less fortunate. Elsewhere, cultural funding for music is being slashed and increasingly articulated to the instrumental logics of the market. Elsewhere, musicology departments are being closed or are under threat of closure resulting from the rationalized logics of university administration. In those situations, where not only musical ideologies but cultural values and personal livelihoods are at stake, it is understandable that people would lean on defenses of music that suggest it is a special form of human relatedness, that they would emphasize its uniqueness compared to other cultural forms, that they would dig in their heels regarding existing musicological expertise. These can be effective fallbacks in the face of real dangers. But they require that we fight fire with fire, to consistently return to music and musicology as such even as we critique and pull away from them. If this conundrum leads scholars such as Deborah Wong "to leave music behind" and to "stop rerouting [her] projects to wrestle music into center place," then the reflexive critique of academic research that it invokes also leads us to question our allegiances to musicological disciplines and departments as they are currently constructed.[35]

Toward the end of her reflection on the pasts and prospects of musicology, Dolan suggests that "material histories" (a category in which she would likely include political ecology) "need not downgrade art, reducing it to the level of all other debris, divested of special human interest; rather, they have the potential to transform everything around us into art. There are more things flourishing in the garden than meets the eye, if only one cares to look."[36] This is a nice image, even if I do not subscribe to the notion that music or art are any better suited to bolstering the potentials of humankind than are sport or science, magic or math, reading or religion. The issue, though, is not just that there is more flourishing in the garden than we realize. It is that there is substantially more suffering, too. And it is apparent that many musicologists and music lovers would rather look the other way, shielding themselves from the trauma by incongruously using the lessons of a sociology without the social to call for a return to a musicology of music.

A musicology without music, by contrast, is an approach to music research that denies itself recourse to and recapitulation of existing constructions of "music" and "musical experience," focusing instead on the conditions of exteriority that allow those categories to present themselves to us in the first place. A musicology without music is therefore not a debit. It is a credit. We do not lose music but, rather, gain it anew. When musicologists coat their reservations about decentering music in the language of departure and loss, they give voice to anxieties that emerged in historically specific cultural and institutional arrangements. Looking at music and musicology from the outside, from the mediatic perspective of political ecology, does mean confronting and deflating the exalted status of this domain we call music. But it does not mean abandoning musical practices or music research altogether. Instead, it is to expand those realms and restore to them a fullness that is paradoxically denied in confronting conventional wisdom with conventional wisdom.[37]

Political ecology's staple commodities and supporting casts may require that we shift our focus away from musical meaning and interpretation (at least as starting points). It may mean looking at debris and suffering. But this is not a zero-sum equation where we must choose *either* music and experience *or* an icy world evacuated of meaning and divested of human interest. The point is that shellac, plastic, and data *are* music and that they instantiate not only recognizably musical experiences but also other forms of musical involvement and human investment that are only arbitrarily and ideologically distinguished from "music" as such. Along with their inaudible laborers, shellac and plastic and data are the material and historical grounds that connect musical values and musical pleasures to the global frictions from which such values and feelings emerge in the first place. The critique of political ecology carried out in this book suggests that those researchers who are most concerned with the centrality, the goodness, and the beauty of music should be the last to bracket music's wider mediatic frictions in favor of returns to familiar aesthetic comforts.

If I have spent some time engaging with the perspectives of Mathew, Smart, and Dolan, it is not because their work is impoverished or idiosyncratic but because it is rich and representative; not because they are lone voices addressing these big issues but because they are struggling with questions that we all deal with. They do so with exemplary earnestness and admirable acuity. Although I confronted similar questions while writing this book, my own answers have led me away from musical experiences as such and away from music per se. But to move away is not necessarily to go astray. In resisting the temptation to foreclose what music and musicology are, we open up new possibilities for what they might be and what they might become—even if what we discover there might make us uncomfortable. Musicology is as musicology does. A critique of political ecology may ask us to rethink our prized but problematic musical values and to rebuild our fought-for but freighted musicological expertise. It may even lead us to consider outright rejecting those categories. But it does so in the interest of achieving something more like an intervention than initiating further turns and returns in our scholarship.[38] It does so in the hopes that music research might do more to help repair our broken world.

What Next?

The third main question I was asked was: What do you propose we do? These conscientious inquisitors presumed that I must have a solution to the problems of recorded music's political ecology. They thought the book should end on a hopeful note. I'm sorry to say that I do not have the answers and I am not especially hopeful. Like Buridan's donkey, I'm stuck. Yet that does not mean we should make asses of ourselves. Publicizing the human and environmental ambiguities and wrongdoings that are distributed along recorded music's supply chains, manufacturing and delivery infrastructures, and waste streams is not the same as fixing the issues. But it's not nothing.

When I failed to offer practical solutions, some people offered ideas of their own. Many suggested that we should go unplugged and off-grid, making music only in local communities and using only "natural" resources such as wood and skin. But rebuilding a political ecology of music in which billions of people harvest trees and animals to make instruments would only serve to shift the problem onto other resources and supply chains, other people and communities. Others jokingly suggested that we might abandon instruments and media altogether, using only our lungs to make music. Even if it is pointless to think that we might revert to a global musical culture guided only by voices, doing so would anyway raise the unserious but mildly interesting question of how much atmospheric carbon dioxide would be released or sequestered by this practice.[39] The real error of these ideas, though, is their primitivism.

Wistful thinking won't get us very far. We cannot retreat to some magical past point in time when music was pure and unsullied by technological mediation or exempt from questions of political ecology. No such time has ever existed. To believe otherwise represents an ideologically problematic and historically inaccurate understanding of the relationship between music and technology—as well as between culture and nature, humans and nonhumans. Paleontologists, science and technology scholars, media philosophers, and music researchers all confirm that culture is never an ontological intrusion on nature, that nonhumans are never ontological intrusions on humans, that technology is never an ontological intrusion on music.[40] These domains are defined by recursion and infinite regress—chickens laying their own eggs, turtles all the way down. Tomlinson makes this point based on a million years of evidence:

> Musicking was always technological. Its modes of cognition were shaped from the first by the extensions of the body that were the earliest tools and weapons, in ways that left a deep imprint on both sociality and the genome. Musical instruments as such came late, but this broader, crucial instrumentality appeared long before there was music.

> Musicking was always social. If the cognitive capacities basic to it emerged from a constant, intimate interplay with available materials, their affordances, and their manipulation, all these took place ... in the context of copresent interactions between individuals and within groups. The technological and the social were always bound together, and this *technosociality* formed the matrix in which musicking took shape.[41]

It follows that if we can choose *which* technologies we use to make and hear music, we cannot choose *whether* we make and hear music through technology. This is as true in the deep time of evolutionary history as it is in more contemporary and localized musical practices. Whatever the solutions to the problems of music's political ecology might be, they will not come from musicologies of retreatism, ideologies of escapism, or anxieties of intrusion. Making headway requires staying with the trouble and recognizing the inextricabilities of relationships—caring for kin of all kinds.[42]

If no recording format has ever conformed to principles of extraction or energy that would qualify as equitable or ethical, and if pastoral returns are nonstarters, what we need is a musicology in the future tense—a musicology of the otherwise.[43] Attending to the material realities of musical production and consumption is only the first step along this path. Solutions to the problems of music's political ecology may come partially in the form of new formats and post-catastrophic media.[44] But if research in the wider worlds of waste and energy tells us anything, it is that techno-fixes are not the only or even the most important ways forward. One reason for this was described by William Stanley Jevons in the nineteenth century. Even if we developed new music formats that were more efficient than previous ones, we would inevitably end up listening to even more music using even more devices. Advancements in resource efficiency seem bound to be overwhelmed by increases in demand. A truly post-catastrophic format would thus require not only a technological development but a shift in culture.

The question, then, is what music looks like after shellac, after oil—even after the internet. It turns out that looking forward might be as unsettling as looking behind the scenes of recorded music's pasts and presents (albeit for different reasons). Looking forward requires that we confront the impossibility of continuing to expect a world made by seemingly unlimited resources in the wake of the recognition that resources are definitely limited.[45] Musically, we may need to question our expectations of instant access and infinite storage. We may need to recognize that recorded music is as finite as everything else. Indeed, music is a microcosm of some of our most general and most deeply held values and practices surrounding wealth, growth, independence, and mobility—values and practices that could only emerge in the context of the perception that resources were inexhaustible.

It is for this reason that notions such as degrowth and sufficiency have become serious suggestions for twenty-first-century culture and beyond. Such notions are difficult to imagine for those in the Global North who are accustomed to unfettered economic growth in the name of unrestrained personal gain, as well as ever-increasing efficiency in the name of evermore consumption. This is why the purpose of future-oriented cultural research is to provide a redescription of the world in a way that both accounts for its own situatedness and "allows us to imagine other—better—possibilities and how we might get to them."[46] A critique of political ecology offers one such material redescription in relation to recorded music's past and present circumstances—one that perhaps encourages us to decouple the idea of better from the expectation of more. And if *Decomposed* is a story about how things are and how they came to be, this is where it opens onto a musicology in the future tense that asks how things might be otherwise.

* * *

Friedrich Kittler once wrote that those who could hear the circuitry in the CD would find happiness. If *Decomposed* attempts something like that—if it searches for reminders of the depths of music's political ecology in the surfaces of recording formats—then I would hesitate to say that such a project leads to happiness. Of course, there is a lot to be gained from research that is defined less by texts and interpretations than by supply chains and waste streams, staple commodities and supporting casts. This is a kind of heightened awareness that might have pleased the pragmatist in Kittler, for with heightened awareness come heightened stakes and heightened critical potential. And here we find ourselves retracing our own steps, back to where this book began: with a version of music research that was less concerned with music as a cultural symbol than the ways that music could be reimagined in terms of its political ecologies, and which could therefore better account for the full range of music's contribution to the dynamics of thriving and suffering on this planet we share.

Every needle we drop, every play button we press, every earbud we insert, every mouse we click, every screen we swipe—every time and every way that we listen to music, we are participating in its political ecology. On this level, it doesn't matter if we curse the sizzle of shellac or the slosh of MP3. Nor does it matter if we adore the cozy crackle of vinyl or the warm hiss of tape. And it does not matter which songs and styles we happen to cherish, or which genetics of influence happen to have shaped which generic constellations. From the perspective of political ecology, what matters are music's generalized systems, its mediatic conditions.

To listen to recorded music is unavoidably to tune into the superhuman scales of time and space that are required to create fossil fuels and undo plastics. It is to encounter the multispecies balletics of trees, insects, and rocks as well as miners, drillers, and IT workers. It is to tap into the topology of local and global stories about petrocapitalism and polymer chemistry, forestry and factories, war and waste, gendered labor and geological laceration. These are the conditions that we encounter in recorded music's political ecology—conditions that are often distinctly *unhappy*. But if we develop ears to hear these conditions, then we may also be motivated to change them. And if developing those ears means thinking about music in terms of decomposition as much as composition, this is the price of admission for those of us who want to recompose a better world.

Notes

Introduction

1. This is beginning to change, as new vinyl pressing technologies and techniques are introduced (e.g., Bregar 2016a, Hogan 2016, Chen 2017, and Lauzon 2017).

2. Some technical clarification is needed for the discussion that follows: PVC *compound* is made by mixing pure PVC *resin* (which typically takes the form of white salt-like particles) with additives such as stabilizers, plasticizers, and lubricants. Exact compound mixtures vary by company and are often trade secrets. TPC produces both pure PVC resin as well as various specialized PVC compounds for numerous applications.

3. PVC compound is shipped in sizes ranging from 25-kilogram bags (typically usually for specialty colored vinyl) to one-ton cardboard boxes known as gaylords (typically used for standard black PVC). The average weight of an LP is 120 to 150 grams.

4. It appears the amount was close to 90 percent around 2014 ("US Vinyl Suppliers Struggling to Keep up with Demand from Pressing Plants," 2014). However, TPC says the figure as of 2018 was more like 60 percent. By volume, record-grade PVC compound is a small portion of TPC's overall business. Another key US supplier of record-grade PVC is the Rimtec Corporation of New Jersey (Reall 2014). In Europe, a company called GZ Media produces its own vinyl compound in the Czech Republic (Higgs 2014, 2015). Other specialized, longstanding PVC

compound suppliers to the European record industry include Dugdale in Britain and CAF in Italy.

5. Since 2012–2013, TPC has been owned and operated by SCG Chemicals (where "SCG" stands for Siam Cement Group). In addition to my discussion with the SCG representative, some of the description that follows is adapted from Fremer (2017).

6. Polymerization refers to the "chemical reactions that link the individual molecules together to form large molecules or materials sometimes called resins that can take the form of liquids, pellets, and powders" (Grossman 2016: 69). The SCG representative I met asked me rhetorically how PVC could be considered toxic, given its use in medical equipment that saves lives.

7. Greenpeace (2004).

8. The process here, known as cracking, is one of several ways that crude oil, which contains hydrocarbons of varying carbon-chain lengths, is separated into longer and shorter molecules.

9. Excell and Moses (2017: 20).

10. For studies of oil pipelines, politics, and industries, see, for example, Marriott and Minio-Paluello (2012), Barry (2013), and Appel et al. (2015). For a more general critique of petrocultures, see the Petrocultures Research Group (2016) and Wilson, Szeman, and Carlson (2017).

11. McLean (2015: 102, 104, 106, 108). McLean shows that one thrift store chain in one Canadian province sends up to 10,000 records to landfill every year. It is impossible to know the total amount of vinyl records that have been sent to garbage dumps or incinerators. But it doesn't take much imagination to see that the number is massive. For additional discussions of the cultural meaning and material intensity of exhausted recorded music commodities, on which I am drawing in this paragraph, see chapter 2 as well as Straw (1999–2000, 2000, 2007, 2009, 2010b).

12. While there have been consistent increases in vinyl sales since about 2005, discourses of vinyl revival extend back to the mid-1990s

(e.g., Rothenbuhler and Peters 1997). Indeed, the relationship between vinyl and digitalization goes back much further than the ten-year period normally discussed in revivalist discourses (i.e., to the introduction of the CD) while there have "been a number of vinyl revivals" since cassette sales first pulled ahead of vinyl in the 1980s (Osborne 2016: 270). For further discussion of the relationship between the vinyl revival and digital audio files, see Barry (2014).

13. Stanley (2015).

14. Sisario (2015).

15. For some examples of the wider reportage and discourse, see Bhaktavatsala (2003), Shedden (2015), "Why South African Millennials Are Buying More Vinyl Records Online?" (2016), Havens (2017), Kwon (2017), Schoop (2017), Dowkes (2018), and Parkin (2018). For coverage within the plastics industry trade paper *Plastics News*, see "Record Growth: The Story Behind the Vinyl Comeback" (2014), Higgs (2014), Reall (2014), Bregar (2016b), and Lauzon (2017).

16. Reynolds (2011). Note that, while Reynolds (and many others) propound a discourse in which the phrase "digital age" refers to the age of the internet, the rise of digital music technology goes back at least to the 1950s and was not in any sense a "revolution" (Théberge 2015: 329, 337) or an absolute rupture with so-called analog technologies (Sterne 2006a). For broader problematizations of the terms digital and analog, and the relationships between the two, see Peters (2016) and Sterne (2016a). While I recognize these issues and therefore do not endorse an oversimplified idea that "digital age" refers only to the rise of the public internet since the 1990s, I do follow the shorthand convention of referring to our contemporary, online moment in terms of "digitalization."

17. Tschmuck (2017); the publication is in German and the translation is mine. Note that similar issues are understood have to influenced the apparently paradoxical boom in the live music industries of concerts, festivals, and touring in the contemporary context of digitalization (Frith et al. 2013: x; cf. Frith 2007, Holt 2010, Kjus and Danielsen 2014). As Brennan (forthcoming) notes, the environmental consequences of

live music are just as problematic, and more so, than recording. See the afterword to this book for further discussion.

18. On the renaissance of cassettes, see Eley (2011), Curran (2016), and Demers (2017). On the potential resurrection of the CD, see Soghomonian (2010), Browne (2016), and Toth (2018).

19. For research attempting to answer the question of why people appreciate LPs and why vinyl sales are rising, see Davis (2007), Katz (2015), Winters (2016), Harper (2018), and Albiez (forthcoming). Bartmanski and Woodward (2013, 2015, 2018) intellectualize but tend to replicate the insider ideologies of the publications and collectors that they study. Although Osborne (2012: 183–186) does romanticize the phenomenology of vinyl to some degree, he also offers the most historically grounded and effective explanation for the staying power of vinyl: "The vinyl record has been responsible for outlining many of music's horizons."

20. For a love letter, in addition to those sources cited above, see Corbett (2017).

21. Marriott and Pinio-Paluello (2013: 172). For a classic essay that describes something similar in terms of automobiles, see Barthes (1972b).

22. To make explicit what is implicit in the preceding paragraph, I am not advocating for a stone-cold demystification of false consciousness among music lovers. The aim is more humble. It is to highlight various facts about the effects of our musical investments, and to redistribute knowledge about those facts and effects. Howard Becker has well summarized this position: "Many social theories start with the premise that reality is hidden from ordinary mortals and that it takes a special competence, perhaps even a magical gift, to be able to see through these obstacles and discover The Truth. I have never believed that. [Everett Hughes] often said that sociologists did not know anything that nobody else knew. Whatever sociologists knew about social life, they had learned from someone who was part of and fully engaged in that area of life. But since … knowledge is not equally distributed, everyone doesn't know everything—not because people are blinded to reality by

illusions, but because things have been kept from them by institutional arrangements (which may or may not have been put in place to achieve that end). Sociologists find out what this one knows and what that one knows so that, in the end, they can assemble the partial knowledge of participants into a more comprehensive understanding" (Becker and Pessin 2006: 285; cf. Sterne 2019).

23. Timothy Taylor has been one of the main voices calling for researchers to address big questions about the commodification and consumption of music under capitalism. He claims that "there has been little advancement in thinking about music and capitalism" and "virtually no thoroughgoing studies of the production and consumption of music that engage substantively with major theories of today's capitalism" (Taylor 2016: 1). In an earlier text, Taylor puts it even more simply: "There haven't been many sustained treatments of music and capitalism at all" (Taylor 2012: 5; see also Taylor 2007a). The exceptions to this, Taylor writes, apart from relatively brief remarks in Karl Marx and Max Weber, are primarily Theodor Adorno and Jacques Attali. Although I certainly agree with Taylor that music scholars should be addressing questions of capitalism, his review of the literature seems selective and his assessment of the state of scholarship seems overstated. For example, a significant foundational and ongoing feature of popular music studies is that it has been defined by a similar mixture of Marxist critique and interactionist empirics that Taylor finds lacking in music research (e.g., Frith 1978; cf. Shepherd 1982, Born 1987). There is also a long-standing focus (more and less directly) on music's capitalist conditions in those studies arising from the sociology of work and organizations (Becker 1963, Peterson and Berger 1975, Faulkner 1978). And there are established literatures on professional music-making in ethnomusicology (Stokes 2002, Cottrell 2004); on music in relation to social class, consumption, and taste (Weber 1975, Peterson 1992, Savage and Gayo 2011); and in the form of reflexive critiques of musicology and music theory (Gramit 2002, Klumpenhouwer 2002). Nevertheless, research into music (and sound) does currently seem buoyed by interest in musical commodities and musical labor under capitalism. See, for example, Straw (1999–2000), Qureshi (2002), Laing (2003), Toynbee (2003), Frith and Marshall (2004), Krims (2007), Sterne (2012), Born (2013), Frith

et al. (2013), Gopinath (2013), Marshall (2013, 2015), Anderson (2014), Beaster-Jones (2014, 2016), Morcom (2015), Morris (2015), Stahl (2013, 2015), Haynes and Marshall (2017), and Hesmondhalgh and Meier (2017). For essays suggesting that music's current attention to labor and commodities has been presaged by work in the studies of the media and cultural industries, which itself owes a debt to the sociology of work, see, for example, Hesmondhalgh (2000), Beck (2003), and Murdock (2003)—from which I borrow the idea that music researchers are going "back to work." For classic studies of factory labor, which have also been influential here, see Buraway (1979, 1985).

24. Williamson and Cloonan (2007, 2013).

25. I am paraphrasing and expanding on Frith (1978: 160).

26. As Sterne (2014a: 52) puts it: "We miss a lot by focusing everything around the musicians–audiences–recordings nexus and we miss even more when we limit our understanding of music as a social practice to the objects sold as 'music' in its wake" (see also Sterne 2014a: 54). Sterne's argument can be seen as an extension of Kittler's "There Is No Software" (2013), where Kittler argues that all software operations resolve into hardware operations and, eventually, voltage differences. For further explanation of Kittler's argument, see note 50 as well as Siegert's (2003) argument that "There Are No Mass Media" and Horn's (2007) argument that "There Are No Media" (cf. Winthrop-Young 2018). Note that while such arguments embody a certain form of reductionism, the point is equally geared toward complexification.

27. Cusick (2008: para. 4) is here summarizing and critiquing this discourse. For additional commentary on musical exceptionalism, see the afterword as well as Beaster-Jones (2014), Spiller (2014), and Wong (2014). A parallel scholarly argument advances a kind of analytical exceptionalism, suggesting that music is an especially complex object of study that demands theoretical and methodological perspectives of its own. While I generally disagree with this form of analytical exceptionalism (is music *really* more complex than anything else?), Shepherd and Wicke (1997) present a nuanced and justified perspective that attempts to understand how music, as an affective and symbolic system that

exists as a sonic medium which, though it is neither more special nor more complex than other cultural forms, nevertheless operates *distinctly* when compared to that other most prominent symbolic and affective sonic medium of human expression and communication: language.

28. Indeed, Marx's (1909: 83) critique of political economy highlighted parallels between the fetishisms described by anthropologists of religion and those observed by commentators on consumer capitalism. However, note that our belief in the power of music, as in any belief in the power of objects, makes these practices and things not less but *more* true. The issue is not exclusively one of critical debunking but also of understanding the processes and motivations for composing particular versions of truth (see Latour 2010a, 2010b). See the afterword for further discussion.

29. The notion of a "deflationary mode" comes from Bruno Latour (1988: 19, 21–22) and is developed by Lisa Gitelman, whose book on documents is not concerned with the inflated notions of print cultures and reading publics that have guided communications research but, rather, with the neglected category of "job printers." As Gitelman (2014: 11) writes: "Job printing was a specialization that accounted for roughly a third of the printing trades in [the late nineteenth century], and for this reason alone its output must have contributed largely to the meanings of letterpress printing ... even though it does not fit neatly within the framework of 'print culture' ... Indeed, because nineteenth-century job printing has so seldom been studied on its own and in any significant detail, it has never been clear the extent to which job printers sidelined the time-honored subjects and agencies that have come to populate generalizations about print media and the history of the book, including authors, readers, publishers, booksellers, and editors. Considered as an admittedly heterogeneous class, telegram blanks, account book headings, menus, meal tickets, stock certificates, and the welter of other documentary forms that issued in such profusion from jobbing houses in the nineteenth century suggest a corrective addition to—or perhaps an additional negation of—the histories of authorship, reading, and publishing." For additional work in a broadly similar deflationary mode, see note 36.

30. On cultural commodities in general, the classic statement is Miège (1979). On various forms of recorded music's commodification, see note 23. Parts of the discussion that follow in this paragraph are paraphrased from Straw (1999–2000).

31. Among the many scholars that convincingly make this point, see, for example, Stokes (1994), Frith (1996), DeNora (2000), Hennion (2007b), and Born (2011).

32. Stahl (2013: 8; cf. 228). On professional musical labor and its industries, see also Ehrlich (1985), Negus (1992), Kraft (1996), Toynbee (2003), Williamson and Cloonan (2016), and Haynes and Marshall (2017). On creative labor in general, see Menger (1999, 2014) and Hesmondhalgh and Baker (2011).

33. On the social life of things, see Appadurai (1986). On the social death of things, see Gabrys (2011). Talking about the social lives and social deaths of artifacts is more like describing the topology of a Möbius strip or an Escher print than it is to describe "product lifecycles," which is an ironically linear understanding of the relations between production, consumption, and waste. Indeed, cultural geographers find "no inherent directionality" in the generative and degenerative matrices of cultural forms; their research instead leads them to "unbracket the architecture of beginnings and endings" that normally guides such thinking (quotes from Lepawsky and Mather 2011: 274, 243; cf. Gregson and Crang 2010). In a significant way, and not purely by coincidence, topology entered cultural studies with Michael Thompson's *Rubbish Theory* (1979), in which he was drawn to geometric mathematical models in attempting to describe the apparently paradoxical relations between the creation and destruction of value under consumer capitalism. For contemporary applications of topology in cultural theory, see Lury et al. (2012) and Hawkins (2013).

34. Sterne (2012: 218; original emphasis).

35. It is necessary to elaborate on staple commodities in relation to fetishism and determinism. In certain readings, the staples theory of Harold Innis (1933, 1970) has been described, not as a Marxist critique of commodity fetishism, but as itself an instantiation of commodity

fetishism. This leads to charges that Innis traded the agency of humans and societies for the determinations of technology and economics. In David McNally's (1981: 38) words: "Innis' work contains the fetish of market relations and the 'technicist' concept of production which, according to Marx, characterize classical political economy.... Innis' work, replete with historical insights though it may be, embodied a crude materialism... which led to a systematic neglect of the role of social relations of production in economic life. The result was a rigidly deterministic interpretation of economic history whose central feature was *commodity fetishism*—the attribution of creative powers in the historical process to the staple commodity as a natural and technical object" (original emphasis). Determinism has become a dirty word in cultural research. All it really means is that a given writer has over-privileged a certain variable as a causal explanation of a certain situation in a particular line of argument. Yet the term has taken on the charge of such a self-evidently damning criticism that its mere mention is enough to automatically short-circuit further discussion (cf. Winthrop-Young 2011a: 120ff and 2017: 208). This is what makes Friedrich Kittler's infamous words—media determine our situation—not only so inflammatory but also so easily mischaracterized and misunderstood. Contemporary music researchers (among many others) are more interested in notions such as co-production, mutual mediation, and affordance (DeNora 2000, Katz 2004, Hennion 2010, Born 2012, and Prior 2018). The technology- and media-focused work of Kittler, as well as others such as Bernhard Siegert, asks us to look instead at how affordances are themselves determined—albeit in recursive processes of determination that do indeed, on some level, look like relations of mutual constitution. Yet the difference is important. Rather than describing a "soft" world of material affordances in a way that attempts to chart a path between caricatured versions of "technological determinism" and "social constructivism," the goal in so-called German media theory is to specify determinations and the challenge is to understand their mixtures. Even though I have focused on staple commodities, the notions of demystification and deflation developed here in relation to them should not therefore be misinterpreted as unwitting embodiments of commodity fetishism or determinism. And even though I do include human supporting casts in this analysis, none of these people make or use the staple commodities that make up music in conditions that are entirely of their choosing (see below). If either of these stances prompts readers to reach for their determinism trump cards, before playing their hands I would encourage them first to read the illuminating historical and conceptual discussion of determinism offered by John Durham Peters (2017: 23–24): "If we want knowledge, we will need some kinds of determination. Distancing this goal by calling it an *-ism* is a kind of bad faith that misses what academic inquiry is about. It simply restates something that no one could disagree with: we want to avoid bad explanations. We desperately need knowledge of cause-and-effect relationships such as between human activity and environmental transformations. We can't afford to not try to tell big stories about data power or infrastructural shape. Disdaining technological determinism is part of a wider political culture shared by the right and the left in which self-evidently bad things that no one will speak up for are zealously attacked. It is a lot easier to denounce government abuse than to make democracy work; to attack fallacies than to figure out what explanation or interpretation really mean; to denounce technological determinism than to write a really good history of technics and civilization."

36. It should be obvious that I am following Becker (1982: 77) in executing a definite epistemological break with the value judgment implied in the designation that certain people and materials are mere supports: "It is unfeeling to speak of the people who cooperate in the production of art works as 'personnel' or, worse yet, 'support personnel,' but that accurately reflects their importance in the conventional art world view. In that view, the person who does the 'real work,' making the choices that give the work its artistic importance and integrity, is the artist.... Everyone else's job is to assist the artist. I do not accept the view of the relative importance of the 'personnel' involved that the term connotes, but I use it to emphasize that it *is* the common view in art worlds" (original emphasis). For Becker's related take on the centrality of unassuming material resources in cultural production, see chapter 3 in *Art Worlds*. For additional work along these lines, which can also be viewed in relation to the deflationary mode mentioned above, see also Small (1998) on roadies and ticket agents in musicking; Molotch (2003) on toasters

and other devices; Darnton (2007) on the everyday operations of book publishing; Mayer (2011) on assembly lines, creativity, and identity in television production; Straw (2011a) on bit parts in cinema as well as Acland (2009, 2012) and Wasson (2015) on additional aspects of screen cultures that do not sit so easily within mainstream film studies; Smith et al. (2006), Nakamura (2014), Maxwell (2016), and Vágnerová (2017) on electronics manufacturing.

37. On world-systems theory, see Wallerstein (2004). For a world-ecology approach to capitalism in the web of life, which is an extension of world-systems theory, see Moore (2015). Additional work that has influenced my thinking here includes Hughes and Reimer (2004) on geographies of commodity chains and Tsing (2009) on supply chains and the human condition. See Morcom (2015) for a music-related discussion of some of these issues.

38. Political ecology has been written about as a corrective outgrowth of certain oversights in Marx's critique of political economy as well as a crucial part of what Marx was doing all along (e.g., Burkett 1999, Foster 2000, Foster and Burkett 2016). In a detailed analysis of Marx's publications and notebooks, Kohei Saito (2017: 14) furnishes a justification for the shift from political economy to political ecology undertaken in this book: "Ecology does not simply exist in Marx's thought—my thesis is a stronger one. I maintain that *it [is] not possible to comprehend the full scope of his critique of political economy if one ignores its ecological dimension*" (original emphasis).

39. One of the best introductions to the broader field political ecology in terms of its intellectual history is found in Biersak (2006). For other commentary and guides to political ecology, see Hayward (1994), Robbins (2012), Neumann (2014), and Bryant (2015). Ecology is also a keyword in contemporary music research. It is found everywhere from ecomusicology to the ecology of live music to acoustic ecologies (or soundscape studies) to ecological music psychology. Although I have found value and inspiration in such work, the particular critique of music's political ecology set out in this book, which I will soon define in terms of a subset of mediality and therefore as a musicology without music, is not yet represented in those studies—though certain

resonances are apparent (e.g., Allen 2012, 2017). Readers are encouraged to consult the insightful and inclusive summaries of ecological music research found in Aaron Allen's and Kevin Dawe's foundational *Current Directions in Ecomusicology: Music, Culture, Nature* (2016). For a guide to the environmental humanities writ large, see Emmett and Nye (2017).

40. For scholarship along these lines, albeit in a book that is about music's media infrastructures rather than a critique of political ecology as such, see various chapters in Devine and Boudreault-Fournier (forthcoming).

41. See, for example, Frith et al. (2013) and Waksman (2018). For examples and discussions of the performance turn (also called the practice turn) in musicology more generally, see Small (1998), Abbate (2004), Born (2010), and Cook (2013).

42. On dispossession, see Lucas (2002).

43. This is another way of refiguring Marx's critique of political economy as a critique of political ecology. The purpose of Marx's work was not only to describe the conditions of capitalism but, equally, to criticize the assumptions of classical political economy that allowed those conditions to become naturalized (see Heinrich 2004: 32–36).

44. The point I am building on suggests that that genre classifications do not merely describe groups of already linked musical styles or practices. Rather, they constitute acts of grouping that perform the categories and, in so doing, operate as political apparatuses that sanction some while silencing others—some forms of music but not others, some means of making music but not others, some people who make music but not others. Genre labels create conditions of belonging. Classification carries consequences. On genres as acts of grouping, I am paraphrasing Piekut (2011: 10). On genres and the politics of exclusion, I am paraphrasing Valiquet (2018: 97), who compares the performativity of genre to that of gender: "Genre, like gender, is not a property of things but a complex political apparatus that uses bodies, behaviours and machines to construct relations of belonging." For earlier work on "music" as a "meta-category" that constructs politics of difference, see Grenier (1990) and Shepherd (1993). For a broader perspective on *Classification and Its Consequences*, see Bowker and Star (1999). Note the similarities between

work on genre and classification, on the one hand, and Becker's (1963, 2017) labeling theory, on the other.

45. A musicology without music is something like a sociology without the social. Whereas conventional sociological wisdom sees the need to provide social explanations for various facts of life and forms of collectivity, other sociologists say that this approach confuses question and answer. It is not "the social" that explains a phenomenon. Rather, it is precisely "the social" that needs to be explained as a phenomenon. See Latour (2005). For related musical discussions, see Hennion (2007a) and Piekut (2014) as well as the afterword.

46. Although mediatic research into music and sound is becoming more common (e.g., Kittler 1999, Sterne 2012, Siegert 2013, Steingo 2015, Straw 2015, Western 2015, Ernst 2016, Moseley 2016, Bohlman and McMurray 2017, Kane 2017, and Rehding 2017), I will add some notes of clarification. In order to define mediality, it is useful to oppose the notion to both the customary objects and approaches of media studies—texts/interpretations, audiences/uses, industries/institutions—as well as customary understandings of mediation—"intersession, filtration, or representation" (see respectively Peters 2008, Sterne 2012: 9). Mediality refers to something other than "the media" or "mediation" in their usual senses. Conventional approaches in media studies and conventional ideas of mediation suggest an interest in the processes by which something passes through something else, and to what mutually transformative and/or constitutive ends—an understanding that can be accompanied by the assumption that mediation is only that which comes between two more or less real inputs or outputs, messages or effects. Mediality, by contrast, "implies no particular historical or ontological priority of communicative forms" (Sterne 2012: 10). Note that, while I am using "conventional" definitions of mediation as the foils for my description of mediality, there is a sophisticated body of work on mediation in music research—work that is not limited to conventional understandings of mediation. In fact, several contemporary uses of mediation in music research offer something similar to the conception of mediality adopted in this book (e.g., Meintjes 2003, Born 2005 and 2012, Hennion 2016, Valiquet 2017, and Prior 2017 and 2018).

It is beyond the scope of my argument to provide a detailed analysis or synthesis these two concepts. Suffice it to say that I am describing and deploying a version of mediality as it exists in media studies, because this is the most straightforward path to the musicology without music that I am proposing here.

47. For a summary of the so-called nonhuman turn, see Grusin (2015a). On the Anglophone reception of German media theory, see the translators's notes in Kittler (1990, 1999) as well as commentaries by Peters (2008, 2015), Winthrop-Young (2011b, 2017), and Sterne (2014c). On the resonances between German media theory and actor-network-theory, see Siegert (2015, 2017) and Pöhnl (2017). For additional background on the materialities of communication, see Gumbrecht and Pfeiffer (1994).

48. For clear-eyed work on the intellectual histories of Kittler and Latour, see Schmidgen (2014, 2018). See also Born and Barry (2018) for a critical discussion of actor-network-theory in music research.

49. See Latour and Woolgar (1986) and Kittler (1990). See also Lenoir (1998).

50. On the politics of turns and interventions in academic scholarship, see Straw (2016) and Sterne (2017). The perspective I am advancing here is indebted to media researchers who, more and less explicitly, have drawn their interests in the materialities of communication into dialog with the materialities of infrastructures and environments. Let me clarify by drawing on Kittler. In the same ways and for the same reasons that this book does not speak of a music industry or even the music industries but, rather, describes a kind of never-ending dispersion of what we think of as the music industry into other sectors, Kittler has written that there is no software (see also note 26). What he means is that the programs we run on our computers—no matter what they may look like or how seemingly unique they may be, and no matter what kind of content we might generate in using them—are surface effects that can be resolved into basic hardware operations and circuitry. Douglas Kahn (2015: 23), Jussi Parikka (2015: 3–4), and Nicole Starosielski and Janet Walker (2016: 12–14) have been instrumental in extending such thinking. For if all software operations can be traced back to their hardware

and circuitry, so can hardware and circuitry be traced back to the staple commodities and supporting casts that make all this possible in the first place (see also Parikka 2013, 2016). Parikka's "geology of media" is related to the thriving fields of infrastructural and environmental media studies, which have been key inspirations for this book (e.g., Gabrys 2011, Maxwell and Miller 2012, Acland 2014, Guins 2014, Maxwell et al. 2014, Parks and Starosielski 2015, Starosielski 2015, Peters 2015, Rossiter 2016, Cubitt 2017, Mattern 2017, Young 2017, Ensmenger 2018, and Stamm 2018). Although such perspectives are gaining traction in music and sound studies (see note 46), with certain exceptions they are not yet well represented in those fields. There are of course many other strands of contemporary materialist thought that could be cited and engaged with, including various neo-vitalisms, object-oriented ontologies, affect theories, thing theories, instrument studies, as well as anthropologies of consumption and heritage (to name but a few). But I will not review those frameworks here, both because they are evidently less relevant to (and sometimes at odds with) the specific critique of music's political ecology attempted in this book (meaning that further engagement would amount to a literature review for the sake of a literature review) and because others have already provided admirable overviews and critical applications of contemporary materialist discourses. For some such overviews and applications in relation to music and sound, see, for example, Weheliye (2005), Leonard (2007), Born (2011), Bates (2012), Straw (2012), Eidsheim (2015), Roy (2015), Smith (2015), Bennett and Rogers (2016), Jasen (2016), Steingo (2017), Thompson (2017), Trippett (2017), Kelly (2018), and James (forthcoming). For some such overviews and applications in cultural research more generally, see Miller (1987), Brown (2001), Barad (2003), Miller (2005), Morton (2007), Bennett (2010), Bennett and Joyce (2010), Brown (2010), Coole and Frost (2010), Sterne (2014c), Richardson and Weszkalnys (2014), Joselit et al. (2016), Dourish (2017), and Rekret (2018).

51. For additional commentary on certain problematic tendencies in environmentalist discourse and eco-critical scholarship, particularly from the perspectives of postcolonialism and American studies, see Nixon (2011: 233–262).

52. For historical and political critiques of "culture" and "nature" as such, see Haraway (1991), Latour (1993, 1998, 2004, 2005), Cronon (1995), and Morton (2007) among others. For a related and valuable discussion of nature as a theme in sociological thought that proceeds from an engagement with Max Weber, see Murphy (1994).

53. Straw (2010a: 215).

54. Hawkins (2013: 51). For problematizations of the cradle-to-grave conception of commodity lifecycle analysis, see Hetherington (2004), Gregson and Crang (2010), and Lepawsky and Mather (2011).

55. On musical consumption, see Peterson (1992), DeNora (2000), Bull (2007), and Savage and Gayo (2011); for broader perspectives see Bourdieu (1984) and Bennett et al. (2009). On time, exhaustion, and waste in relation to recorded music commodities, see Straw (1999, 1999–2000, 2000, 2007, 2009); for broader discussions of cultural practices and meanings of waste and secondhand cultures, see Strasser (1999), Lucas (2002), Gregson and Crewe (2003), Hetherington (2004), and Hawkins (2006).

56. Ingold (2012: 431). Although, as below, I use the word "flow" here because it appears in the Ingold quote, see chapter 3 for a critique of this notion. Note also that whereas Ingold (2007) tends to favor materials such as stone, which may be understood as more "natural" or "raw" than those such as plastic or data, the focus here is on mass produced and mass consumed materials and commodities (cf. Miller 2007).

57. See Behr (2015) for a summary.

58. See, for example, Bottrill et al. (2008).

59. See, for example, Born and Hesmondhalgh (2000), Cusick (2008), Johnson and Cloonan (2009), Fast and Pegley (2012), Daughtry (2015), and Pieslak (2015).

60. As discussed in the afterword, the phrase slow violence of music is adapted from Nixon (2011). For other scholarship that has influenced my thinking in this and the next paragraph, see Frith (2008), Povinelli (2011, 2014, 2016), Cheng (2016), Haraway (2016), Nooshin (2016),

Gómez-Barris (2017), Mezzadra and Neilson (2017), Puig de la Bellacasa (2017), and Sterne (2017).

61. Hesmondhalgh (2013: 6). The next quote is also from Hesmondhalgh (2013: 10).

62. Auslander (2001: 82).

63. On the materiality of data and "the stuff of bits," see Kirschenbaum (2008), Sterne (2012), Morris (2015), and Dourish (2017).

64. Frith (1987: 73; cf. 57). See also Frith and Marshall (2004).

65. For explorations of this state of affairs, see David (2010: 138–139), Winseck (2011: 43–44), Taylor (2012: 197–229), and Marshall (2013: 67–68).

66. For related arguments, albeit ones that either do not focus on political ecology or are only marginally concerned with it, see Frith (1988), Théberge (1997: 243–245), Taylor (2007a: 283), Winseck (2011), Sterne (2014a: 52–53), Morris (2015: 11), and Hesmondhalgh and Meier (2017). For more general perspectives on "the myth of immateriality" in relation to digital labor, see Maxwell (2016) and Schulz (2017: 97–99). All of this is discussed in more detail in chapter 3.

67. Residual media is a term introduced by Acland (2007), which is drawn from Williams's (1977) dominant–residual–emergent model of cultural history.

68. Shekhar (1996).

69. Renewed media should not be confused with the notion of "zombie media" (Hertz and Parikka 2012). Zombie media implies, not the widespread social renewal of a format on a general level, but the DIY cultural practices that breathe new life into specific dead devices. While DIY, hacker, tinkerer, and maker movements do of course have widespread appeal, they typically designate acts of repurposing that can be distinguished from the logics of renewal and revival that surround vinyl and cassettes. For additional studies of repurposing formats and devices in artistic and musical practice, see Flood (forthcoming) and Roy

(forthcoming). As a final point here, note that the idea of the zombie derives from Haitian folklore and voodoo, and that to nonchalantly use the term as a metaphor for media is to disregard its historical roots in slavery and colonialism (cf. Flood [forthcoming]).

70. Williams (1977: 122) is of course not referring to media as such but to more general cultural and historical processes. I nevertheless am adapting the widespread application of Williams's model in media studies (e.g., Acland 2007 and Jenkins et al. 2013).

71. Straw (2007: 4).

72. Nowak (2014a: 150).

73. Roy (2015: 1). See also Granjon and Combes (2007) as well as Barry (2014), who notes: "Today's vinyl collector has his [sic] musical cake, collecting LPs, and eats it too, via digital media."

74. Jevons (1865: 103–104): "*It is wholly a confusion of ideas to suppose that the economical use of fuel is equivalent to a diminished consumption. The very contrary is the truth.* As a rule, new modes of economy will lead to an increase of consumption.... The economy of labour effected by the introduction of new machinery, for the moment, throws labourers out of employment. But such is the increased demand for the cheapened products, that eventually the sphere of employment is greatly widened. Often the very labourers whose labour is saved find their more efficient labour more demanded than before" (original emphasis).

75. See Sellen and Harper (2001), York (2006), and Gitelman (2014).

76. Smil (2014: 130).

77. For the audit report, see Stentiford et al. (2007). The sales figures of the deluxe album were reported in *Rolling Stone* ("Radiohead Reveal 'In Rainbows' Sales," 2008a; cf. "Did Radiohead's 'In Rainbows' Honesty Box Actually Damage the Music Industry?" 2017).

78. Morris (2015: 161–162, 207–213).

79. Indeed, with digital music "there is still a desire for making exceptional objects and for finding creative ways of propagating them" (Morris 2015: 212; on re-materialization, see 12; on splintering, see 161–162).

80. On the ideological questions of mechanical reproduction and mass culture, see Benjamin (1973) and Horkheimer and Adorno (2002) as well as Frith (1978, 1988). For outstanding conceptual work on liveness and deadness in relation to mediated music, see Mowitt (1987), Auslander (2002), Sterne (2006b), and Stanyek and Piekut (2010).

81. Lucas (2002: 19). For broadly related discussions of "compositionism" and "decompositionism," see Latour (2010b) and Sterne (2012).

82. The quoted definition of "music industry" is found in Frith (2004: 176). Although I use the word flow in this context, to mirror Frith's statement, again see chapter 3 for a historical critique of this notion.

Chapter 1

1. Shapes ranged from cylindrical tubes to flat round discs, with diameters from under 15 centimeters (5 inches) to 50 centimeters (20 inches). Speeds generally ranged from 60 to 130 rpm. For more information about Condensite and celluloid, see below.

2. On chocolate, see Rondeau (2002). On cheese, see a letter from Joseph Sanders to B.L. Aldridge (24 April 1953), where Aldridge responds as follows: "I am sorry I cannot help on the question of cheese, as having been used in the record material. I have never heard of it and I can not imagine that such an unstable material would hardly have been used in either the dis [sic] records or the wax records, though in the latter ones a great many different materials were compounded in the so-called wax mixture." The correspondence between Sanders and Aldridge, which lasted from April 1953 to July 1956, is held at the Library of Congress, Emile Berliner Collection—RPA 00851—Box 34, Series 15 (Joseph Sanders materials). The correspondence is not listed in the bibliography. For a broader perspective on edible recordings, see VanCour and Barnett (2017).

3. These stories have been told and retold. See, for example, Read and Welch (1976: 127). Note that Berliner's company was still experimenting with wax throughout the 1910s. Although such experiments had to do with the mastering process, rather than record pressing, this nevertheless confirms that recording interests were constantly experimenting

with various materials even while shellac became most widely used (see Berliner n.d.).

4. Osborne (2012: 18) explains: "Following the introduction of electric recording Victor's speed of 78.26 rpm was adopted as the industry standard in America and the Gramophone Company's speed of 77.92 rpm was adopted in Britain. The reason for the difference is that early constant speed motors in America (with its mains frequency of 60 Hz) ran at 3,600 rpm (using a gearing of 46:1 leaves the 78.26 rpm figure) whereas in Britain the mains frequency is 50 Hz (therefore with the same gearing the standard speed dropped to 77.92 rpm)."

5. In the discourses of sound reproduction, the issue of sonic definition is often framed in terms of "fidelity"—a problematic notion with a long history of social construction. See, for example, Thompson (1995) and Sterne (2003a) among others, as well as the afterword for brief additional comments.

6. Michel Pastoureau's art histories of blue, black, green, and red are exemplary in this regard (2001, 2008, 2014, 2016).

7. Ball (2001: 11–12).

8. Ball (2001: 10–11).

9. The lyrics here and the quotations that follow are found in Peterson (2013: 111–112).

10. Oliver (2001).

11. Quote from "Jefferson, Blind Lemon" (1995: 2153).

12. Rust (1978: 8).

13. Petrusich (2014: 17).

14. The point is not that aesthetically oriented music researchers should fully shift their attention to such issues to the detriment of other forms of aesthetic analysis. Rather, it is to highlight that surface noises serve as a constant reminder of wider political-ecological conditions—and that such noises are therefore worthy of their own attention. This point is a

version of Sterne's (2012) "format theory," which is a type of "media analysis beyond content" that focuses on "the morphology of media over what they carry" (Sterne 2014b: 102; cf. Roy 2016–2017). The broader references here are to figures such as Kittler (1999) and Siegert (2015). For related discussions of "sonic markers" and "sonic signatures," albeit with an emphasis on how surface features function as experiential properties in musical consumption as well as aesthetic imperatives in musical production, see Askerøi (2016), Brøvig-Hanssen and Danielsen (2016), and Brøvig-Hanssen (2018). The difference here is important. Whereas Askerøi, Brøvig-Hanssen, and Danielsen study how surface textures can function as meaningful texts, the emphasis in this book is on how textures index broader global frictions (Tsing 2005) regardless of what they signify in their contexts of production or reception.

15. Meadowcroft (1921: 228). Edison's labs at Menlo Park and West Orange were both well stocked with almost every imaginable material. The case for Edison as a chemist is made in Vanderbilt (1971). Note that part of the subtitle for this section is also used by Sterne (2003a: 292), albeit in a different context (namely in relation to chemical embalming).

16. Rondeau (2001: 129).

17. "Wax" is technically something of a misnomer: "True natural waxes available in the 19th century, known to be esters of both a high molecular weight fatty acid and an alcohol, were beeswax, carnauba, montan wax, and spermaceti. The mineral wax, ozocerite, associate with coal deposits, is not a true wax, but is designated a wax because its physical properties closely resemble those of beeswax" (Burt 1977: 731). Other experiments with "wax" during this period were carried out by the Volta Laboratory, which was started by Alexander Graham Bell and staffed by his cousin, a chemist named Chichester Bell, as well as a machinist named Charles Tainter (see, for example, Wile 1990). Note also that carnauba wax, derived from a Brazilian palm tree, was widely used in the cylinder industry and eventually also used to create the master recordings from which metal stampers were made and shellac discs were pressed. The story of carnauba wax, as told by Michael Silvers (2018), parallels the recording industry's extractivist relationship with Indian shellac that is told in the pages below.

18. For discussions of mastering and molding, see Berliner (1895), Berliner (n.d.), and Read and Welch (1976), among many others.

19. Vanderbilt (1971: 120–122). See also Burt (1977).

20. Celluloid, a flammable semi-natural plastic, was already widely used in photography and cinema. For excellent work on celluloid, see Bijker (1995), Meikle (1995), and Rossell (1998).

21. On the story of Condensite as a forerunner of Bakelite, and the patent war between the two firms, see Bijker (1995) and Meikle (1995).

22. Meadowcroft (1921: 296). See also Vanderbilt (1971: 246–247).

23. The Great Phenol Plot is described in Jeffreys (2005: 109–114).

24. Read and Welch (1976: 102). See also Vanderbilt (1971).

25. On V-Discs, see Kenney (1999: 193ff) as well as chapter 2.

26. The main reason Edison favored this format was that the record maintained a constant speed under the stylus at the surface of the rotating cylinder. On discs, by contrast, the effective speed of the record slows as it reaches the center of the disc, which results in lower-definition sound. This problem is known as inner-groove distortion.

27. Meikle (1995: 2). See also Bensaude-Vincent (2013).

28. Berliner (1913: 191).

29. Berliner (1913: 191–192). The way that Berliner recounts this eureka moment should be treated with healthy scepticism.

30. Sanders (1906: 2 April). Quotation has been edited for clarity and consistency of style.

31. Sanders (1907: 1 January). Quotation has been edited for clarity and consistency of style.

32. Berliner (1913: 192).

33. Berliner (1913: 192).

34. Aldridge (1964: 4).

35. Walker and Steele (1922: 278).

36. See "Shellac for Talking Machine" (1906) and Bryson (1935). For additional background on the shellac trade in India, see Walker and Steele (1922), Parthasarathi (2007), Melillo (2014), Smith (2015), and Roy (forthcoming). For broader environmental histories of the British Empire, see Beinart and Hughes (2007) and Beattie et al. (2014).

37. Isom (1977: 719).

38. "Shellac Importers Are Worried" (1919: 42).

39. "The Shellac Market—Conditions Affecting Supply" (1920: 69).

40. Government of India (1946: 381).

41. James Hough, manager of the Winner record label, quoted in Sturdy (1920a).

42. "Proposed Tax on Shellac and Copal Gum" (1913). See also "Marion Dorian Speaks on Tariff" (1912).

43. "Important Tariff Rulings" (1921).

44. Lionel Sturdy's column in *Talking Machine World* closely followed the market (1913, 1919a, 1919b, 1920a, 1920b, 1920c, 1920d, 1920e, 1921a, 1921b, 1921c). See also "Shellac High in Price" (1903), "Shellac for Talking Machine" (1906), Shellac Importers Are Worried" (1919), "Shortage of Shellac" (1920), "Record Demand Steadily Expanding" (1920), "Cost of Shellac Rises 1,212%" (1920), "The Shellac Market—Conditions , Affecting Supply" (1920), "Indian Shellac and Mica Trade" (1920), "Slump in Demand for Shellac" (1921), and "London Shellac Stocks Increase" (1922). For an analysis, see Martland (2013: 201, 271).

45. "Shortage of Shellac" (1920). See also Walker and Steele (1922: 280) and Martland (2013).

46. Martland (2013: 210, 271, 276).

47. Swadeshi International (2011) puts the peak annual yield at approximately 40 million kilograms. Berenbaum (1993: 27) provides the figure that between 1921 and 1928 in Europe, 16 million kilograms of shellac were

used to press 260 million records. Gronow (1983: 63, 66) indicates that, before the Stock Market Crash of 1929, and again with the recovery of the industry approaching 1950, global *annual* record sales could have met or exceeded the 260 million mark. Thus my estimate that, in 1940, record companies were purchasing about half of India's yearly shellac gross.

48. Victor Talking Machine Company (1924, 1928b). It was usual to sell shellac in burlap bags of two "maunds" each. As a measurement, the amount contained in a maund has varied with time and place. But the standard amount delivered to the recording industry—two maunds—equaled 164 pounds, or about 75 kilograms.

49. For example, "Shellac High in Price" (1903) and Chatterja (1924).

50. Musso (2017).

51. Estimates on the number of beetles required to produce a kilogram of shellac range from about 10,000 to 100,000 (*The Story of Shellac* 1913, Berenbaum 1993: 27, and Freinkel 2011: 22). Some estimates put the early total of lac beetles in the trillions ("Bug Juice," 1955).

52. The amount is about 1000 square kilometers. On average yields, see Singh (2007). The cultivation and exportation of shellac were governed by the British Empire through this period of Indian history (see Mahapatra 2004 and Meillo 2014).

53. *The Story of Shellac* (1913).

54. Lindsay and Harlow (1921: 13).

55. Lindsay and Harlow (1921: 18).

56. Lindsay and Harlow (1921: 30).

57. Isom (1977: 719).

58. Lindsay and Harlow (1921: 81, 118).

59. Putting the overall production of shellac discs in the billions is an extrapolation from Gronow's (1983) excellent work, though it should be noted that production figures and sales records are difficult in general and particularly patchy before World War I.

60. On the relationship between conservation and deforestation in relation to the violin—particularly the Italian spruce used to make soundboards and the Brazilian pernambuco used to make bows—see Allen (2012). On the relationship between Fijian landowners and the plantation-grown mahogany used in contemporary guitar production, see Martínez-Reyes (2015 and forthcoming). On supply-chain capitalism, see Tsing (2009).

61. Government of India (1946). The work of this body continues today and is now known as the Indian Labour Conference, a section of the Ministry of Labour and Employment.

62. The quotations and general overview are found in Government of India (1946: 11, 17–18, 35, 74, 92, 120, 133, 150, 266, 380). Mica was also among the lowest-paid industries. For a striking assessment of mica in the history of sound reproduction, see Bronfman (forthcoming).

63. RCA Victor (1944: 1). This document exists in various drafts and was republished in the shellac era and beyond (e.g., Warrender 1947, "The Making of a Record" ca. 1951).

64. See Parthasarathi (2007) as well as Roy (forthcoming). For a broader critique of colonialism and extractivism, see Gómez-Barris (2017). The extractive colonial or imperial situations that took shape after record companies abandoned this natural plastic in favour of synthetic polymers around 1950, and even in today's digital economy, are not so different. Such issues are explored in later chapters.

65. Isom (1977: 720).

66. The paper label reduction was reported by the Victor Talking Machine Company (1928a).

67. Part of the decline in the stone industry was due to technological change (mechanical planers and diamond power saws replaced chisels and mallets) and, later, the development of other limestone-producing regions as well as improvements in other building materials. See Batchelor (1944).

68. Cowie (2001: 41–50; quote from 48).

69. Cowie (2001: 50).

70. Cowie (2001: 17–18).

71. Cowie (2001: 19).

72. On women in electronic media and electronics manufacturing, see Martin (1991), Smith et al. (2006), Mayer (2011), Nakamura (2014), Maxwell (2017), Vágnerová (2017), and Bronfman (forthcoming). See also chapter 2 and chapter 3.

73. Bronfman (forthcoming).

74. Howley (2005: 88).

75. For a preservation-motivated study that uses infrared spectroscopy and gas chromatography to reverse-engineer the composition of shellac recordings produced by Pathé Records, see Nguyen et al. (2011).

76. The reasons carbon black was used are debated. See Angus (1974) and Osborne (2012: 68).

77. Isom (1977: 720).

78. Isom (1977: 720).

79. Isom (1977: 720–721).

80. Eisenberg (2005: 18). See also Osborne (2012: 70).

81. Frith (1988: 14–15).

82. Description compiled from Sarlan (1924) and Aldridge (1964).

83. "A Real Captain of Industry" (1910: 24).

84. Warrender (1947: 31). As noted above, the same text was also used in RCA Victor (1944) and "The Making of a Record" (ca. 1951: 8–9).

85. RCA Victor (n.d.).

86. Sturdy (1919a: 167–168).

87. The Adorno, Claire, and Orwell examples are presented in Osborne (2012: 70–71).

88. "On a Ruined Farm near the His Master's Voice Gramophone Factory," by George Orwell (Copyright © George Orwell, 1934). Reprinted by permission of Bill Hamilton as the Literary Executor of the Estate of the Late Sonia Brownell Orwell.

89. Crowther (1945: 23).

90. On the relationships between music and consumer electronics sectors, see Frith (1988), Théberge (1997), Taylor (2007a), Morris (2015), Hesmondhalgh and Meier (2017), and chapter 3.

91. See Victor Talking Machine Company (1924–1928).

92. On globalization and hybrid musical aesthetics and identity formations, see, for example, Born and Hesmondhalgh (2000), Kassabian (2004), and Taylor (2007b). For studies of the global recording industry in terms of the sale of finished products, see, for example, Gronow (1983) and Marshall (2013).

93. Keightley (2011).

94. Appadurai (1986: 13).

95. Smith (2015: 38).

Chapter 2

1. On phonograph effects, see Katz (2004: 3–6, 189–191). For a study of the LP, from which parts of the summary history in the preceding paragraph are drawn, see Osborne (2012). For a broader theoretical perspective on the mutually mediating factors that influence cultural production, see Born (2010b).

2. On the affordances of tape, see Brøvig-Hanssen (2012). See also Bohlman (2017), Kane (2017), and McMurray (2017), all of whom add considerable nuance and complexity to the story that I am outlining here. On compact discs, see Downes (2010) and Straw (2009, 2011) among others.

3. Keightley (2004: 378). The subtitle of this section comes from Kenney (1999: 195).

4. Stanley (1947: 107).

5. Previous three quotations from, respectively, Stanley (1947: 107), Read and Welch (1976: 324), and Gelatt (1977: 290–291).

6. Osborne (2012: 67).

7. Respectively, the quotes are from "Diskers Ready New Plans" (1942: 68) and "WPB Sharply Curtails Music Industry" (1942: 5). For a discussion of rubber on the development of bebop, see DeVeaux (1997: 240–244).

8. Goldsmith Bros. to Columbia (11 November 1943). Letter held at the New York Public Library for the Performing Arts, A.F.R. Lawrence Papers—*L (Special) 89.21—Box 5.

9. General Phonograph president Allan Fritzsche to Columbia's James Hunter (6 December 1943). See also John R. Kennedy (Columbia's materials manager) to General Phonograph Manufacturing (11 November 1943). Both held at the New York Public Library for the Performing Arts, A.F.R. Lawrence Papers—*L (Special) 89.21—Box 5.

10. Winner (1944: 55).

11. "Diskers Ready New Plans." (1942: 68).

12. Respectively: "Diskers Ready New Plans" (1942: 68) and "Diskers Still Fear Shellac Grab by Govt" (1942: 62).

13. "Diskers Eye WPB Action" (1942: 70).

14. "WPB Announce No New Shellac After November" (1942: 20).

15. "Diskers Still Fear Shellac Grab by Govt" (1942: 62).

16. "Diskers Still Fear Shellac Grab by Govt" (1942: 62).

17. Chasins (1943: 83).

18. Chasins (1943: 83).

19. "Old Records Yield Valuable Shellac" (1942), Osborne (2012: 67).

20. Hunter to Donner (10 June 1942). The correspondence between Hunter and Donner, which lasted from March 1942 to January 1942,

is held at the New York Public Library for the Performing Arts, A.F.R. Lawrence Papers—*L (Special) 89.21—Box 5. These letters are not listed in the bibliography but are cited by date in the notes that follow.

21. Hunter to Donner (14 September 1942).

22. Donner to Hunter (7 December 1942).

23. Both the correspondence on needle materials and the memorandum between Edward Wallerstein and James H. Hunter (2 December 1942) are held at the New York Public Library for the Performing Arts, A.F.R. Lawrence Papers—*L (Special) 89.21—Box 4.

24. Memorandum from Earl Graham of the Consumer Durable Goods Section of the OPA, to William MacLeod of the WPB's Office of Civilian requirements. See Graham (1943).

25. Letter from Glenn Henry of the Radio and Radar Division of the WPB to the Columbia Recording Corporation. See Henry (1944).

26. As discussed below, some records were in fact made of vinyl during this transitionary period. The unpredictability surrounding shellac supplies, as well as the advances in sciences and chemical industries spawned by the War, meant that synthetic plastics had achieved a certain level of industrial momentum and their price was on a relatively equal footing with shellac.

27. On the recording industry as an early plastics industry, see "A Decade of Plastics" (1950), "The Record-Setting Business of Records" (1961), Emmerson (1978), and Magoun (2000).

28. Respectively, Bensaude-Vincent and Simon (2008: 1) and Meikle (1995: xiii). See also Fenichell (1996: 5), Freinkel (2011: 1), and Gabrys et al. (2013) among others.

29. These various early consumer applications of plastic have been compiled from the trade journal *Plastics* (1944–1949), DuBois (1972), Meikle (1995), and others.

30. Beall (n.d.: 4, 6). See also Spitzer et al. (1946) and Cooling and Clements (1959).

31. These examples, including *The Graduate*, are discussed in Meikle (1997); cf. Meikle (1995).

32. See "Call to Plastics" (1945), "More Music for Millions" (1945), "How Emerson Combines Beauty and Utility in the 1946 Radio" (1945), "Plastics in Accordions" (1947), "A Growing Industry" (1948), "Plastics in the Making of Phonograph Records" (1949) and Schack (1946) as well as Meikle (1995).

33. B.F. Goodrich also carried out foundational research around 1930. See Dubois (1972: 281–282)

34. Emmerson (1978: 132).

35. Sutherland quoted in Emmerson (1978: 111). Additionally, "Duncan Douglass of Goodrich Canada recalls that in the late 1940s its vinyl co-polymer resin had a large share of this business in Canada. The company sold first to RCA Victor, some with Compo, then Spartan in London, and later to Quality Records in Toronto" (Emmerson (1978).

36. Stanley (1947: 108).

37. On radio transcription discs, see Isom (1977: 722) and Fenichell (1996: 254–257); on Muzak, see Lanza (2004: 40–41); on film sound, see Barton (1932). For additional background on Victrolac, the RCA trade name used for licensing Vinylite, see Magoun (2000: 328–329) and Bonner (2008: 15–18). For additional applications of RCA's pre-LP vinyl discs, which included uses in advertising home appliances as well as background music in funeral parlors, see Fagan (1981).

38. The V-Disc program outlasted the war because various military personnel were still stationed overseas.

39. Kenney (1999: 198).

40. On the use of Formvar in V-Discs, see Helbig (1966) and Sears (1980: lxxv–lxxvii). Formvar was used throughout the war, while companies switched back to Vinylite when the material was taken off the restricted list after the War.

41. Isom (1977: 722).

42. "More Music for Millions" (1945: 84, 86).

43. Fenichell (1996: 255).

44. Bonner (2008: 31).

45. Bonner (2008: 31).

46. Quote from "One Record Holds Entire Symphony" (1948: 39).

47. Wallerstein quoted in Columbia Records (1948: 3).

48. Marmorstein (2007: 158).

49. Fenichell (1996: 255).

50. Columbia Records (1948: 1).

51. For additional information on Bozo the Clown, the mascot that Capitol Records invented to market storytelling and read-along records to children, see Bonner (2008) and Smith (2011). For a detailed study of the uptake of vinyl in the German Democratic Republic, see Ó Callanáin (2019).

52. Magoun (2000: 396–399). For a brief take on RCA's underlying ideology of the 45, see Magoun (2002).

53. Sterne (2012: 12).

54. Scaping (1979: 136).

55. Porter (1980: 6), writing for *The Mix*, notes that the main supplier of vinyl compounds during this period, Keysor-Century Inc. (Saugus, California), annually produced over 30 million kilograms of "record vinyl." This accounted "for about 40 percent of domestic production." As early as 1957, record companies in smaller countries such as Peru were consuming 10,000 kilograms of plastic annually to produce 45s (Cooling and Clements 1959: 56).

56. "The Record-Setting Business of Records" (1961: 1).

57. This had its own devastating effects for workers based in India (see Smith 2015).

58. See Scaping (1979: 136), Duston (1974: 3), and Martin (1951: 78).

59. Isom (1977: 723).

60. Cook (1954: 38, 40; emphasis in original).

61. Khanna (1977: RS-86).

62. Allied representative quoted in Sippel (1974: 8).

63. Khanna (1977: RS-86).

64. Théberge (1997: 58). For additional studies of transectorial innovation in relation to music, see Gay (1999), Sterne (2012), and Morris (2015). To anticipate the point that follows, note that Théberge (1997: 61) understands how "transectorial innovation has not simply been a one-way street." Indeed, he shows that integrated circuits initially developed for specifically musical purposes in Yamaha organs (as early as 1969) eventually spread to the wider digital electronics industry (e.g., in Atari computers).

65. Graham (1986: 4, 7, 26, 70).

66. Graham (1986: 28).

67. Fox (1973: 3).

68. Fox 1973: 3).

69. Fox (1973: 4).

70. Fox and Ryan (1979: 1–2).

71. Weisberg (1979: 1).

72. Keating and Weisberg (1980: 4).

73. RCA sold only 100,000 of a projected 200,000 VideoDisc playback devices in the year of its release. By contrast, VHS players were found in 20 million US homes by 1984. See Graham (1986: 213–214).

74. Philip Race of PR Records quoted in Smith (1985: 20).

75. Rodia (1985: 28).

76. Smith (1985: 19).

77. Whitman (1987: 46).

78. Whitman (1987: 46).

79. See, for example, Egen (2015).

80. The information in the following paragraphs is summarized from Hemmingsen (2015: 336–379). For an account of Canada as the gateway of the British Invasion, see Jennings (2000).

81. There is a growing range of research that supplements established studies of the music industry (which have paid scant attention to women) as well as existing feminist interventions in the historiography of electronic music (which focus on exceptional women) in order to show that "unexceptional," everyday women's labor has played an equally central role in music history (e.g., Vágnerová 2017). For parallel interventions into media history more generally, see, for example, Hill's (2016) *Never Done: A History of Women's Work in Media Production* (focused on the film industry) and Evans's (2018) *Broad Band: The Untold Story of the Women Who Made the Internet.*

82. Sippel (1973: 1).

83. Holt (2017).

84. Environmental Protection Agency (1978).

85. Environmental Protection Agency (2004).

86. Fausset (2002).

87. Environmental Protection Agency (2004).

88. For an account of the Atari story, which includes a discussion of the much-derided game *E.T. The Extra-Terrestrial*, see Guins (2014).

89. On the early history of magnetic recording, see Kusisto (1977), Clark (1993), and Morton (1993).

90. Athey (1966: 5–6) and Isom (1977: 722), respectively.

91. Hung and Morencos (1990: 65). The figures in the next sentence are from Hung and Morencos (1990: 75, 77).

92. See, for example, Laing (1990, 2013). On cassette cultures in the global south, see, for example, Manuel (1993, Hirschkind (2006), and Impey (2013).

93. Savicky (1987: 10).

94. Nor is it to account for the prevalence of magnetic tape recording as a mode of data storage in military and oil industry applications—as well as space exploration (see Athey 1966, Clark 1993, and Morton 1993).

95. McMurray (2017: 27). For other work on magnetic tape, see, for example, Bohlman and McMurray (2017) and Demers (2017).

96. Strauss (1995).

97. Türk et al. (2003: 16).

98. Bottrill et al. (2008: 31), Weber et al. (2010: 759).

99. "Robbie Williams to Pave Chinese Roads" (2008). For a description of overstocking CDs, see Witt (2015: 137).

100. McClure (1999: 114).

101. These estimates are extrapolated from Environmental Protection Agency (2012: 14) and Freinkel (2011: 7). See also Thompson et al. (2009).

102. These figures do not account for freight, distribution, or retail (see Türk et al. 2003, Bottrill et al. 2008, and Weber et al. 2010). And this is not even to mention the production of discs for software installation and DVD films, or CD-Rs for data storage and backup. For more on the Anthropocene as an epoch in the history of the planet distinct from the earlier Holocene, see Chakrabarty (2009) and Haraway et al. (2016).

103. Clair Patterson developed ultraclean lab technology in his quest to determine the age of the Earth, which he did by measuring lead deposits—thereby inadvertently also discovering the dangers of leaded gasoline (Reilly 2017). The lab technologies used to press CDs are descendants of Patterson's lab purification techniques.

104. Snape (1987: 27).

105. Fox (1988: 59).

106. Fox (1988: 59).

107. Givens (1990). See also Holden (1990), Goldstein (1990), and Straw (2009). For outstanding studies of the environmental effects of paper in the media industries, see Maxwell and Miller (2012) and Stamm (2018). For a mediatic and environmental assessment of paper in relation to music publishing, see Devine and Boudreault-Fournier (forthcoming).

108. Clark-Meads (1997).

109. Meikle (1995: 189).

110. Block (1998).

111. Respectively: Kirsch (1973) and Partridge and Irwin (1973). As the *Melody Maker* title indicates, the industry was also facing a paper shortage at this time, which is of course necessary for record packaging.

112. Quoted in Partridge and Irwin (1973: 39).

113. See, for example, Lees (1974), Kozack (1976), and Thomas (1980).

114. Hung and Morencos (1990: 75); quotation from Scaping (1979: 136).

115. Scaping (1979: 136); quotation from Porter (1980: 6).

116. Lees (1974: 69).

117. Osborne (2012: 81–82).

118. Traiman (1979).

119. Traiman (1995). See also Köster (1993).

120. Block (1998).

121. See Kirsch (1973), "Tape Industry Shortage Eases; Benefits Gained" (1974), Traiman (1979), and Traiman (1995).

122. Quotes from Humphries (1992: 129–133) as well as his appearance on the BBC's *Desert Island Discs* (24 November 1973). Thanks to Julie

Brown for sharing her archival work on *Desert Island Discs*. Note that the subheading for this section is borrowed from Lucas (2002).

123. Sterne (2003a: 287).

124. Sterne (2008: 59).

125. LeMahieu (1988: 88).

126. LeMahieu (1988: 88–89).

127. Shuker (2010).

128. LeMahieu (1982: 379).

129. On "Collector's Corner," see LeMahieu (1982: 379). On collector guides and discographies, see Shuker (2010: 25–27). On libraries, see Almquist (1987: 13–16).

130. On jazz, see Millard (2005: 252). On collection and distinction, see Shuker (2010: 17–21).

131. On the "patrimonialization" of music that occurred with the rise of recording, see Maisonneuve (2001). On the sociological theory of attachment, see Hennion (2007b).

132. Library staff and heads of music departments relay stories of widows attempting to donate substantial collections of 78s, only to be told that there is neither the space to house nor the resources to process them. Some libraries and departments would agree out of pity to accept certain collections, only to eventually throw them away.

133. See Shuker (2010: 27ff) on contemporary 78 collectors. See also Petrusich (2014).

134. Strasser (1999: 173).

135. Lucas (2002).

136. Straw (1999–2000: 162).

137. Keightley (2004: 386).

138. Keightley (2004: 383).

139. Meikle (1995, 1997). Note the contrast here with the ways that early recorded music and the songsheet industry were articulated to the anxieties of modernity through the symbolism of other contemporary industrial goods: "canned" music and "tin pan alley" (see Sterne 2003a, Keightley 2012).

140. Keightley (2001: 109). See also Frith (1981b).

141. See also Osborne (2012: 72): "artists were as likely to reject standardization as they were to embrace it. Correspondingly, audiences tended to emphasize the presence of standardization when it came to music they disliked, but aimed to dissolve the bond between mass manufacture and recordings when it came to music they admired. The music industry was similarly conflicted: the assembly line could be their ideal or something to disguise."

142. Ríos (2011).

143. Wittchen (2012).

144. Gabrys (2011).

145. On piracy, see Jones (1977) and Yamamoto (1977). See also Marshall (2003) and Sterne (2012: 209ff). On romance and nostalgia, see Harrison (2006), Jansen (2008), Eley (2011), and Demers (2017).

146. Hegerty (2007: para. 6).

147. Hegerty (2007: para. 6).

148. Hegerty (2007: para. 6).

149. See Thompson (1979).

150. Witkin (2011).

151. Türk et al. (2003: 20).

152. Straw (2009: 82). For another argument about the "paradox of the CD," namely "that its success led to its decline"—albeit an argument that stems from melancholic audiophilic concerns that are very different from those of Straw and from those in this book—see Rothenbuhler (2012: 49).

153. Taussig (1993: 232–233).

154. See Adorno (1991) and Horkheimer and Adorno (2002). For a clear explanation of Adorno's position here, see Bowman (1998: 318ff).

155. As suggested in chapter 1, Adorno's critiques of standardization are in many ways more to the point. However, his focus on symbolic cultural production meant that he did not pursue the kind of material critique under consideration here.

156. Frith (1981a: 62): "The music business is organized around the realities of overproduction—its daily practices reflect not the problems of creating needs but of responding to them.... In general, the rock business was built on two great market discoveries: the discovery of working-class teenagers in the 1950s and middle-class youth in the 1960s. The industry had to *learn* about these audiences and their demands, and the musical results followed rather than led youthful tastes and choices" (original emphasis). See also Frith (1978: 160).

157. Hennion (1983: 191).

158. The quotes and the paraphrasings on complicity are drawn from Hennion (1983: 191).

Chapter 3

1. Energy intensity, which I return to below, is defined as the amount of electricity it takes to transmit a specified amount of data.

2. Smith (2012). Note also that Smith is here tapping into a widespread sentiment whereby the superabundance and convenience of digital music has produced an equal but opposite reaction in which listeners seek "forms of music which are *not* available to any individual, anytime and everywhere" (Fleisher 2015: 256; original emphasis).

3. This is from Hansen's preface to the *Song Reader*, which was also published in the *New Yorker* (Hansen 2012). For a broader reflection on notation in popular music culture, see also Maxwell's (2016) discussion of the *Song Reader*.

4. “Tenner” is UK slang for a £10 note.

5. The origins of sound reproduction were marked by similarly anxious discourses in which the introduction of a new form of music technology supposedly threatened established aspects of musical culture (see, for example, Sousa 1906; cf. Sterne 2003a).

6. See Benjamin (1973) and Crary (1999). For a specifically musical take on distracted listening, see Goodman (2010).

7. Sterne (2006b: 338).

8. Electromagnetic radiation involves particles, wave actions, and energy propagation—all of which are themselves material and thus also affected by the material environment. Who has not lost a signal on a subway or traveling through a tunnel of some sort? On the materiality of digital files and information, see also note 23.

9. See, for example, Hu (2015), Morris (2015), and Peters (2015).

10. Taylor (2016: 18; cf. 146ff).

11. See Morris (2015: 13ff) for a clear articulation of this point.

12. The new-Apple aroma, for example, is such a distinctive aspect of the purchasing ritual that a group of artists teamed up with a perfume company to synthesize the smell (Aamoth, 2012).

13. Cubitt et al. (2011: 156). See also Gabrys (2015).

14. Roy (2014).

15. On the rise of the listener turned consumer, see Hennion (2001, 2015). On the ways that making music has become inseparable from consuming technology, see Théberge (1997).

16. These morphologies could be seen to parallel Kittler’s (1990, 1999) version of media history. If scores and notations correspond to Discourse Network 1800, and recordings to Discourse Network 1900, then the digital media morphology could be seen as a part of Discourse Network 2000 (which, although not a phrase favored by Kittler, nevertheless has

some validity as a description of his project; see Winthrop-Young 2011a and Sale and Salisbury 2015).

17. Quotations from Straw (2012: 234) and Straw (2010c: 21).

18. Coroama et al. (2015).

19. Achachlouei and Moberg (2015).

20. Quote from Burrington (2015). For further discussions of DVDs versus streaming, see also Seetharam et al. (2010) and Shehabi et al. (2014).

21. Mayers et al. (2014).

22. Mayers et al. (2014: 413).

23. McCourt (2005: 249). For details of the materiality of software formats and information infrastructures, see Sterne (2012: 6–7, 194ff), Kirschenbaum (2008), Morris (2015), and Dourish (2017).

24. Morris (2013: 2)

25. Türk et al. (2003: 34) and Weber et al. (2010: 763).

26. According to the International Federation of the Phonographic Industries: "YouTube is the most used music service: 82% of all YouTube visitors use it for music" (IFPI 2016: 3).

27. See Morris (2015: 180, 207–208) as well as Arditi (2017) on the politics of "unending consumption."

28. Morris (2008). This means that a large proportion of digital music's resource and energy quotients come from "indirect sources" (Bottrill et al. 2008: 7).

29. Carruth (2014: 358).

30. Morris (2011: 3). See also Morris (2015, chapter 5) for an insightful critique of the cloud metaphor. For an entertaining account of the material geography of the internet writ large, see Blum (2012).

31. Maguadda (2011: 19). The US headphone industry, for example, is a $3 billion industry that showed an annual growth rate of 10 percent between 2011 and 2016, according to IBISWorld.

32. Hogg and Jackson (2009: 338). See also Berkhout and Hertin (2004) and *The Carbon Impacts of Recorded Music Products in a Time of Transition* (2009).

33. Scholz (2017: 97). On the "social factory" and web 2.0, see Terranova (2013).

34. Straw (2012: 229). See also Straw (1999–2000).

35. Millard (2005: 405).

36. Hinkes (2009).

37. Roy (2013). See also Morris (2015: 180) on the role of the market here: "While it may seem convenient to keep all our music, email, and other documents on someone else's server, data in the cloud become at least partly the property of the companies that manage the service. The information is entirely dependent on the unregulated whims of the record labels and technology companies who manage it."

38. Sterne (2008: 64).

39. Sterne (2008: 65).

40. Morris (2010: 32) argues similarly that the "fetish logic" of the digital music commodity is "displaced to other aspects of the commodity" (see also Morris 2015). For additional reflection on archives, memory, and digitalization, see Chun (2008), Ernst (2013), and Blom et al. (2017).

41. Frith (1988, 2001).

42. Théberge (1997: 243, 245).

43. On "convergence culture" surrounding content and branding in contemporary media, see Jenkins (2006). On software and hardware convergence, see Kittler (1999).

44. Indeed, according to the International Federation of the Phonographic Industry, "Smartphones are moving towards replacing computers as the most used device for music consumption" (IFPI 2016: 3). See also Morris (2015: 190), who outlines "the increasing technological and social interdependence of music and the devices of its production,

distribution, and consumption." Sterne (2012) and Nowak (2014b) both make a similar point.

45. Quotes from Slade (2006: 106, 113).

46. See Sterne (2007).

47. Qui (2015: 5). For another forceful critique of slavery and racism in what he calls the international division of digital labor, see Fuchs (2016, 2017).

48. The aluminum and cobalt examples (and more) are paraphrased and quoted from Merchant (2017b: 63).

49. Merchant (2017a).

50. On plastic water bottles, see Hawkins (2013).

51. EPA (2011: 1).

52. The contributions of smaller polluters, down to the level of the individual consumer, may seem insignificant—an ineffective starting point for change. "But," say Maxwell and Miller (2012: 30), "we should note the premise of Greenpeace's strategy: it assumes the futility of consumer decision making as a basis for massive change."

53. Quotation from Taussig (1993: 232). The actual amount of electronic waste that is shipped from the Global North to the Global South is uncertain. The most widely cited figure indicates that the South receives 50 to 80 percent of the North's e-waste—a figure that is typically traced back to a 2002 report called *Exporting Harm*, published by the Basel Action Network (cf. Gabrys 2011: 129). Josh Lepawsky has recently challenged and nuanced these figures on both empirical and epistemological grounds. Lepawsky (2018: 27–45, 107–127) notes that the amount of e-waste moving from the North to the South actually decreased significantly between 1996 and 2012, while e-waste shipments moving the other way, from the South the North, have been increasing. What is more, the most substantial international traffic in e-waste actually occurs *within* the Global North, from industrialized country to industrialized country. All of this of course depends on what

we mean by e-waste. It reminds us that any form of waste is a complex topological function of the permanence and ephemerality of value that characterizes all cultural artifacts.

54. See Rai (2013), Manuel (2014), and Deo and Duggal (2017).

55. Quotation from Kumar and Parikh (2013: 2863). On the earlier cassette culture, see Manuell (1993).

56. On pirate modernity and media urbanism, see Sundaram (2010). On the connection here to e-waste, see Borthakur and Sinha (2013).

57. Mohammed Moinuddin quoted in Gallagher (2014).

58. Eisenberg (2012).

59. See IFPI (2014) and Matinde (2014).

60. On licensing and piracy, see Eisenberg (2012). For a broader critique of the political economy of ringtones, see Gopinath (2013).

61. Hesmondhalgh and Meier (2017: 12). See also Morris (2015).

62. These figures were current as of 15 December 2015. Spotify received a passing grade of D in Greenpeace's 2017 report. At that time, it was using about 50 percent clean energy, 50 percent gas, coal, and nuclear. Although this discussion is about everyday music listening, the issues apply to musician-oriented sites such as SoundCloud, which also fails the most recent Greenpeace test.

63. It should be noted that Equinix has recently committed to transitioning to 100 percent clean energy (Cook and Pomerantz 2015). Note also that in 2018, as this book was completed and sent to press, Spotify decommissioned all but one of its own data centers, thus completing the migration of its infrastructure to the Google Cloud Platform. Google claims that the corporation has been carbon-neutral since 2007 and that in 2017 its Cloud Platform matched 100 percent of their yearly electricity consumption with renewable energy procurements. This does not mean, however, that Google uses 100 percent renewable energy. Like everyone else, Google is dependent on the forms of energy used to generate electricity for a given grid—which means that in many regions,

the Google Cloud uses mainly coal, gas, and nuclear power to power its facilities. As such, Google's claim to carbon neutrality means that the corporation buys renewable energy in amounts that are equivalent to the total amount of energy they use—but they nevertheless use dirty energy in the first place. Being climate neutral is not the same as being carbon free. This is not to suggest that Google isn't doing some good work in terms of renewable energy (see Google 2018). It is simply to note that the problems of powering the internet are not so easily resolved.

64. Dormon (2016).

65. Columbia's 1946 coal bill for its plant in Bridgeport, Connecticut was $102,264, while the average price of coal was $8.64 per ton—thus my estimate of 12,000 tons of coal (Myers and Addington 1947: 8–9, 31).

66. "Radio-Phonograph Making Halted" (1942: 5).

67. See Eriksson et al. (2019). It must be mentioned that Spotify (2017, 2018) has started to publish information about its electricity usage and carbon emissions. This is a positive step. That said, they provide information only for their own data centers, which excludes energy usage by the Google Cloud and by Spotify's content delivery network. So the numbers should be significantly higher than those actually reported. Additionally, while Spotify has a stated goal of achieving carbon neutrality, they have not to my knowledge committed to carbon-free energy.

68. The scandalized tone of the reportage on these inflated figures apparently forgets that payola (the practice of bribing radio stations and DJs for increased airtime for particular musicians) has been the norm throughout the history of recording.

69. One possibility that was especially exciting for Tidal in the fall of 2015 was MQA (Master Quality Authenticated), which was described to me as the audiophile's audio file (provided listeners have the requisite decoder). For an argument about "the persistence of compression" despite changes in internet infrastructure, see Sterne (2012: 230ff): "Every time a potential expansion of definition, storage, and bandwidth occurs, it is matched by a new set of compression schemes that attempt to wring more efficiency out of the system." Note that this is something Jevons might have predicted.

70. On the CD smugglers, see Witt (2015). On Spotify, see Wallenberg (2017) and Eriksson et al. (2019). For a comparative study of an anonymous P2P music-sharing community, see Durham (2017).

71. Harteau quoted in Henderson (2016).

72. The classic statement on time-biased versus space-biased media is Innis (2008). For good summaries and discussions of the implications of Innis's ideas, see Carey (2006: 109–132, 155–177) and Peters (2015: 306–313). On the relationships between wired and wireless media, see Mackenzie (2010) and Starosielski (2015).

73. Lees (1974: 69).

74. Whyte (1979: 29).

75. Moore (1979: 18). For contemporary research on the networked studio, see Théberge (2004).

76. Owen (2017).

77. Cook and Pomerantz (2015: 11). For the electricity figure, see Aslan et al. (2017: 1).

78. Cubitt et al. (2011: 155).

79. On the notion of genuine extended producer responsibility, see Lepawsky (2018). Saito (2017: 55–56) reminds us of the underlying distinction here between idealism and materialism: "According to Marx, Feuerbach's critique of religion may be able to educate the masses about God being a mere illusion.… The problem is that Feuerbach's critique ends there without posing a more substantial question: 'How did it come about that people "got" these illusions "into their heads"?' In other words, God is not a mere illusion that would disappear after its falseness was recognized. Rather, the illusion is an objective appearance produced by social relations.… Without a radical transformation of the social relations, the religious 'illusion' will be repeatedly reproduced as an objective force through social practice." Something similar could be said about the political ecology of music listening.

80. The *Times* of London initially reported the kettle statistic, which was based on the research of computer scientist Alexander Wissner-Gross.

Although this stat was widely republished, its accuracy was also quickly contested—by both Wissner-Gross and Google. I reproduce the kettle statistic here regardless of its validity, because it seems to have attained a place in popular discourse and so serves as a gateway to the wider issue. None of the estimates that follow is based on the *Times* reportage itself.

81. Aslan et al. (2017: 1).

82. Because the Recording Industry Association of America has published seemingly thorough statistics from the US industry, the United States will serve as the basis of comparison (see https://www.riaa.com/u-s-sales-database/). See also notes 83, 84, and 85 for further background information and caveats about the research in this section.

83. These figures have been reached by noting the total sales across each format in the three years and multiplying them by the average weight of each format.

84. To come up with these numbers, I have used standard contemporary figures that state greenhouse gas equivalents per kilogram of plastic production, as well as standard weight figures for LPs, 45s, cassettes, and CDs (including cases). I have not adjusted for historical greenhouse gas equivalents per kilogram of plastic production, which means that these amounts are almost certainly higher. The numbers that follow, on carbon dioxide equivalents in relation to downloading and streaming, are extrapolations based on several assumptions and averages. Part of the basis for these calculations is the 0.06 kilowatt-hours figure from Aslan et al. (2017). Their number is based on data transmission infrastructures (e.g., core internet protocol networks and the access networks that connect users to the wider internet). The number excludes data processing and storage infrastructures (e.g., data centers and undersea cables) as well as on-site networking equipment and user devices. The number is also based on the energy efficiency of data infrastructures in so-called developed countries in the year 2015. All of this means that the total amount of electricity required for, and pollution generated by, downloading data is likely higher—both in developed countries and around the world. My next step was to average the amount of data required for downloading and streaming songs and albums. This

allowed me to approximate both the amount of data transmitted and the amount of electricity used in the transmission of streamed and downloaded music around the years 2015–2016. Finally, knowing from the Click Clean Scorecard something about what types of power sources are used to generate electricity for services such as Spotify, I was able to convert electricity usage into approximate carbon dioxide equivalents. See also note 85 for additional variables and factors that could influence these figures.

85. To mention just a few examples: How long is the song or album? What's its file resolution? What type of server is used to store, process, and transmit the data? By what means is the electricity that powers a given server generated? How many different servers are used to back-up the data? Is it a high-speed connection? How long is the signal path? Is the listening device a computer or a phone? The list goes on. Note also that none of these figures accounts for the electricity used in powering various playback devices, which would add further variables. For additional estimates on energy usage in recorded music production and consumption, see George and McKay (2019).

86. For inflation-adjusted figures suggesting that an album costs less today than in the past, see Hogan (2015). Some of the research in the section features in a documentary called *The Cost of Music* (Brennan and O'Hara 2019), part of which I helped write and in which I appear as an interviewee and narrator. The documentary also shows that recorded music is less expensive now than in previous times. Thanks to Matt Brennan for sharing his research and for inviting me to collaborate in *The Cost of Music*.

87. In fact, this relationship has been understood at least since Adorno, though current research has refined our understanding of the point.

88. I am here paraphrasing Winthrop-Young (2014: 385).

89. Quotations from, respectively, Hennion (2015: 270) and Hennion (2005: 139; original emphasis). In speaking in these terms, Hennion indirectly acknowledges a broader and longstanding interest in social "morphology" that is found in the work of Durkheim, Mauss, Simmel, Benjamin, Elias, and others.

90. Hennion et al. quoted in Granjon and Combes (2007: 295). The article is in French and the translations are mine. See also Hennion (2001). On how notation "prepared the social, cultural, and economic ground for sound reproduction," see Théberge (1997: 176). And see Théberge (2013) on how the preponderance of digital visualization techniques and technologies in popular music production (which offer a variety of novel "material engagements with sound" and "many other forms of musical 'literacy'") continues to be rooted in notation. Indeed, in Théberge's analysis "the production of pop may now be as dependent on graphical notations as any other genre."

91. Granjon and Combes (2007). It is not possible here to fully describe the extent and character of these changes that fall under the umbrella of digitamorphosis. Georgina Born and Christopher Haworth (2017: 601) note some other shifts with music's digitalization: "the changing nature of the musical object; the effects of new modes of internet-based distribution, circulation, and disintermediation on the music industries; the novel possibilities for internet-based musical performance; and the potential for music recommendation and discover systems presented by online databases."

92. Granjon and Combes (2009: 287).

93. Granjon and Combes (2007: 295; the translation is mine).

94. Steingo (2015: 103). For additional commentary on ubiquity and mobility, see Kassabian (2013) and Gopinath and Stanyek (2014).

95. Sedgewick (2014: 143). See also Starosielski (2015) for an analysis of global internet infrastructure that is also "against flow." For a keyword discussion of flow in terms of information, see Braman (2016). For a similar critique of the cloud as a metaphor for storage, see Morris (2015, chapter 5). For other critiques of waterborne metaphors in audiotechnical discourse, see Rodgers (2010) and Shiga (2015). Tsing's (2005: 4) work on friction—"the awkward, unequal, unstable, and creative qualities of interconnection across difference"—offers a better foundation for understanding movement and attachment than does flow.

96. Although Castells (2000), from whom I am borrowing the term network society, does describe the rise of the network society in terms

of a space of flows, he sees such flows in material terms rather than as strictly electronic digital spaces. For a discussion of networks in relation to contemporary music studios, which puts Castells into conversation with Appadurai, see Théberge (2004).

97. See Morris (2015: 176).

98. For a nuanced introduction to networks and "historical ecology" in relation to music research, see Piekut (2014). See also Latour (2005). In an earlier essay, Latour (1999: 15) noted the extent to which the meaning of the word network that emerged alongside the World Wide Web served to undermine the purpose of that notion in his scholarship: "At the time, the word network … clearly meant a series of transformations—translations, transductions—which could not be captured by any of the traditional terms of social theory. With the new popularization of the word network, it now means transport without transformation, an instantaneous, unmediated access to every piece of information. That is exactly the opposite of what we meant."

99. See Steingo (forthcoming), where he shows how power cuts were purposefully orchestrated by the South African government. This observation leads him to subtly rethink the trope of "invisibility" in infrastructure studies: "I used to think I that I could hear the crumbling infrastructure every time a desktop went silent or the lights went out. Or I thought that I could hear scarcity, could hear a kind of national lack in those audio glitches created by power cuts. But we know now that the cuts themselves were multiply mediated and even deliberately plotted. Failure, in this context, does not disclose the truth of the system, nor does it reveal the materiality of media beyond a cultural veneer. It points, rather, to multiple layers of material, cultural, technological, and political mediation rooted in South Africa's specific history and present" (cf. Steingo 2015, 2016, 2017). See also Boudreault-Fournier (forthcoming), where she describes how electronic musicians in Cuba, an island where digital infrastructures have been scarce and unreliable, have developed systems for making and listening to music that are "about alternative local intranets as much as the official global internet, hand-to-hand data sharing as much as peer-to-peer file transfers, human 'servers' as much as computer servers."

Afterword

1. See Sterne (2003a) for a thorough critique of "fidelity" in terms of its social construction. In outlining their theory of the social construction of reality in 1966, Berger and Luckman (1991) draw implicitly on the "theorem" (Merton 1948) of Dorothy Thomas and William Thomas (1928: 571–572) that I have paraphrased here: "If [people] define situations as real, they are real in their consequences." For further background on how this "theorem" developed in sociology, and how it was also articulated in different terms by George Herbert Mead and Erving Goffman, see Merton (1995) and Vera (2016: 8).

2. A concert setting is of course never "immediate" but is always a fully mediated situation. In Grusin's (2015b: 135) terms, "*mediation is itself immediate*" (original emphasis). For additional background on the experiences and ideologies of concertgoers in relation to contemporary digital media, see Frith (2007), Holt (2010), and Kjus and Danielsen (2014).

3. Brennan (forthcoming). See also Pedelty (2012, 2016).

4. On hat-tipping and mediality, see Sterne (2012: 15). On bagels and mediality, see Straw (2015: 128). On "the quiet work of the generative matrix," see Straw (2010a: 215).

5. McClary (2011).

6. This opinion comes from the comment thread on Slipped Disc, a UK music website where Cheng's book was willfully misread and unfortunately maligned (http://slippedisc.com/2016/08/what-musicology-is-for-in-2016/).

7. Cusick (2008: para. 4; original emphasis). For additional work on music, violence, and war that confronts similar issues, see Johnson and Cloonan (2009), Fast and Pegley (2012), Daughtry (2015), and Pieslak (2015). See also Hesmondhalgh (2013: 4) for a broader "*critical defense* of music" that accounts for "the way that music is imbricated with society and the self, with all their problems" (original emphasis).

8. Nixon (2011: 2).

9. Although my discussion is routed through musicology, similar worries about decentering cultural works are expressed in most of the humanities and social science fields that have met the perspectives I am drawing on in this discussion. When media philosophy developed out of literature departments in the 1980s, for example, it became known as a form of "Literary Studies +/– Literature" (Griffin 1996) that "was disturbing for some people" (Kittler in Armitage 2006: 21). As interest in the post-hermeneutic materialities of communication spread to other fields, Bernhard Siegert (2015: 3) describes the negative reaction: "the many literature scholars, philosophers, anthropologists, and communication experts who were suddenly forced to realize how much there was beyond the hermeneutic reading of texts when it came to understanding the medial conditions of literature and truth or the formation of humans and their souls, were much too offended by this sudden assault on their academic habitat to ask what theoretical justification [or, I would add, ethical imperative] lay behind this invasion." Film scholarship is also characterized by these debates. Compare, for example, Andrew (2009) with Wasson (2015).

10. Tomlinson (1993: 23).

11. Tomlinson (1993: 24). Note that whereas Tomlinson is partly criticizing the tendency to value the music of the Western concert tradition above others, the same critical mind set ought to inform research in popular music studies and ethnomusicology—indeed all music (cf. Beaster-Jones 2014, Spiller 2014). It is interesting to note how Tomlinson's argument here can be seen to prefigure his recent book, *A Million Years of Music* (2015)—which itself contains no analyses of particular musics or musical experiences but, rather, is an examination of what I would describe as the generalized conditions of music's mediality.

12. This and previous quotes from Kramer (1993: 32, 27 respectively). For another example of the concern surrounding the decentering of music, this time from the perspective of gender theory, see Citron (1993: 74–75): "Of course there are risks [to the infiltration of gender theory into musicology]. … We could become so wrapped up in critical theory that we lose sight of the *raison d'être* of our efforts: music itself. Many

believe this has already happened with literature. One hopes that our roots in musical performance and the sheer aesthetic pleasure of music will temper any disciplinary tendencies toward theoretical excess."

13. Kramer (1993: 27). Although I am focusing on this debate as it has played out among major US-based musicologists, a similar tension has animated the international field of popular music studies from the beginning: scholars have been pigeonholed as working from *either* sociological *or* musicological perspectives, with each group of scholars pointing out inadequacies in the other's theories and methods. Sociologists are seen to decenter musical specificity while musicologists are seen to focus too tightly on musical specificity. The same questions have animated the sociology of art. For a summary of these debates, see Prior (2011).

14. Piekut (2014: 213).

15. For explanations of these perspectives from sociology, ecology, and media studies, see respectively Latour (2005), Morton (2007), and Sigert (2015; cf. Sterne 2014b).

16. See Sterne (2003b), who is developing a foundational premise of Pierre Bourdieu's approach to sociology.

17. Mathew and Smart (2014: 61) do not provide much detail about why there is now a "suspicion of close reading" or an uncertainty surrounding "the status of the 'texts' (musical works, as notated or performed) whose interpretation and explanation traditionally anchored much musicological writing." In addition to Tomlinson's above-mentioned perspective, for further background on these issues see various critiques from musicologists and sociologists engaged with both classical and popular music: Hennion (1983, 1995, 2003), DeNora (1986, 2003), Martin (1995, 2006), Frith (1996), and Hooper (2006).

18. Mathew and Smart (2015: 63). One of the most insightful issues covered by Mathew and Smart (2015: 72) is their recognition that quirk historicism has been compounded by Google searches, which is to recognize (with discomfort) the mediatic constitution of contemporary musicology (see also Walton 2015). Yet they do not completely pursue where this reflexivity might lead: namely toward a full-blown mediatic

critique of musicology as a whole (cf. Sterne 2015). On chatter in media and academic research, see Winthrop-Young (2017: 216–217): "Any full account of the Kittler effect needs to pay attention to the *theory chatter* of social media (remember that in the intelligence context *chatter* is not a disparaging term). This, needless to say, is not just another indication of the decline of authority suffered by traditional academic gatekeepers.... Media—social media—determine the situation of our media theorists, also and especially of those who had little to say about social media" (original emphases).

19. Mathew and Smart (2015: 63, 73).

20. Mathew and Smart (2015: 73).

21. Mathew and Smart (2015: 72).

22. Mathew and Smart (2015: 72).

23. Indeed, the near total absence of Born, DeNora, and Hennion (not to mention others) here is conspicuous, especially given that each scholar has been influenced to greater and lesser degrees by the Latourian perspectives that Mathew and Smart are engaging with. The sociological theories developed by Hennion, for example, emerged partly out of a specific disagreement with Durhkheim and Bourdieu. Whereas Bourdieu's (1984) anti-Kantian sociology of taste and aesthetics has been criticized for "conceptually eradicat[ing] the specific and distinctive qualities of individual art works by reducing them to the conditions of reflective social symbols" in games of distinction played by ostensibly naïve believers (Shepherd and Devine 2015: 10), Hennion wishes to draw attention to the ongoing and mutual constitution of particular objects and particular subjects in observable cultural practices. This is also, in a somewhat similar way, the direction for musicology that Mathew and Smart wish to pursue. For other pioneering music scholarship more or less along these lines, see Shepherd and Wicke (1997), DeNora (2003), and Prior (2011), as well as Born's essay on "The Social and the Aesthetic" (not cited in the bibliography). See also Felski (2015) for a related view from literary studies.

24. Hennion (2016: 302).

25. Dolan (2015: 88).

26. Dolan (2015: 88). See also Dolan (2011).

27. Dolan (2015: 89): "often, the turn to music's materiality risks being antidialogical; it has sometimes involved unearthing oddities and curious objects... without prompting or even allowing for further critical discussion." Sterne and Leach (2006: 189) are similarly dissatisfied with constructivist work in science and technology studies: "We felt that a story about social construction was being told over and over, regardless of the artifact in question... object 'X' turns out to be constructed instead of natural. By narrating the process of constriction... the author uncovers a range of interested social actors and, in some cases, the actions of material factors themselves in a web of interconnected causes and effects.... Having restored the artifact to its fullness, the story ends happily." See also Sterne (2014c) for a measured consideration of the material turn.

28. Dolan (2015: 91).

29. Mathew and Smart (2015: 72).

30. For the beginnings of an answer to this question, see Tomlinson (1999: 344): "The problem with 'music' is on familiar to us from other naturalized constructs. It tends to stand outside our thought, directing it but inaccessible. Music's transparency gives it power to determine our discourse while remaining invisible to it. In this it operates together with another construct, the aesthetic, that emerged in the eighteenth century just as music (again, the cultural category) was attaining its modern form. Together, aesthetics and music came, across the 1700s, to cast a new light on concepts hallowed in the West—beauty, for example, or the sublime. Together they informed a new conception of emotion expressed in new terms such as sentiment, sensibility.... Together still, a century later, the underwrote a fundamental articulation in European thought that could, at its culminating moment in Schopenhauer, the early Nietzsche, and Wagner, encompass in music metaphysical or transcendental realms all told." See also Kerman (1980) for additional background. Note again that, although Tomlinson and Kerman (and others) were primarily concerned to trace these notions as they developed

from and influenced the world of art music, these same notions have been translated in various ways into popular music (see Frith 1996 and Keightley 2001).

31. Hennion (2007a: 330–331).

32. Mathew and Smart (2015: 72). See also Dolan (2015) and Richardson (2016). The staying power of all this is remarkable. Similar questions were posed to McClary (1990: 9) in the 1980s, when she was asked "by a well-meaning, liberal musicologist … 'How is the work of art to survive the social critique? Is there a remedy that does not violate the work?'" Additionally, see Subotnik (1991: 3), reflecting on her early musicology training going back to the 1970s: "Some time ago, an established American musicologist complained to me that I approached the study of music with a philosophical orientation and was therefore bound to falsify music and music history."

33. I am here adapting Winthrop Young (2015: 81–82): "Kittler readers will … recall that he was a great promoter of unknown quotations. Among the best-known is the observation by the newly mechanized Friedrich Nietzsche, who, reflecting on the impact that his [typewriter] had on his style, noted in a letter: … 'our writing tools too are working on our thoughts.' … The obvious self-reflexive twist—our writing tools are also working on our thoughts about our writing tools—contains in a nutshell the recursive epistemological dilemma that has haunted media theory since the early days of Harold Innis."

34. These last three sentences refer to Raymond Williams's (1989) perspective on culture. A similar notion is expressed in the work of Tami Gadir, whose critical response to utopian and exceptionalist rave discourses is forthcoming with Bloomsbury.

35. Wong (2014: 351–352).

36. Dolan (2015: 92–93).

37. I am adapting from and expanding on McClary (2000).

38. On the politics of turns and interventions in cultural research, see respectively Straw (2016) and Sterne (2017).

39. See Palmer (2009): "The human race breathes out about 8.5 percent as much carbon as we burn. Experts are quick to point out that this figure is meaningless, since human respiration is part of a 'closed loop cycle' in which our carbon dioxide output is matched by the carbon dioxide take in by the wheat, corn, celery, and Ugli fruit that we eat.... In fact, the loop is not entirely closed.... The human body—like all animals—is a very modest carbon sequestration device." Note also that every breath and every voice is an essentially technical, mediatic phenomenon (Peters 2018, Prior 2018).

40. Haraway (1991), Leroi-Gourhan (1993), Stiegler (1998), Latour (2002), Mackenzie (2002), Peters (2015), and Siegert (2015). For a summary that traces the notion of "originary technicity" from Marx to Derrida and beyond, see Bradley (2011). For related perspectives from music and sound studies, see Born (2005), Gallope (2011), Sterne (2012), Steingo (2015), Sterne (2016b), Prior (2018), and Steingo and Sykes (2019).

41. Tomlinson (2015: 48–49; original emphasis).

42. On staying with the trouble and making kin, see Haraway (2016).

43. The phrase *musicology in the future tense* builds on Grossberg (2010). A similar notion—ecomusicology in the future tense—has been developed by Størvold (forthcoming). The notion of a *musicology of the otherwise* is loosely adapted from Povinelli (2011, 2014, 2016). See also Born and Barry (2018), who connected Born's fourfold theory of musical mediation to what we might call an anthropology of the possible (cf. Holbraad, Pederson, and Viveiros de Castro 2014).

44. Thanks to Jonathan Sterne for suggesting the phrase *post-catastrophic media*.

45. I am paraphrasing the Petrocultures Research Group (2016: 68). See also Wilson, Szeman, and Carlson (2017). On degrowth in relation to the electronics industries, see Lepawsky (2018).

46. The paraphrasing and quotation in this sentence are from Grossberg (2010: 294).

Bibliography

Aamoth, Dough. 2012. "Like the Smell of New Apple Gadgets? There's a Fragrance for That." *Time* (17 April): online.

Abbate, Carolyn. 2004. "Music: Drastic or Gnostic?" *Critical Inquiry* 30(3): 505–536.

Achachlouei, Mohammad Ahmadi, and Åsa Moberg. 2015. "Life Cycle Assessment of a Magazine, Part II." *Journal of Industrial Ecology* 19(4): 590–606.

Acland, Charles. 2007. "Introduction: Residual Media." In *Residual Media*, edited by Charles Acland, xiii–xxvii. Minneapolis: University of Minnesota Press.

Acland, Charles. 2009. "Curtains, Carts, and the Mobile Screen." *Screen* 50(1): 148–166.

Acland, Charles. 2012. "The Crack in the Electric Window." *Cinema Journal* 51(2): 167–171.

Acland, Charles. 2014. "Dirt Research for Media Industries." *Media Industries Journal* 1(1): 6–10.

Adorno, Theodor. 1991. *The Culture Industry: Selected Essays on Mass Culture*. New York: Routledge.

Albeiz, Sean. Forthcoming. "Vinyl." In *The Bloomsbury Encyclopedia of Popular Music of the World*, edited by David Horn and John Shepherd. New York: Bloomsbury.

Aldridge, B.L. 1964. *The Victor Talking Machine Company: A Candid History*. Camden: RCA Sales Corporation. [Box 1, RCA Victor Camden / Frederick O. Barnum III collection (Accession 2069). Hagley Museum and Library, Wilmington, DE.]

Allen, Aaron. 2012. "Fatto di Fiemme: Stradivari and the Musical Trees of the Paneveggio." In *Invaluable Trees: Cultures of Nature, 1660–1880*, edited by Laura Auricchio, Elizabeth Heckendorn Cook, and Giulia Pacini, 301–315. Oxford: Voltaire Foundation.

Allen, Aaron. 2017. "Greening the Curriculum: Beyond a Short Music History in Ecomusicology." *Journal of Music History Pedagogy* 8(1): 91–109.

Allen, Aaron, and Kevin Dawe, eds. 2016. *Current Directions in Ecomusicology: Music, Culture, Nature*. New York: Routledge.

Almquist, Sharon. 1987. "Sound Recordings and the Library." Occasional Paper No. 179. Graduate School of Information Sciences: University of Illinois.

Anderson, Tim. 2014. *Popular Music in a Digital Music Economy: Practices, Problems, and Solutions for an Emerging Service Industry*. New York: Routledge.

Andrew, Dudley. 2009. "The Core and the Flow of Film Studies." *Critical Inquiry* 35(4): 879–915.

Angus, Robert. 1974. "Why Do Records Have to Be Black Anyway?" *High Fidelity* 24(7): 68.

Appadurai, Arjun, ed. 1986. *The Social Life of Things: Commodities in Cultural Perspective*. Cambridge: Cambridge University Press.

Appel, Hanna, Arthur Mason, and Michael Watts, eds. 2015. *Subterranean Estates: Life Worlds of Oil and Gas*. Ithaca: Cornell University Press.

Arditi, David. 2017. "Digital Subscriptions: The Unending Consumption of Music in the Digital Era." *Popular Music and Society* (online prepublication version): 1–17.

Armitage, John. 2006. "From Discourse Networks to Cultural Mathematics: An Interview with Friedrich A. Kittler." *Theory, Culture, and Society* 23(7–8): 17–38.

Askerøi, Eirik. 2016. "Who Is Beck? Sonic Markers as a Compositional Tool in Pop Production." *Popular Music* 35(3): 380–395.

Aslan, Joshua, Kieren Mayers, Jonathan Koomey, and Chris France. 2017. "Electricity Intensity of Internet Data Transmission: Untangling the Estimates." *Journal of Industrial Ecology* (online prepublication version): 1–14.

Athey, Skipwith. 1966. *Magnetic Tape Recording*. Washington: National Aeronautics and Space Administration.

Auslander, Philip. 2001. "Looking at Records." *The Drama Review* 45(1): 77–83.

Auslander, Philip. 2002. *Liveness: Performance in a Mediatized Culture*, 2nd ed. New York: Routledge.

Ball, Philip. 2001. *Bright Earth: The Invention of Colour*. London: Viking.

Barry, Andrew. 2013. *Material Politics: Disputes along the Pipeline*. Oxford: Wiley.

Barry, Eric. 2014. "Digilog Culture and the Vinyl Revival of the Early 21st Century." *American History Now* (30 April): online.

Barthes, Roland. 1972a. "Plastic." In *Mythologies*. New York: Hill and Wang.

Barthes, Roland. 1972b. "The New Citroën." In *Mythologies*. New York: Hill and Wang.

Bartmanski, Dominik, and Ian Woodward. 2013. "The Vinyl: The Analogue Medium in the Age of Digital Reproduction." *Journal of Consumer Culture* 15(1): 3–27.

Bartmanski, Dominik, and Ian Woodward. 2015. *Vinyl: The Analogue Record in the Digital Age*. New York: Bloomsbury.

Bartmanski, Dominik, and Ian Woodward. 2018. "Vinyl Record: A Cultural Icon." *Consumption Markets and Culture* 21(2): 171–177.

Barton, F.C. "Victrolac Motion Picture Records." *Journal of the Society of Motion Picture Engineers* 18(4): 452–460.

Batchelor, Joseph. 1944. *An Economic History of the Indiana Oolitic Limestone Industry*. Bloomington: Indiana University.

Bates, Eliot. 2012. "The Social Life of Musical Instruments." *Ethnomusicology* 56(3): 363–395.

Beall, Glen. No date. *The Evolution of Plastics in America (Occasional Paper No. 1)*. New York: Plastics Historical Society.

Beaster-Jones, Jayson. 2014. "Beyond Musical Exceptionalism: Music, Value, and Ethnomusicology." *Ethnomusicology* 58(2): 334–340.

Beaster-Jones, Jayson. 2016. *Music Commodities, Markets, and Values: Music as Merchandise*. New York: Routledge.

Beattie, James, Edward Melillo, and Emily O'Gorman. 2014. "Introduction: Eco-Cultural Networks and the British Empire, 1837–1945." In *Eco-Cultural Networks and the British Empire: New Views on Environmental History*, edited by James Beattie, Edward Melillo, and Emily O'Gorman, 3–20. New York: Bloomsbury.

Beck, Andrew. 2003. "Introduction: Cultural Work, Cultural Workplace—Looking at the Cultural Industries." In *Cultural Work: Understanding the Cultural Industries*, edited by Andrew Beck, 1–11. New York: Routledge.

Becker, Howard. 1963. *Outsiders: Studies in the Sociology of Deviance*. New York: The Free Press.

Becker, Howard. 1982. *Art Worlds*. Berkeley: University of California Press.

Becker, Howard. 2017. "Creativity Is Not a Scarce Commodity." *American Behavioral Scientist* 61(12): 1597–1588.

Becker, Howard, and Alain Pessin. 2006. "A Dialogue on the Ideas of 'World' and 'Field.'" *Sociological Forum* 21(2): 275–286.

Behr, Adam. 2015. "Cultural Policy and the Creative Industries." In *The Routledge Reader on the Sociology of Music*, edited by John Shepherd and Kyle Devine, 277–286. New York: Routledge.

Beinart, William, and Lotte Hughes. 2007. *Environment and Empire*. Oxford: Oxford University Press.

Bennett, Jane. 2010. *Vibrant Matter: A Political Ecology of Things*. Durham: Duke University Press.

Bennet, Tony, and Patrick Joyce, eds. 2010. *Material Powers: Cultural Studies, History, and the Material Turn*. New York: Routledge.

Bennett, Tony, Mike Savage, Elizabeth Bortolaia Silva, Alan Warde, Modesto Gayo-Cal, David Wright. 2009. *Culture, Class, Distinction*. New York: Routledge.

Berenbaum, May. 1993. *Ninety-Nine More Maggots, Mites, and Munchers*. Champaign: University of Illinois Press.

Berger, Peter, and Thomas Luckmann. 1991. *The Social Construction of Reality: A Treatise in the Sociology of Knowledge*. New York: Penguin Books.

Berkhout, Frans, and Julia Hertin. 2004. "De-Materialising and Re-Materialising: Digital Technologies and the Environment." *Futures* 36(8): 903–920.

Berliner, Edgar. No date (ca. 1912–1919). "Laboratory Notebook" (NAC: 3100.0010). Montreal: Emile Berliner Sound and Image Archive.

Berliner, Emile. 1895. "Technical Notes on the Gramophone." *Journal of the Franklin Institute* 140(6): 419–437.

Berliner, Emile. 1913. "The Development of the Talking Machine." *Journal of the Franklin Institute* 176(2):189–200.

Benjamin, Walter. 1973. "The Work of Art in the Age of Mechanical Reproduction." In *Illuminations*, 211–244. London: Fontana Press.

Bennett, Andy, and Ian Rogers. 2016. "Popular Music and Materiality: Memorabilia and Memory Traces." *Popular Music and Society* 39(1): 28–42.

Bensaude-Vincent, Bernadette. 2013. "Plastics, Materials, and Dreams of Dematerialization." In *Accumulation: The Material Politics of Plastic*, edited by Jennifer Gabrys, Gay Hawkins, and Mike Michael, 17–29. New York: Routledge.

Bensaude-Vincent, Bernadette, and Jonathan Simon. 2008. *Chemistry: The Impure Science*. London: Imperial College Press.

Bhaktavatsala, M. 2003. "Mr Shellac and Miss Vinyl." *The Hindu* (3 February): online.

Biekrsack, Aletta. 2006. "Reimagining Political Ecology: Culture/Power/Nature/History." In *Reimagining Political Ecology*, edited by Aletta Biersack and James Greenberg, 3–40. Durham: Duke University Press.

Bijker, Wiebe. 1995. *Of Bicycles, Bakelites, and Bulbs: Toward a Theory of Sociotechnical Change*. Cambridge: MIT Press.

Block, Debbie Galante. 1998. "The Raw-Material World: Polycarbonate Supply Barely Meets Demand." *Billboard* (15 August): 60, 62, 64.

Blom, Ina, Trond Lundemo, and Eivind Røsaak, eds. 2017. *Memory in Motion: Archives, Technology, and the Social*. Amsterdam: Amsterdam University Press.

Blum, Andrew. 2012. *Tubes: Behind the Scenes at the Internet*. Harmandsworth: Penguin.

Bohlman, Andrea. 2017. "Making Tapes in Poland: The Compact Cassette at Home." *Twentieth-Century Music* 14(1): 119–134.

Bohlman, Andrea, and Peter McMurray. 2017. "Tape: Or, Rewinding the Phonographic Regime." *Twentieth-Century Music* 14(1): 3–24.

Bonner, David. 2008. *Revolutionizing Children's Records: The Young People's Records and Children's Record Guild Series, 1946–1977*. Lanham: Scarecrow Press.

Born, Georgina. 1987. "Modern Music Culture: On Shock, Pop, and Synthesis." *New Formations* 2: 51–78.

Born, Georgina. 2005. "On Musical Mediation: Ontology, Technology, and Creativity." *Twentieth-Century Music* 2(1): 7–36.

Born, Georgina. 2010. "For a Relational Musicology: Music and Interdisciplinarity, Beyond the Practice Turn." *Journal of the Royal Musical Association* 135(2): 205–243.

Born, Georgina. 2011. "Music and the Materialization of Identities." *Journal of Material Culture* 16(4): 376–388.

Born, Georgina. 2012. "Music and the Social." In *The Cultural Study of Music: A Critical Introduction,* edited by Martin Clayton, Trevor Herbert, and Richard Middleton, 261–274. New York: Routledge.

Born, Georgina, ed. 2013. *Music, Sound, and Space: Transformations of Public and Private Experience*. Cambridge: Cambridge University Press.

Born, Georgina, and Andrew Barry. 2018. "Introduction: Music, Mediation Theories, and Actor-Network Theory." *Contemporary Music Review* 37(5–6): 443–487.

Born, Georgina, and Christopher Haworth. 2017. "From Microsound to Vaporwave: Internet-Mediated Musics, Online Methods, and Genre." *Music and Letters* 98(4): 601–647.

Born, Georgina, and David Hesmondhalgh, eds. 2000. *Western Music and Its Others: Difference, Representation, and Appropriation in Music*. Berkeley: University of California Press.

Borthakur, Anwesha, and Kunal Sinha. 2013. "Generation of Electronic Waste in India: Current Scenario, Dilemmas, and Stakeholders." *African Journal of Environmental Science and Technology* 7(9): 899–910.

Bottrill, Catherine, Geoff Lye, Max Boykoff, and Diana Liverman. 2008. *First Step: UK Music Industry Greenhouse Gas Emissions for 2007*. Oxford: Julie's Bicycle.

Bourdieu, Pierre. 1984. *Distinction: A Social Critique of the Judgement of Taste*. Cambridge: Harvard University Press.

Boudreault-Fournier, Alexandrine. Forthcoming. "Street Net and Electronic Music in Cuba." In *Audible Infrastructures: Music, Sound, Media,* edited by Kyle Devine and Alexandrine Boudreault-Fournier. New York: Oxford University Press.

Bowker, Geoffrey, and Susan Leigh Star. 1999. *Sorting Things Out: Classification and Its Consequences*. Cambridge: MIT Press.

Bowman, Wayne. 1998. *Philosophical Perspectives on Music*. Oxford: Oxford University Press.

Bradley, Arthur. 2011. *Originary Technicity: The Theory of Technology from Marx to Derrida*. Basingstoke: Palgrave Macmillan.

Bregar, Bill. 2016a. "Germany's Newbilt Machinery Tackles the Niche for Vinyl Record Presses." *Plastics News* (7 October): online.

Bregar, Bill. 2016b. "It's Not about the Machines, It's the Music." *Plastics News* (17 October): online.

Braman, Sandra. 2016. "Flow." In *Digital Keywords: A Vocabulary of Information Society and Culture*, edited by Benjamin Peters, 118–131. Princeton: Princeton University Press.

Brennan, Matt. Forthcoming. "The Infrastructure and Environmental Consequences of Live Music." In *Audible Infrastructures: Music, Sound, Media*, edited by Kyle Devine and Alexandrine Boudreault-Fournier. New York: Oxford University Press.

Brennan, Matt, and Graeme O'Hara. 2019. *The Cost of Music*. Glasgow: Bob's Trainset Productions.

Bronfman, Alejandra. Forthcoming. "Glittery: Unearthed Histories of Music, Mica, and Work." In *Audible Infrastructures: Music, Sound, Media*, edited by Kyle Devine and Alexandrine Boudreault-Fournier. New York: Oxford University Press.

Brown, Bill. 2001. "Thing Theory." *Critical Inquiry* 28(1): 1–22.

Brown, Bill. 2010. "Materiality." In *Critical Terms for Media Studies*, edited by W.J.T. Mitchell and Mark Hansen, 49–63. Chicago: University of Chicago Press.

Browne, David. 2016. "In Defense of the CD." *Rolling Stone* (4 February): online.

Brøvig-Hanssen, Ragnhild. 2012. "The Magnetic Tape Recorder: Recording Aesthetics in the New Era of Schizophonia." In *Material Culture and Electronic Sound*, edited by Frode Weium and Tim Boon, 135–161. Washington: Smithsonian Institution Scholarly Press.

Brøvig-Hanssen, Ragnhild. 2018. "Listening To or Through Technology: Opaque and Transparent Mediation in Popular Music." In *Critical Approaches to the Production of Music and Sound*, edited by Samantha Bennett and Eliot Bates, 195–210. New York: Bloomsbury.

Brøvig-Hanssen, Ragnhild, and Anne Danielsen. 2016. *Digital Signatures: The Impact of Digitization on Popular Music Sound*. Cambridge: MIT Press.

Bryant, Raymond, ed. 2015. *The International Handbook of Political Ecology*. Cheltenham: Edward Elgar Publishing.

Bryson, H. Courtney. 1935. *The Gramophone Record*. London: Ernest Benn Ltd.

"Bug Juice." 1955. *Journal of the Franklin Institute* 260(4): 312.

Bull, Michael. 2007. *Sound Moves: iPod Culture and Urban Experience*. New York: Routledge.

Buraway, Michael. 1979. *Manufacturing Consent: Changes in the Labor Process under Monopoly Capitalism*. Chicago: University of Chicago Press.

Buraway, Michael. 1985. *The Politics of Production: Factory Regimes Under Capitalism and Socialism*. London: Verso.

Burkett, Paul. 1999. *Marx and Nature: A Red and Green Perspective*. New York: Palgrave Macmillan.

Burrington, Ingrid. 2015. "The Environmental Toll of a Netflix Binge." *The Atlantic* (16 December): online.

Burt, Leah. 1977. "Chemical Technology in the Edison Recording Industry." *Journal of the Audio Engineering Society* 25(10–11): 712–717.

"Call to Plastics." 1945. *Plastics* 3(2): 64, 91–92.

The Carbon Impacts of Recorded Music Products in a Time of Transition. 2009. Oxford: Julie's Bicycle.

Carey, James. 2006. *Communication as Culture: Essays on Media and Society*. New York: Routledge.

Carruth, Allison. 2014. "The Digital Cloud and the Micropolitics of Energy." *Public Culture* 26(2): 339–364.

Castells, Manuel. 2000. *The Rise of the Network Society*, 2nd ed. Malden: Blackwell.

Caulfield, Keith. 2018. "U.S. Vinyl Album Sales Hit Nielsen Music-Era Record High in 2017." *Billboard* (3 January): online.

Chakrabarty, Dipesh. 2009. "The Climate of History: Four Theses." *Critical Inquiry* 35: 197–222.

Chasins, Gladys. 1943. "Scrap Fights: Two Ways." *Billboard 1943 Music Year Book*. New York: Billboard.

Chatterja, J. 1924. "Rogers-Pyatt Shellac & Co. vs Secretary of State for India." Calcutta High Court (28 May).

Chen, Rene. 2017. "Meet the Record-Pressing Robot Fueling Vinyl's Comeback." *Wired* (2 September): online.

Cheng, William. 2016. *Just Vibrations: The Purpose of Sounding Good*. Ann Arbor: University of Michigan Press.

Chun, Wendy Hui Kyong. 2008. "The Enduring Ephemeral, or the Future Is Memory." *Critical Inquiry* 35(1): 148–171.

Citron, Marcia. 1993. "Gender and the Field of Musicology." *Current Musicology* 53: 66–75.

Clark, Duncan. 2011. "Google Discloses Carbon Footprint for the First Time." *The Guardian* (8 September): online.

Clark, Mark. 1993. "Suppressing Innovation: Bell Laboratories and Magnetic Recording." *Technology and Culture* 34(3): 516–538.

Clark-Meads, Jeff. 1997. "Polymer Suppliers Are Called On To Help Curb Piracy." *Billboard* (27 September): 1, 119.

Columbia Records. 1948. "Long Playing Microgroove Disc Demonstrated by Columbia Records." New York: Columbia Records Press Department.

Cook, Emory. 1954. "The Grooves Are Full of Gremlins." *High Fidelity* (April): 38–40.

Cook, Nicholas. 2013. *Beyond the Score: Music as Performance*. Oxford: Oxford University Press.

Cook, Gary, and David Pomerantz. 2015. *Clicking Clean: A Guide to Building the Green Internet*. Washington: Greenpeace.

Coole, Diana, and Samantha Frost, eds. 2010. *New Materialisms: Ontology, Agency, and Politics*. Durham: Duke University Press.

Cooling, B.F., and Norma Clements. 1959. *World Survey of Plastics: 1954–1957*. Washington: Department of Commerce (Business and Defense Services Administration.

Corbett, John. 2017. *Vinyl Freak: Love Letters to a Dying Medium*. Durham: Duke University Press.

"Cost of Shellac Rises 1,212%." 1920. *Talking Machine World* 16(4): 60.

Cottrell, Stephen. 2004. *Professional Music-Making in London: An Ethnography*. Abingdon: Ashgate.

Cowie, Jefferson. 2001. *Capital Moves: RCA's Seventy-Year Quest for Cheap Labor*. New York: The New Press.

Crandall, Elizabeth Brownell. 1924. *Shellac: A Story of Yesterday, Today, and Tomorrow*. Chicago: James B. Day & Co.

Crary, Jonathan. 1999. *Suspensions of Perception: Attention, Spectacle, and Modern Culture*. Cambridge: MIT Press.

Cronon, William. "The Trouble with Wilderness; or, Getting Back to the Wrong Nature." In *Uncommon Ground: Rethinking the Human Place in Nature*, edited by William Cronon, 69–90. New York: W.W. Norton.

Crowther, Bosley. 1945. "'Duffy's Tavern,' a Sprawling Film Revue." *New York Times* (6 September): 23.

Cubitt, Sean. 2017. *Finite Media: Environmental Implications of Digital Technologies*. Durham: Duke University Press.

Cubitt, Sean, Robert Hassan, and Ingrid Volkmer. 2011. "Does Cloud Computing Have a Silver Lining?" *Media, Culture, and Society* 33(1): 149–158.

Curran, Kieran. 2016. "On Tape: Cassette Culture in Edinburgh and Glasgow Now." In *21st Century Perspectives on Music, Technology, and Culture*, edited by Richard Purcell and Richard Randall, 33–54. London: Palgrave Macmillan.

Cusick, Suzanne. 2008. "Musicology, Torture, Repair." *Radical Musicology* 3: online.

Darnton, Robert. 2007. "'What Is the History of Books?' Revisited." *Modern Intellectual History* 4(3): 495–508.

Daughtry, J. Martin. 2015. *Listening to War: Sound, Music, Trauma, and Survival in Wartime Iraq*. Oxford: Oxford University Press.

Davenport, Matt. 2016. "Groovy Chemistry: The Materials Science Behind Records." *Chemical and Engineering News* 94(24): 16–19.

David, Matthew. 2010. *Peer to Peer and the Music Industry: The Criminalization of Sharing*. London: Sage.

Davis, John. 2007. "Going Analog: Vinylphiles and the Consumption of the 'Obsolete' Vinyl Record." In *Residual Media*, edited by Charles Acland, 222–236. Minneapolis: University of Minnesota Press.

"A Decade of Plastics." 1950. *Modern Plastics Encyclopedia and Engineer's Handbook*. New York: Plastics Catalogue Corporation.

Demers, Joanna. 2017. "Cassette Tape Revival as Creative Anachronism." *Twentieth-Century Music* 14(1): 109–117.

DeNora, Tia. 1986. "How Is Extra-Musical Meaning Possible? Music as a Place and Space for 'Work.'" *Sociological Theory* 4(1): 84–94.

DeNora, Tia. 2000. *Music and Everyday Life*. Cambridge: Cambridge University Press.

DeNora, Tia. 2003. *After Adorno: Rethinking Music Sociology*. Cambridge: Cambridge University Press.

Deo, Aditi, and Vebhuti Duggal. 2017. "Radios, Ringtones, and Memory Cards or, How the Mobile Phone Became Our Favourite Music Playback Device." *South Asian Popular Culture* 15(1): 41–56.

DeVeaux, Scott. 1997. *The Birth of Bebop: A Social and Musical History*. Berkeley: University of California Press.

Devine, Kyle. 2015. "Decomposed: A Political Ecology of Music." *Popular Music* 34(3): 367–389.

Devine, Kyle. 2016a. "L'intensité matérielle de l'écoute musicale sous forme de données." In *Où va la musique? Numérimorphose et nouvelles experiences d'écoute*, edited by Philippe Le Guern, 47–64. Paris: Presses des Mines.

Devine, Kyle. 2016b. "Sound Media Research Report." Ottawa: Canada Science and Technology Museum.

Devine, Kyle. 2019. "Musicology without Music." In *On Popular Music and Its Unruly Entanglements*, edited by Kai Arne Hansen and Nick Braae. Basingstoke: Palgrave Macmillan.

Devine, Kyle, and Alexandrine Boudreault-Fournier. Forthcoming. "Making Infrastructures Audible: An Introduction." In *Audible Infrastructures: Music, Sound, Media*, edited by Kyle Devine and Alexandrine Boudreault-Fournier. New York: Oxford University Press.

"Did Radiohead's 'In Rainbows' Honesty Box Actually Damage the Music Industry?" 2017. *NME* (9 October): online.

"Diskers Eye WPB Action." 1942. *Billboard* 54(26): 70.

"Diskers Ready New Plans." 1942. *Billboard* 54(17): 68, 74.

"Diskers Still Fear Shellac Grab by Govt." 1942. *Billboard* 54(36): 62.

Dolan, Emily. 2011. "Editorial." *Eighteenth-Century Music* 8(2): 175–177.

Dolan, Emily. 2015. "Musicology in the Garden." *Representations* 132: 88–94.

Dourish, Paul. 2017. *The Stuff of Bits: An Essay on the Materialities of Information*. Cambridge: MIT Press.

Dowkes, Olav. 2018. *Changing Listening Habits in Norway: The Album Format, Vinyl Revival, and Transformations in the Music Industry*. Master's thesis, Norwegian University of Science and Technology.

Downes, Kieran. 2010. "Perfect Sound Forever: Innovation, Aesthetics, and the Re-making of Compact Disc Playback." *Technology and Culture* 51(2): 305–331.

DuBois, J. Harry. 1972. *Plastics History U.S.A.* Boston: Cahners Publishing.

Durham, Blake. 2017. *Regulating Dissemination: A Comparative Digital Ethnography of Licensed and Unlicensed Spheres of Music Circulation*. DPhil diss., University of Oxford.

Duston, A. 1974. "PVC Ad Brings Bootleg Offers Asking 3 Times Regular Price." *Billboard* (11 May): 3.

Egen, Kelly. 2015. "Every Beatles Tune Began in Smiths Falls." *Ottawa Citizen* (16 November): online.

Ehrlich, Cyril. 1989. *The Music Profession in Britain since the Eighteenth Century: A Social History*. Oxford: Oxford University Press.

Eidsheim, Nina Sun. 2015. *Sensing Sound: Singing and Listening as Vibrational Practice*. Durham: Duke University Press.

Eisenberg, Andrew. 2012. "M-Commerce and the (Re)making of the Music Industry in Kenya." Presented at the Association of Social Anthropologists Meeting, Jawaharlal Nehru University, April.

Eisenberg, Evan. 2005. *The Recording Angel*. New Haven: Yale University Press.

Eley, Craig. 2011. "Technostalgia and the Resurgence of Cassette Culture." In *The Politics of Post-9/11 Music: Sound, Trauma, and the Music Industry in the Time of Terror*, edited by Joseph Fisher and Brian Flota, 43–54. Farnham: Ashgate.

Emmerson, Donald. 1978. *Canadian Inventors and Innovators, 1885–1950: Pioneering in Plastic*. Scarborough: Canadian Plastics Pioneers.

Emmett, Robert, and David Nye. 2017. *The Environmental Humanities: A Critical Introduction*. Cambridge: MIT Press.

Ensmenger, Nathan. 2018. "The Environmental History of Computing." *Technology and Culture* 59(4): S7–S33.

Environmental Protection Agency. 1978. *Survey of Vinyl Chloride Levels in the Vicinity of Keysor-Century, Sagus, California*. Denver: National Enforcement Investigations Center.

Environmental Protection Agency. 2004. "California PVC Firm Pays $4.3 Million Fine for Multiple Environmental Violations." EPA News Release (17 June): online.

Environmental Protection Agency. 2011. *Electronics Waste Management in the United States through 2009: Executive Summary*. Washington: EPA.

Environmental Protection Agency. 2012. *Climate Change Indicators in the United States, 2012*, 2nd ed. Washington: EPA.

Eriksson, Maria, Rasmus Fleischer, Anna Johansson, Pelle Snickars, and Patrick Vonderau. 2019. *Spotify Teardown: Inside the Black Box of Streaming Music*. Cambridge: MIT Press.

Ernst, Wolfgang. 2013. *Digital Memory and the Archive*. Minneapolis: University of Minnesota Press.

Ernst, Wolfgang. 2016. *Sonic Time Machines: Explicit Sound, Sirenic Voices, and Implicit Sonicicity*. Amsterdam: Amsterdam University Press.

Esposito, Frank. 2004. "Keysor-Century Pleads Guilty." *Plastics News* (28 June): online.

Evans, Claire. 2018. *Broad Band: The Untold Story of the Women Who Made the Internet*. New York: Portfolio/Penguin.

Excell, Carole, and Elizabeth Moses. 2017. *Thirsting for Justice: Transparency and Poor People's Struggle for Clean Water in Indonesia, Mongolia, and Thailand*. Washington: World Resources Institute.

Fagan, Ted. 1981. "Pre-LP Recordings of RCA at 33 1/3 rpm. through 1931 to 1934." *ASRC Journal* 13(1): 20–42.

Fast, Susan, and Kip Pegley, eds. 2012. *Music, Politics, and Violence*. Middletown: Wesleyan University Press.

Faulkner, Robert. 1978. "Swimming with Sharks: Occupational Mandate and the Film Composer in Hollywood." *Qualitative Sociology* 1(2): 99–129.

Fausset, Richard. 2002. "Sagus Firm Is Focus of Probe by U.S. Agencies." *Los Angeles Times* (14 February): online.

Felski, Rita. 2015. *The Limits of Critique*. Chicago: University of Chicago Press.

Fenichell, Stephen. 1996. *Plastic: The Making of a Synthetic Century*. New York: HarperCollins.

Fleischer, Rasmus. 2015. "Towards a Postdigital Sensibility: How to get Moved by too Much Music." *Culture Unbound* 7: 255–269.

Flood, Laruen. Forthcoming. "The Sounds of Zombie Media: Waste and the Sustainable Afterlives of Repurposed Technologies." In *Audible Infrastructures: Music, Sound, Media*, edited by Kyle Devine and Alexandrine Boudreault-Fournier. New York: Oxford University Press.

Foster, John Bellamy. 2000. *Marx's Ecology: Materialism and Nature*. New York: Monthly Review Press.

Foster, John Bellamy, and Paul Burkett. 2016. *Marx and the Earth: An Anti-Critique*. Leiden: Brill.

Fox, Barry. 1988. "The Changing Face of CD Production." *One-to-One* (January): 58–59.

Fox, Leonard. 1973. SelectaVision Processing. Unpublished research report. [Box M&A 881 / Folder 28, David Sarnoff Research Center Records (Accession 2464.09). Hagley Museum and Library, Wilmington, DE.]

Fox, Leonard, and Robert Ryan. 1979. "Conductive Polymer Composites for the VideoDisc." Presented at Society of Plastics Engineers Inc., New Orleans (May). [Box M&A 881 / Folder 29, David Sarnoff Research Center Records (Accession 2464.09). Hagley Museum and Library, Wilmington, DE.]

Freinkel, Susan. 2011. *Plastic: A Toxic Love Story*. New York: Houghton Mifflin Harcourt.

Fremer, Michael. 2017. "In a Thai Vinyl Noodle Factory (TPC—Thai Plastic Company)." *Analog Planet* (1 August): online.

Frith, Simon. 1978. *The Sociology of Rock*. London: Constable.

Frith, Simon. 1981a. *Sound Effects: Youth, Leisure, and the Politics of Rock 'n' Roll*. New York: Pantheon.

Frith, Simon. 1981b. "The Magic that Can Set You Free: The Ideology of Folk and the Myth of the Rock Community." *Popular Music* 1: 159–168.

Frith, Simon. 1987. "Copyright and the Music Business." *Popular Music* 7(1): 57–75.

Frith, Simon. 1988. "The Industrialization of Music." In *Music for Pleasure*. New York: Routledge.

Frith, Simon. 1996. *Performing Rites: On the Value of Popular Music*. Cambridge: Harvard University Press.

Frith, Simon. 2001. "The Popular Music Industry." In *The Cambridge Companion to Pop and Rock*, edited by Simon Frith, Will Straw, and John Street, 26–52. Cambridge: Cambridge University Press.

Frith, Simon. 2004. "Music and the Media." In *Music and Copyright*, edited by Simon Frith and Lee Marshall, 171–188. New York: Routledge.

Frith, Simon. 2007. "Live Music Matters." *Scottish Music Review* 1(1): 1–17.

Frith, Simon. 2008. "Why Music Matters." *Critical Inquiry* 50(1–2): 165–179.

Frith, Simon, Matt Brennan, Martin Cloonan, and Emma Webster. 2013. *The History of Live Music in Britain, Volume I: 1950–1967*. Farnham: Ashgate.

Frith, Simon, and Lee Marshall. 2004. "Making Sense of Copyright." In *Music and Copyright* (second edition), edited by Simon Frith and Lee Marshall, 1–18. New York: Routledge.

Frow, George. 2001. *The Edison Disc Phonographs and the Diamond Discs*. Los Angeles: Mulholland Press.

Fuchs, Christian. 2016. "Digital Labor and Imperialism." *Monthly Review* 67(8): 14–24.

Fuchs, Christian. 2017. "Capitalism, Patriarchy, Slavery, and Racism in the Age of Digital Capitalism and Digital Labour." *Critical Sociology* (online pre-publication version): 1–26.

Gabrys, Jennifer. 2011. *Digital Rubbish: A Natural History of Electronics*. Ann Arbor: University of Michigan Press.

Gabrys, Jennifer. 2015. "Powering the Digital: From Energy Ecologies to Electronic Environmentalism." In *Media and the Ecological Crisis*, edited by Richard Maxwell, Jon Raundalen, and Nina Lager Vestberg, 3–18. New York: Roultedge.

Gabrys, Jennifer. 2016. "Re-Thingifying the Internet of Things." In *Sustainable Media: Critical Approaches to Media and Environment*, edited by Nicole Starosielski and Janet Walker, 180–195. New York: Routledge.

Gabrys, Jennifer, Gay Hawkins, and Mike Michaels, eds. 2013. *Accumulation: The Material Politics of Plastic*. New York: Routledge.

Gallagher, S. 2014. "India: The Rising Tide of e-Waste." Pulitzer Center on Crisis Reporting: online.

Gallope, Michael. 2011. "Technicity, Consciousness, and Musical Objects." In *Music and Consciousness: Philosophical, Psychological, and Cultural Perspectives*, edited by David Clarke and Eric Clarke, 47–64. Oxford: Oxford University Press.

Gay, Leslie C. 1999. "Before the Deluge: The Technoculture of Song-Sheet Publishing Viewed from Late Nineteenth-Century Galveston." *American Music* 17(4): 396–421.

Gelatt, Roland. 1977. *The Fabulous Phonograph, 1877–1977*. New York: Collier Books.

George, Sharon, and Deirdre McKay. 2019. "The Environmental Impact of Music: Digital, Records, CDs Analysed." *The Conversation* (10 January): online.

Gitelman, Lisa. 2014. *Paper Knowledge: Toward a Media History of Documents*. Durham: Duke University Press.

Givens, Ron. 1990. "Trash the Longbox?" *Entertainment Weekly* (20 April): online.

Goldstein, Patrick. 1990. "The CD Long Box: Victim or Villain?" *Los Angeles Times* (8 July): online.

Goodman, David. 2010. "Distracted Listening: On Not Making Sound Choices in the 1930s." In *Sound in the Age of Mechanical Reproduction*, edited by David Suisman and Susan Strasser, 15–46. Philadelphia: University of Pennsylvania Press.

Google. 2018. *Moving toward 24x7 Carbon-Free Energy at Google Data Centers: Progress and Insights*. Mountain View: Google.

Gopinath, Sumanth. 2013. *The Ringtone Dialectic: Economy and Cultural Form*. Cambridge: MIT Press.

Gopinath, Sumanth, and Jason Stanyek, eds. 2014. *The Oxford Handbook of Mobile Music Studies* (Volume 1). Oxford: Oxford University Press.

Gómez-Barris, Macarena. 2017. *The Extractive Zone: Social Ecologies and Decolonial Perspectives*. Durham: Duke University Press.

Government of India. 1946. *Labour Investigation Committee: Main Report*. Delhi: Manager of Publications.

Graham, Earl. 1943. "Phonograph Records: Quality Deterioration." Memorandum from the Office of Price Administration to William MacLeod of the War Production Board (14 December). [New York Public Library for the Performing Arts, A.F.R. Lawrence Papers—*L (Special) 89.21—Box 5.]

Graham, Margaret. 1986. *The Business of Research: RCA and the VideoDisc*. Cambridge: Cambridge University Press.

Gramit, David. 1999–2000. "The Roaring Lion: Critical Musicology, the Aesthetic Experience, and the Music Department." *Repercussions* 7–8: 29–53.

Gramit, David. 2002. "Music Scholarship, Musical Practice, and the Act of Listening." In *Music and Marx: Ideas, Practice, Politics*, edited by Regula Qureshi, 3–22. New York: Routledge.

Granjon, Fabien, and Clément Combes. 2007. "La Numérimorphose des pratiques de consummation musicale: le cas de jeunes amateurs." *Réseaux* 145–146: 291–334.

Granjon, Fabien, and Clément Combes. 2009. "Digitamorphosis of Music Consumption Practices: The Case of Young Music Lovers." *French Cultural Studies* 20(3): 287–314.

Greenpeace. 2004. "Plastics Company Dumps Toxic Chemicals into Chao Praya River." *Greenpeace News* (8 July): online.

Gregson, Nicky, and Mike Crang. 2010. "Materiality and Waste: Inorganic Vitality in a Networked World." *Environment and Planning A: Economy and Space* 42: 1026–1032.

Gregson, Nicky, and Louise Crewe. 2003. *Second-Hand Cultures*. Oxford: Berg.

Grenier, Line. 1990. "The Construction of Music as a Social Phenomenon: Implications for Deconstruction." *Canadian University Music Review* 10(2): 27–47.

Griffin, Matthew. 1996. "Literary Studies +/–Literature: Friedrich A. Kittler's Media Histories." *New Literary History* 27(2): 709–716.

Gronow, Pekka. 1983. "The Record Industry: The Growth of a Mass Medium." *Popular Music* 3: 53–75.

Grossberg, Lawrence. 2010. *Cultural Studies in the Future Tense*. Durham: Duke University Press.

Grossman, Elizabeth. 2016. "The Body Burden: Toxics, Stresses, and Biophysical Health." In *The Routledge Companion to Labor and Media*, edited by Richard Maxwell, 65–77. New York: Routledge.

"A Growing Industry." 1948. *Plastics* 8(12): 6.

Grusin, Richard, ed. 2015a. *The Nonhuman Turn*. Minneapolis: University of Minnesota Press.

Grusin, Richard. 2015b. "Radical Mediation." *Critical Inquiry* 42(1): 124–148.

Guins, Raiford. 2014. *Game After: A Cultural Study of Video Game Afterlife*. Cambridge: MIT Press.

Gumbrecht, Hans Ulrich, and K. Ludwig Pfeiffer, eds. 1994. *Materialities of Communication*. Stanford: Stanford University Press.

Hansen, Beck. 2012. "A Preface to 'Song Reader.'" *The New Yorker* (12 November): online.

Haraway, Donna. 1991. *Simians, Cyborgs, and Women: The Reinvention of Nature*. New York: Routledge.

Haraway, Donna. 2016. *Staying with the Trouble: Makin Kin in the Chthulucene*. Durham: Duke University Press.

Haraway, Donna, Noboru Ishikawa, Gilbert Scott, Kenneth Olwig, Anna Tsing, and Nils Bubandt. 2016. "Anthropologists Are Talking—About the Anthropocene." *Ethnos* 81(3): 535–564.

Harper, Adam. 2018. "To Have and To Hold: Touch and the Vinyl Resurgence." *Tempo* 73(287): 52–61.

Harrison, Antony Kwame. 2006. "Cheaper Than a CD, Plus We Really Mean It: Bay Area Underground Hip Hop Tapes as Subcultural Artefacts." *Popular Music* 25(2): 283–301.

Havens, Lindsey. 2017. "Sony Music to Open Vinyl Pressing Plant in Japan." *Billboard* (29 June): online.

Hawkins, Gay. 2006. *The Ethics of Waste: How We Relate to Rubbish*. Lanham: Romwan and Littlefield.

Hawkins, Gay. 2013. "Made to be Wasted: PET and Topologies of Disposal." In *Accumulation: The Material Politics of Plastic*, edited by Jennifer Gabrys, Gay Hawkins, and Mike Michael, 49–66. London: Routledge.

Haynes, Jo, and Lee Marshall. 2017. "Reluctant Entrepreneurs: Musicians and Entrepreneurship in the 'New' Music Industry." *British Journal of Sociology* (online pre-publication version): 1–24.

Hegerty, Paul. 2007. "The Hallucinatory Life of Tape." *Culture Machine* 9: online.

Helbig, Otto Henry. 1966. *A History of Music in the U.S. Armed Forces during World War II*. New York: M.W. Lads.

Hemmingsen, Piers. 2015. *The Beatles in…Canada: The Origins of Beatlemania!* Canada: Hemmingsen Publishing.

Henderson, Nicole. 2016. "Spotify Ditches Own Data Centers in Favor of Google Cloud." *Data Center Knowledge* (26 February): online.

Hennion, Antoine. 1983. "The Production of Success: An Anti-Musicology of the Pop Song." *Popular Music* 3: 159–193.

Hennion, Antoine. 1995. "The History of Art: Lessons in Mediation." *Réseaux* 3(2): 233–262.

Hennion, Antoine. 2001. "Music Lovers: Taste as Performance." *Theory, Culture, and Society* 18(5): 1–22.

Hennion, Antoine. 2003. "Music and Mediation: Toward a New Sociology of Music." In *The Cultural Study of Music: A Critical Introduction*, edited by Martin Clayton, Trevor Herbert, and Richard Middleton, 80–91. New York: Routledge.

Hennion, Antoine. 2005. "Pragmatics of Taste." In *The Blackwell Companion to the Sociology of Culture*, edited by Mark Jacobs and Nancy Weiss Hanrahan, 131–144. Oxford: Blackwell.

Hennion, Antoine. 2007a. "Rewriting History from the Losers' Point of View: French Grand Opera and Modernity." In *Opera and Society in Italy and France from Monteverdi to Bourdieu*, edited by Victoria Johnson, Jane Fulcher, and Thomas Ertman, 330–350. Cambridge: Cambridge University Press.

Hennion, Antoine. 2007b. "Those Things That Hold Us Together: Taste and Sociology." *Cultural Sociology* 1(1): 97–114.

Hennion, Antoine. 2010. "Loving Music: From a Sociology of Mediation to a Pragmatics of Taste." *Comunicar* 34(8): 25–33.

Hennion, Antoine. 2015. *The Passion for Music: A Sociology of Mediation.* Farnham: Ashgate.

Hennion, Antoine. 2016. "From ANT to Pragmatism: A Journey with Bruno Latour at the CSI." *New Literary History* 47(2–3): 289–308.

Henry, Glenn. 1944. Letter from the War Production Board to the Columbia Recording Corporation (14 January). [New York Public Library for the Performing Arts, A.F.R. Lawrence Papers—*L (Special) 89.21—Box 5.]

Hertz, Garnet, and Jussi Parikka. 2012. "Zombie Media: Circuit Bending Media Archaeology into an Art Method." *Leonardo* 45(5): 424–430.

Hesmondhalgh, David. 2000. "Alternative Media, Alternative Texts? Rethinking Democratization in the Cultural Industries." In *Media Organizations in Society*, edited by James Curran, 107–125. London: Arnold.

Hesmondhalgh, David. 2009. "The Digitalisation of Music." In *Creativity, Innovation, and the Cultural Economy*, edited by Andy Pratt and Paul Jeffcutt, 57–73. London: Routledge.

Hesmondhalgh, David. 2013. *Why Music Matters*. Oxford: Wiley-Blackwell.

Hesmondhalgh, David, and Sarah Baker. 2011. *Creative Labour: Media Work in Three Cultural Industries*. London: Routledge.

Hesmondhalgh, David, and Leslie Meier. 2017. "What the Digitalisation of Music tells Us about Capitalism, Culture, and the Power of the Information Technology Sector." *Information, Communication, and Society* (online pre-publication version): 1–16.

Hetherington, Kevin. 2004. "Secondhandedness: Consumption, Disposal, and Absent Presence." *Environment and Planning D: Society and Space* 22: 157–173.

Hicks, Edward. 1962. *Shellac: Its Origin and Applications*. London: MacDonald.

Higgs, Richard. 2014. "Czech Disc Maker Cashes in on Vinyl Record Revival." *Plastics News* (14 August): online.

Higgs, Richard. 2015. “Pressing Demand for Vinyl sees GZ Expand Record Output.” *Plastics News* (18 December): online.

Hill, Erin. 2016. *Never Done: A History of Women’s Work in Media Production*. New Brunswick: Rutgers University Press.

Hirschkind, Charles. 2006. *The Ethical Soundscape: Cassette Sermons and Islamic Counterpublics*. New York: Columbia University Press.

Hogan, Marc. 2015. “How Much Is Music Really Worth?” *Pitchfork* (16 April): online.

Hogan, Marc. 2016. “Can Brand-New Record Presses Solve Vinyl’s Supply Problem?” *Pitchfork* (13 June): online.

Holbraad, Martin, Morten Axel Pederson, and Eduardo Viveiros de Castro. 2014. “The Politics of Ontology: Anthropological Positions.” *Cultural Anthropology* (13 January): online.

Holden, Stephen. 1990. “CD Packaging Attacked as Wasteful.” *New York Times* (25 December): 28.

Holt, Fabian. 2010. “The Economy of Live Music in the Digital Age.” *European Journal of Cultural Studies* 13(2): 243–261.

Holt, Jim. 2017. “Company’s Woes Still Plague SCV.” *The Signal* (3 May): online.

Hooper, Giles. 2006. *The Discourse of Musicology*. Aldershot: Ashgate.

Horkheimer, Max, and Theodor Adorno. 2002. *Dialectic of the Enlightenment: Philosophical Fragments*. Stanford: Stanford University Press.

Horn, Eva. 2007. “There Are No Media.” *Grey Room* 29: 6–13.

“How Emerson Combines Beauty and Utility in the 1946 Radio.” 1945. *Plastics* 3(5): 40, 42, 98.

Howley, Kevin. 2005. *Community Media: People, Places, and Communication Technologies*. Cambridge: Cambridge University Press.

Hu, Tung-Hui. 2015. *A Prehistory of the Cloud*. Cambridge: MIT Press.

Hughes, Alex, and Susanne Reimer, eds. 2004. *Geographies of Commodity Chains*. New York: Routledge.

Humphries, Barry. 1973. Appearance on *Desert Island Discs*. BBC (24 November).

Humphries, Barry. 1992. *More Please*. London: Viking.

Hung, Michele, and Esteban Morencos, eds. 1990. *World Recording Sales, 1969–1990: A Statistical History of the World Recording Industry*. London: International Federation of the Phonographic Industry.

Impey, Angela. 2013. "Keeping in Touch via Cassette: Tracing Dinka Songs from Cattle Camp to Transnational Audio-Lecture." *Journal of African Cultural Studies* 25(2): 197–210.

"Important Tariff Rulings." 1921. *Talking Machine World* 17(7): 157.

"Indian Shellac and Mica Trade." 1920. *Talking Machine World* 16(7): 10.

Ingold, Tim. 2007. "Materials against Materiality." *Archaeological Dialogues* 14(1): 1–16.

Ingold, Tim. 2012. "Toward an Ecology of Materials." *Annual Review of Anthropology* 41: 427–442.

Innis, Harold. 1933. *Problems of Staple Production in Canada*. Toronto: Ryerson Press.

Innis, Harold. 1970. *The Fur Trade in Canada: An Introduction to Canadian Economic History*. Toronto: University of Toronto Press.

Innis, Harold. 2008. *The Bias of Communication*. Toronto: University of Toronto Press.

International Federation of the Phonographic Industries. 2014. *Digital Music Report*. London: IFPI.

International Federation of the Phonographic Industries. 2016. *Music Consumer Insight Report 2016*. London: IFPI.

Isom, Warren Rex. 1977. "Record Materials." *Journal of the Audio Engineering Society* 25(10–11): 718–723.

James, Robin. Forthcoming. *The Sonic Episteme: Acoustic Resonance, Neoliberalism, and Biopolitics*. Durham: Duke University Press.

Jansen, Bas. 2008. "Tape Cassettes and Former Selves." In *Sound Souvenirs: Audio Technologies, Memory, and Cultural Practices*, edited by Karin Bijsterveld and José van Dijck, 43–54. Amsterdam: Amsterdam University Press.

Jasen, Paul. 2016. *Low End Theory: Bass, Bodies, and the Materiality of Sonic Experience*. New York: Bloomsbury.

"Jefferson, Blind Lemon." 1995. In *The Guinness Encyclopedia of Popular Music*, edited by Colin Larkin, 2152–2153. Enfield: Guinness Publishing.

Jeffreys, Diarmuid. 2005. *Aspirin: The Remarkable Story of a Wonder Drug*. New York: Bloomsbury.

Jenkins, Henry. 2006. *Convergence Culture: Where Old and New Media Collide*. New York: New York University Press.

Jenkins, Henry, Sam Ford, and Joshua Green. 2013. *Spreadable Media: Creating Value and Meaning in a Networked Culture*. New York: New York University Press.

Jennings, Nicholas. 2000. *Fifty Years of Music: The Story of EMI Music Canada*. Toronto: Macmillan.

Jevons, W. Stanley. 1865. *The Coal Question: An Inquiry Concerning the Progress of the Nation, and the Probable Exhaustion of Our Coal-Mines*. London: Macmillan & Co.

Johnson, Bruce, and Martin Cloonan. 2009. *Dark Side of the Tune: Popular Music and Violence*. Farnham: Ashgate.

Jones, Peter. 1977. "The Record Industry in Europe." *Journal of the Audio Engineering Society* 25(10–11): 789–794.

Joselit, David, Carrie Lambert-Beatty, and Hal Foster, eds. 2016. "A Questionnaire on Materialisms." *October* 155: 3–110.

Kahn, Douglas. 2013. *Earth Sound Earth Signal: Energies and Earth Magnitude in the Arts*. Berkeley: University of California Press.

Kane, Brian. 2017. "Relays: Audiotape, Material Affordances, and Cultural Practice." *Twentieth-Century Music* 14(1): 65–75.

Kassabian, Anahid. 2004. "Would You Like Some World Music with Your Latte? Starbucks, Putumayo, and Distributed Tourism." *Twentieth-Century Music* 1(2): 209–223.

Kassabian, Anahid. 2013. *Ubiquitous Listening: Affect, Attention, and Distributed Subjectivity*. Berkeley: University of California Press.

Katz, Mark. 2004. *Capturing Sound: How Technology Has Changed Music*. Berkeley: University of California Press.

Katz, Mark. 2015. "The Persistence of Analogue." In *Musical Listening in the Age of Technological Reproduction*, edited by Gianmario Borio, 275–287. New York: Routledge.

Keating, J.P., and H. Weisberg. 1980. "Akzo Review March 12 and 13." Unpublished RCA Internal Correspondence. [Box M&A 881 / Folder 28, David Sarnoff Research Center Records (Accession 2464.09). Hagley Museum and Library, Wilmington, DE.]

Keightley, Keir. 2001. "Reconsidering Rock." In *The Cambridge Companion to Pop and Rock*, edited by Simon Frith, Will Straw, and John Street, 109–142. Cambridge: Cambridge University Press.

Keightley, Keir. 2004. "Long Play: Adult-Oriented Popular Music and the Temporal Logics of the Post-War Sound Recording Industry in the USA." *Media, Culture, and Society* 26(3): 375–391.

Keightley, Keir. 2011. "Un Voyage via Barquinho: Global Circulation, Musical Hybridization, and Adult Modernity, 1961–9." In *Migrating Music*, edited by Jason Toynbee and Bryon Dueck, 112–126. Abingdon: Routledge.

Keightley, Keir. 2012. "Tin Pan Allegory." *Modernism/Modernity* 19(4): 717–736.

Kelly, Caleb. 2018. "Materials of Sound: Sound As (More Than) Sound." *Journal of Sonic Studies* 16: online.

Kenney, William. 1999. *Recorded Music in American Life: The Phonograph and Popular Memory, 1890–1945*. Oxford: Oxford University Press.

Kerman, Joseph. 1980. "How We Got into Analysis, and How to Get out." *Critical Inquiry* 7(2): 311–331.

Kerman, Joseph. 1985. *Contemplating Music: Challenges to Musicology*. Cambridge: Harvard University Press.

Khanna, Sarwan K. 1977. "Vinylly a Better Record." *Billboard* (21 May): RS-86.

Kittler, Friedrich. 1990. *Discourse Networks, 1800/1900*. Stanford: Stanford University Press.

Kittler, Friedrich. 1999. *Gramophone, Film, Typewriter*. Stanford: Stanford University Press.

Kittler, Friedrich. 2013. "There Is No Software." In *The Truth of the Technological World: Essays on the Genealogy of Presence*, 219–229. Stanford: Stanford University Press.

Kirsch, Bob. 1973. "Industry Tackles Plastics Shortage." *Billboard* (6 October): 1, 12.

Kirschenbaum, Matthew. 2008. *Mechanisms: New Media and the Forensic Imagination*. Cambridge: MIT Press.

Kjus, Yngvar, and Anne Danielsen. 2014. "Live Islands in the Seas of Recordings: The Music Experience of Visitors at the Øya Festival." *Popular Music and Society* 37(5): 660–679.

Klumpenhauwer, Henry. 2002. "Commodity-Form, Disavowel, and Practices of Music Theory." In *Music and Marx: Ideas, Practice, Politics*, edited by Regula Qureshi, 23–44. New York: Routledge.

Kozak, Roman. 1976. "If Oil Prices Ascend, Expect a PVC Jump." *Billboard* (27 November): 73, 90.

Kraft, James. 1996. *Stage to Studio: Musicians and the Sound Revolution, 1890–1950*. Baltimore: Johns Hopkins University Press.

Kramer, Lawrence. 1993. "Music Criticism and the Postmodernist Turn: In Contrary Motion with Gary Tomlinson." *Current Musicology* 53: 25–35.

Krims, Adam. 2007. *Music and Urban Geography*. New York: Routledge.

Kumar, Neha, and Tapan Parikh. 2013. "Mobiles, Music, and Materiality." *Computer–Human Interaction* (27 April–02 May): 2863–2872.

Kusisto, Oscar. 1977. "Magnetic Tape Recording: Reels, Cassettes, or Cartridges?" *Journal of the Audio Engineering Society* 25(10–11): 828–835.

Kwon, Mee-yoo. 2017. "Vinyl-Pressing Plant Breathes New Life into Record Industry." *The Korea Times* (23 June): online.

Köster, E. 1993. "Trends in Magnetic Recording Media." *Journal of Magnetism and Magnetic Materials* 120: 1–10.

Laing, Dave. 1990. "Record Sales in the 1980s." *Popular Music* 9(2): 235–236.

Laing, Dave. 2003. "Music and the Market: The Economics of Music in the Modern World." In *The Cultural Study of Music: A Critical Introduction*, edited by Martin Clayton, Trevor Herbert, and Richard Middleton, 309–320. New York: Routledge.

Laing, Dave. 2013. "The Recording Industry in the Twentieth Century." In *The International Recording Industries*, edited by Lee Marshall, 31–52. Abingdon: Routledge.

Lanza, Joseph. 2004. *Elevator Music: A Surreal History of Muzak, Easy-Listening, and Other Moodsong*. Ann Arbor: University of Michigan Press.

Latour, Bruno. 1988. "Drawing Things Together." In *Representation and Scientific Practice*, edited by Michael Lynch and Steve Woolgar, 19–68. Cambridge: MIT Press.

Latour, Bruno. 1993. *We Have Never Been Modern*. Cambridge: Harvard University Press.

Latour, Bruno. 1998. "To Modernize or Ecologize? That's the Question." In *Remaking Reality: Nature at the Millennium*, edited by Bruce Braun and Noel Castree, 221–242. New York: Routledge.

Latour, Bruno. 1999. "On Recalling ANT." In *Actor Network Theory and After*, edited by John Law and John Hassard, 15–25. Oxford: Blackwell.

Latour, Bruno. 2002. "Morality and Technology: The Ends of Means." *Theory, Culture, and Society* 19(5–6): 247–260.

Latour, Bruno. 2004. *Politics of Nature: How to Bring the Sciences into Democracy*. Cambridge: Harvard University Press.

Latour, Bruno. 2005. *Reassembling the Social: An Introduction to Actor-Network-Theory*. Oxford: Oxford University Press.

Latour, Bruno. 2010a. *On the Modern Cult of the Factish Gods*. Durham: Duke University Press.

Latour, Bruno. 2010b. "An Attempt at a 'Compositionist Manifesto.'" *New Literary History* 41(3): 471–490.

Latour, Bruno, and Steve Woolgar. 1986. *Laboratory Life: The Construction of Scientific Facts*. Princeton: Princeton University Press.

Lauzon, Michael. 2017. "Toronto Company Using New Technology to Press Vinyl Records." *Plastics News* (27 January): online.

Lees, Gene. 1974. "The Vinyl Shortage: Does It Mean Poorer and Fewer Records?" *High Fidelity* 24(7): 69–72.

LeMahieu, Daniel. 1982. "The Gramophone: Recorded Music and the Cultivated Mind Between the Wars." *Technology and Culture* 23(3): 372–391.

LeMahieu, Daniel. 1988. *A Culture for Democracy: Mass Communication and the Cultivated Mind in Britain Between the Wars*. Oxford: Clarendon.

Lenoir, Timothy. 1990. "Inscription Practices and Materialities of Communication." In *Inscribing Science: Scientific Texts and the Materiality of Communication*, edited by Timothy Lenoir, 1–19. Stanford: Stanford University Press.

Leonard, Marion. 2007. "Constructing Histories through Material Culture: Popular Music, Museums, and Collecting." *Popular Music History* 2(2): 147–167.

Lepawsky, Josh. 2018. *Reassembling Rubbish: Worlding Electronic Waste*. Cambridge: MIT Press.

Lepawsky, Josh, and Charles Mather. 2011. "From Beginnings and Endings to Boundaries and Edges: Rethinking Circulation and Exchange through Electronic Waste." *Area* 43(3): 242–249.

Leroi-Gourhan, André. 1993. *Gesture and Speech*. Cambridge: MIT Press.

Lindsay, H.A.F., and C.M. Harlow 1921. *The Indian Forest Records: Report on Lac and Shellac*. Allahabad: The Pioneer Press.

"London Shellac Stocks Increase." 1922. *Talking Machine World* 18(2): 6.

Lucas, Gavin. 2002. "Disposability and Dispossession in the Twentieth Century." *Journal of Material Culture* 7(1): 5–22.

Lury, Celia, Luciana Parisi, and Tiziana Terranova. 2012. "Introduction: The Becoming Topological of Culture." *Theory, Culture, and Society* 29(4–5): 3–35.

Mackenzie, Adrian. 2002. *Transductions: Bodies and Machines at Speed*. New York: Continuum.

Mackenzie, Adrian. 2010. *Wirelessness: Radical Empiricism in Network Cultures*. Cambridge: MIT Press.

Magoun, Alexander. 2000. *Shaping the Sound of Music: The Evolution of the Phonograph Record, 1877–1950*. PhD diss., University of Maryland.

Magoun, Alexander. 2002. "The Origins of the 45-rpm Record at RCA Victor, 1939–1948." In *Music and Technology in the Twentieth Century*, edited by Hans-Joachim Braun, 148–157. Baltimore: Johns Hopkins University Press.

Maguadda, Paolo. 2011. "When Materiality 'Bites Back': Digital Music Consumption Practices in the Age of Dematerialization." *Journal of Consumer Culture* 11(1): 15–36.

Mahapatra, Richard. 2004. "Steep Lack." *Down To Earth* (15 May): online.

Maisonneuve, Sophie. 2001. "Between History and Commodity: The Production of a Musical Patrimony through the Record in the 1920s–1930s." *Poetics* 29: 89–108.

"The Making of a Record." ca. 1951. Unpublished RCA Victor manuscript. [Box 3 / Folder 25, RCA Victor Camden / Frederick O. Barnum III collection (Accession 2069). Hagley Museum and Library, Wilmington, DE.]

Manuel, Peter. 1993. *Cassette Culture: Popular Music and Technology in North India*. Chicago: University of Chicago Press.

Manuel, Peter. 2014. "The Regional North Indian Popular Music Industry in 2014: From Cassette Culture to Cyberculture." *Popular Music* 33(3): 389–412.

"Marion Dorian Speaks on Tariff." 1912. *Talking Machine World* 8(4): 6.

Marmorstein, Gary. 2007. *The Label: The Story of Columbia Records*. New York: Thunder's Mouth Press.

Marriott, James, and Mika Minio-Paluello. 2012. *The Oil Road: Journeys from the Caspian Sea to the City of London*. London: Verso.

Marriott, James, and Mika Minio-Paluello. 2013. "Where Does this Stuff Come From? Oil, Plastic, and the Distribution of Violence." In *Accumulation: The Material Politics of Plastic*, edited by Jennifer Gabrys, Gay Hawkins, and Mike Michael, 171–183. New York: Routledge.

Marshall, Lee. 2003. "For and against the Record Industry: An Introduction to Bootleg Collectors and Tape Traders." *Popular Music* 22(1): 57–72.

Marshall, Lee. 2013. "The Recording Industry in the Twenty-First Century." In *The International Recording Industries*, edited by Lee Marshall, 53–74. New York: Routledge.

Marshall, Lee. 2015. "'Let's Keep Music Special. F— Spotify': On-Demand Streaming and the Controversy over Artist Royalties." *Creative Industries Journal* 8(2): 177–189.

Martin, Michèle. 1991. *"Hello, Central?" Gender, Technology, and Culture in the Formation of the Telephone System*. Montreal: McGill-Queen's University Press.

Martin, J. 1951. "51 Record Outlook for Ops Brightens." *Billboard* (17 March): 78.

Martin, Peter. 1995. *Sounds and Society: Themes in the Sociology of Music.* Manchester: Manchester University Press.

Martin, Peter. 2006. *Music and the Sociological Gaze: Art Worlds and Cultural Production.* Manchester: Manchester University Press.

Martínez-Reyes, José. 2015. "Mahogany Intertwined: Enviromateriality between Mexico, Fiji, and the Gibson Les Paul." *Journal of Material Culture* 20(3): 313–329.

Martínez-Reyes, José. Forthcoming. "Timber to Timbre: Fijian Mahogany Plantations and Gibson Guitars." In *Audible Infrastructures: Music, Sound, Media,* edited by Kyle Devine and Alexandrine Boudreault-Fournier. New York: Oxford University Press.

Martland, Peter. 2013. *Recording History: The British Recording Industry, 1888–1931.* Lanham: Scarecrow Press.

Marx, Karl. 1909. *Capital: A Critique of Political Economy, Volume 1.* Chicago: Charles H. Kerr and Co.

Mathew, Nicholas, and Mary Ann Smart. 2015. "Elephants in the Room: The Future of Quirk Historicism." *Representations* 132: 61–78.

Matinde, Vincent. 2014. "Can Mobile Digital Music Help African Musicians?" *IDG Connect* (12 June): online.

Mattern, Shannon. 2017. *Code and Clay, Data and Dirt: Five Thousand Years of Urban Media.* Minneapolis: University of Minnesota Press.

Maxwell, Kate. 2016. "Beck's Song Reader: An Unbound Music Book." *Mémoires du livre* 8(1): online.

Maxwell, Richard, ed. 2016. *The Routledge Companion to Media and Labor.* New York: Routledge.

Maxwell, Richard, and Toby Miller. 2012. *Greening the Media.* Oxford: Oxford University Press.

Maxwell, Richard, Jon Raundalen, and Nina Lager Vestberg, eds. *Media and the Ecological Crisis.* New York: Routledge.

Mayer, Vicki. 2011. *Below the Line: Producers and Production Studies in the New Television Economy*. Durham: Duke University Press.

Mayers, Kieran, Jonathan Koomey, Rebecca Hall, Maria Bauer, Chris France, and Amanda Webb. 2014. "The Carbon Footprint of Games Distribution." *Journal of Industrial Ecology* 19(3): 402–415.

McClary, Susan. 2000. *Conventional Wisdom: The Content of Musical Form*. Berkeley: University of California Press.

McClary, Susan. 2002. "*Feminine Endings* in Retrospect." In *Feminine Endings: Music, Gender, and Sexuality*. Minneapolis: University of Minnesota Press.

McClary, Susan. 2011. "*Feminine Endings* at Twenty." *Transcultural Music Review* 15: online.

McClure, S. 1999. "Violence Doesn't Faze Piracy Fighters." *Billboard* (4 December): 110, 114.

McLean, Jacob. 2015. *Tough Vinyl: Packing in Our Record Collections*. Master's thesis, York University.

McCourt, Tom. 2005. "Collecting Music in the Digital Realm." *Popular Music and Society* 28(2): 249–252.

McMurray, Peter. 2017. "Once Upon Time: A Superficial History of Early Tape." *Twentieth-Century Music* 14(1): 25–48.

McNally, David. 1981. "Staple Theory as Commodity Fetishism: Marx, Innis, and Canadian Political Economy." *Studies in Political Economy* 6: 35–63.

Merchant, Brian. 2017a. "Were the Raw Materials in Your iPhone Mined by Children in Inhumane Conditions?" *Los Angeles Times* (23 July): online.

Merchant, Brian. 2017b. *The One Device: The Secret History of the iPhone*. London: Bantam Press.

Meadowcroft, William. 1921. *The Boys' Life of Edison*. New York: Harper & Brothers.

Meikle, Jeffrey. 1995. *American Plastic: A Cultural History*. New Brunswick: Rutgers University Press.

Meikle, Jeffrey. 1997. "Material Doubts: The Consequences of Plastic." *Environmental History* 2(3): 278–300.

Meintjes, Louise. 2003. *Sound of Africa! Making Music Zulu in a South African Studio*. Durham: Duke University Press.

Melillo, Edward. 2014. "Global Entomologies: Insects, Empires, and the 'Synthetic Age' in World History." *Past and Present* 223(1): 233–270.

Menger, Pierre-Michel. 1999. "Artistic Labor Markets and Careers." *Annual Review of Sociology* 25: 541–574.

Menger, Pierre-Michel. 2014. *The Economics of Creativity: Art and Achievement under Uncertainty*. Cambridge: Harvard University Press.

Merton, Robert K. 1948. "The Self-Fulfilling Prophesy." *Antioch Review* 8(2): 193–210.

Merton, Robert K. 1995. "The Thomas Theorem and the Matthew Effect." *Social Forces* 74(2): 379–424.

Mezzadra, Sandro, and Brett Neilson. 2017. "On the Multiple Frontiers of Extraction: Excavating Contemporary Capitalism." *Cultural Studies* 31(2–3): 185–204.

Miège, Bernard. 1979. "The Cultural Commodity." *Media, Culture, and Society* 1: 297–311.

Millard, André. 2005. *America on Record: A History of Recorded Sound*. Cambridge: Cambridge University Press.

Miller, Daniel. 1987. *Material Culture and Mass Consumption*. Oxford: Basic Blackwell.

Miller, Daniel, ed. 2005. *Materiality*. Durham: Duke University Press.

Miller, Daniel. 2007. "Stone Age or Plastic Age?" *Archaeological Dialogues* 14(1): 23–27.

Molotch, Harvey. 2003. *Where Stuff Comes From: How Toasters, Toilets, Cars, Computers and Many Other Things Come to Be as They Are*. New York: Routledge.

Moore, Jason. 2015. *Capitalism in the Web of Life: Ecology and the Accumulation of Capital*. London: Verso.

Moore, Richie. 1979. "The Fiber Optic Connection." *The Mix* 3(3): 18.

Morcom, Anna. 2015. "Locating Music in Capitalism: A View from Exile Tibet." *Popular Music* 34(2): 274–295.

"More Music for Millions." 1945. *Plastics* 3(3): 94, 96, 146.

Morris, J.A. 2008. "The Energy Nightmare of Web Server Farms." *Synthesis/Regeneration* 45: online.

Morris, Jeremy. 2010. *Understanding the Digital Music Commodity*. PhD diss., McGill University.

Morris, Jeremy. 2011. "Sounds in the Cloud: Cloud Computing and the Digital Music Commodity." *First Monday* 16(5): 1–12.

Morris, Jeremy. 2013. "The Person Behind the Music We Adore: Artists, Profiles, and the Circulation of Music." *Wi: Journal of Mobile Media* 7(1): 1–9.

Morris, Jeremy. 2015. *Selling Digital Music, Formatting Culture*. Berkeley: University of California Press.

Morton, David. 1993. "The Rusty Ribbon: John Herbert Orr and the Making of the Magnetic Recording Industry, 1945–1960." *Business History Review* 67(4): 589–622.

Morton, Timothy. 2007. *Ecology without Nature: Rethinking Environmental Aesthetics*. Cambridge. Harvard University Press.

Moseley, Roger. 2016. *Keys to Play: Music as a Ludic Medium from Apollo to Nintendo*. Berkeley: University of California Press.

Mowitt, John. 1987. "The Sound of Music in the Era of Its Electronic Reproducibility." In *Music and Society: The Politics of Composition,*

Performance, and Reception, edited by Richard Leppert and Susan McClary, 173–197. Cambridge: Cambridge University Press.

Murdock, Graham. 2003. "Back to Work: Cultural Labor in Altered Times." In *Cultural Work: Understanding the Cultural Industries*, edited by Andrew Beck, 15–36. New York: Routledge.

Murphy, Raymond. 1994. *Rationality and Nature: A Sociological Inquiry into a Changing Relationship*. Oxford: Westview Press.

Musso, Anthony. 2017. "Rhinebeck's Shellac Factory, Although Lucrative, Cause of Many Concerns." *Poughkeepsie Journal* (25 July): online.

Myers, David, and Herbert Addington. 1947. *Report on Steam Power Supply at the Bridgeport (Conn.) Plant of the Columbia Recording Corporation*. New York: Myers, Fuller, and Addington Consulting Engineers. [AFR Lawrence Papers—*L (Special) 89.21—Box 9. New York Public Library for the Performing Arts.]

Nakamura, Lisa. 2014. "Indigenous Circuits: Navajo Women and the Racialization of Early Electronic Manufacture." *American Quarterly* 66(4): 919–941.

Negus, Keith. 1992. *Producing Pop: Culture and Conflict in the Popular Music Industry*. London: Arnold.

Neumann, Roderick. 2014. *Making Political Ecology*. New York: Routledge.

Nguyen, Thi-Phuong, Xavier Sene, Emilie Le Bourg, and Stephane Bouvet. 2011. "Determining the Composition of 78-rpm Records: Challenge or Fantasy?" *ARSC Journal* 42(1): 27–42.

Nixon, Rob. 2011. *Slow Violence and the Environmentalism of the Poor*. Cambridge: Harvard University Press.

Nooshin, Laudan. 2016. "Happy Families? Convergence, Antagonism, and Disciplinary Identities or 'We're All God Knows What Now' (Cook 2016)." Presented at Are We All Ethnomusicologists Now?, City University of London.

Nowak, Raphaël. 2014a. "Understanding Everyday uses of Music Technologies in the Digital Age." In *Mediated Youth Cultures: The Internet,*

Belonging, and New Cultural Configurations, edited by Andy Bennett and Brady Robards, 146–161. New York: Palgrave Macmillan.

Nowak, Raphaël. 2014b. "Investigating the Interactions between Individuals and Music Technologies within Contemporary Modes of Music Consumption." *First Monday* 19(10): online.

"Old Records Yield Valuable Shellac." 1942. *Hamilton Spectator* (18 August): n.p.

Oliver, Paul. 2001. "Jefferson, Blind Lemon." In *The Grove Dictionary of Music and Musicians*, 2nd ed. New York: Macmillan.

"One Record Holds Entire Symphony." 1948. *Life* (26 July): 39–40.

Osborne, Richard. 2012. *Vinyl: A History of the Analogue Record*. Farnham: Ashgate.

Osborne, Richard. 2016. "Review of *Vinyl: The Analogue Record in the Digital Age*, by Dominik Bartmanski and Ian Woodward." *Popular Music* 35(2): 270–272.

Owen, David. 2017. "The World Is Running Out of Sand." *The New Yorker* (29 May): online.

Ó Callanáin, Cormac. 2019. *Sound Infrastructures of the German Democratic Republic: Renewing Sound Technology during State Socialism*. PhD diss., University of Edinburgh.

Palmer, Brian. 2009. "7 Billion Carbon Sinks: How Much Does Breathing Contribute to Climate Change?" *Slate* (13 August): online.

Parikka, Jussi. 2013. "Green Media Times: Friedrich Kittler and Ecological Media History." *Archiv für Mediengeschichte* 13: 69–78.

Parikka, Jussi. 2015. *A Geology of Media*. Minneapolis: University of Minnesota Press.

Parikka, Jussi. 2016. "So-Called Nature: Friedrich Kittler and Ecological Media Materialism." In *Sustainable Media: Critical Approaches to Media and Environment*, edited by Nicole Starosielski and Janet Walker, 196–211. New York: Routledge.

Parkin, Nick. 2018. "Brazil's Musicians Are Reviving Their Lost Vinyl Industry and 'Rescuing Old Values of Our Music.'" *ABC News* (27 September): online.

Parks, Lisa, and Nicole Starosielski, eds. 2015. *Signal Traffic: Critical Studies of Media Infrastructures*. Champaign: University of Illinois Press.

Parry, Ernest. 1935. *Shellac: Its Production, Manufacture, Chemistry, Analysis, Commerce, and Uses*. London: Sir Isaac Pitman & Sons.

Parthasarathi, Vibodh. 2007. "Not Just Mad Englishmen and a Dog: The Colonial Tuning of 'Music on Record,' 1900–1908." Working Paper no. 02/2008. New Delhi: Jamia Millia Islamia.

Pastoureau, Michel. 2001. *Blue: The History of a Color*. Princeton: Princeton University Press.

Pastoureau, Michel. 2008. *Black: The History of a Color*. Princeton: Princeton University Press.

Pastoureau, Michel. 2014. *Green: The History of a Color*. Princeton: Princeton University Press.

Pastoureau, Michel. 2016. *Red: The History of a Color*. Princeton: Princeton University Press.

Pedelty, Mark. 2012. *Ecomusicology: Rock, Folk, and the Environment*. Philadelphia: Temple University Press.

Pedelty, Mark. 2016. "Pop Ecology: Lessons from Mexico." In *Current Directions in Ecomusicology: Music, Culture, Nature,* edited by Aaron Allen and Kevin Dawe, 200–211. New York: Routledge.

Peters, Benjamin. 2016. "Digital." In *Digital Keywords: A Vocabulary of Information Society and Culture,* edited by Benjamin Peters, 93–108. Princeton: Princeton University Press.

Peters, John Durham. 2008. "Strange Sympathies: Horizons of German and American Media Theory." In *American Studies as Media Studies*, edited by Frank Kelleter and Daniel Stein, 3–23. Heidelberg: Winter.

Peters, John Durham. 2015. *The Marvelous Clouds: Toward a Philosophy of Elemental Media*. Chicago: University of Chicago Press.

Peters, John Durham. 2017. "'You Mean My Whole Fallacy Is Wrong': On Technological Determinism." *Representations* 140: 10–26.

Peters, John Durham. 2018. "The Media of Breathing." In *Atmospheres of Breathing*, edited by Lenart Škorf and Petri Berndtson, 179–195. Albany: State University of New York Press.

Peterson, Richard. 1992. "Understanding Audience Segmentation: From Elite and Mass to Omnivore and Univore." *Poetics* 21: 243–258.

Peterson, Richard, and David Berger. 1975. "Cycles in Symbol Production: The Case of Popular Music." *American Sociological Review* 40(2): 158–173.

Peterson, Robert. 2013. "'Mosquito Moan,' by Blind Lemon Jefferson." *American Entomologist* 59(2): 110–112.

Petrocultures Research Group. 2016. *After Oil*. Edmonton: Petrocultures Research Group.

Petrusich, Amanda. 2014. *Do Not Sell at Any Price: The Wild, Obsessive Hunt for the World's Rarest 78 rpm Records*. New York: Scribner.

Pohlman, Ken. 1989. *The Compact Disc: A Handbook of Theory and Use*. Madison: A-R Editions.

Pöhnl, Veronika. 2017. "Mind the Gap: On Actor-Network Theory and German Media Theory." In *Applying the Actor-Network Theory in Media Studies*, edited by Markus Spöhrer and Beate Ochsner, 249–265. Pennsylvania: IGI Global.

Piekut, Benjamin. 2011. *Experimentalism Otherwise: The New York Avant-Garde and Its Limits*. Berkeley: University of California Press.

Piekut, Benjamin. 2014. "Actor-Networks in Music History: Clarifications and Critiques." *Twentieth-Century Music* 11(2): 191–215.

Pieslak, Jonathan. 2015. *Radicalism and Music*. Middletown: Wesleyan University Press.

"Plastic Music." 1945. *Time* (22 October): 84, 86.

"Plastics Crisis Hits Records." 1972. *Melody Maker* (20 October): 5.

"Plastics in Accordions." 1947. *Plastics* 7(2): 11–13, 71.

"Plastics in the Making of Phonograph Records." 1949. *Plastics* 9(2): 5.

"Plastics Shortage Affecting Audio Industry." 1973. *Studio Sound* 15(12): 34, 36.

Porter, Martin. 1980. "Vinyl Considerations: Cost vs Quality." *The Mix* 4(2): 6.

Povinelli, Elizabeth. 2011. "Routes/Worlds." *e-flux* 27 (September): online.

Povinelli, Elizabeth. 2014. "Geontologies of the Otherwise." *Cultural Anthropology* (13 January): online.

Povinelli, Elizabeth. 2016. *Geontologies: A Requiem to Late Liberalism*. Durham: Duke University Press.

Prior, Nick. 2011. "Critique and Renewal in the Sociology of Music: Bourdieu and Beyond." *Cultural Sociology* 5(1): 121–138.

Prior, Nick. 2017. "On Vocal Assemblages: From Edison to Miku." *Contemporary Music Review* (online pre-publication version): 1–19.

Prior, Nick. 2018. *Popular Music, Digital Technology, and Society*. London: SAGE.

"Proposed Tax on Shellac and Copal Gum." 1913. *Talking Machine World* 9(1): 26.

Puig de la Bellacasa, María. 2017. *Matters of Care: Speculative Ethics in More Than Human Worlds*. Minneapolis: University of Minnesota Press.

Qiu, Jack Linchuan. 2016. *Goodbye iSlave: A Manifesto for Digital Abolition*. Urbana: University of Illinois Press.

Qureshi, Regula Burckhardt, ed. 2002. *Music and Marx: Ideas, Practice, Politics*. New York: Routledge.

"Radiohead Reveal 'In Rainbows' Sales." 2008. *Rolling Stone* (13 November): online.

"Radio-Phonograph Making Halted." 1942. *Music Trades* 90(3): 5.

Rai, Amit. 2013. "Sound Perception and Mobile Phones in India." In *Ubiquitous Musics: The Everyday Sounds That We Don't Always Notice*, edited by Marta García Quiñones, Anahid Kassabian, and Elena Boschi, 75–88. Farnham: Ashgate.

RCA Victor. No date. "A Compact Summary of Freight Rates and Traffic Rules as they Apply to Radio Receivers, Phonographs, and Records." Unpublished RCA Victor Representative's Bulletin. [Box 9 / Folder 28, RCA Victor Camden / Frederick O. Barnum III collection (Accession 2069). Hagley Museum and Library, Wilmington, DE.]

RCA Manufacturing Company. 1940 (ca.). *Student's Sales Manual*. Camden: RCA Educational Department. [Box 10 / Folder 6, RCA Victor Camden / Frederick O. Barnum III collection (Accession 20169). Hagley Museum and Library, Wilmington, DE.]

RCA Victor. 1944. "Facts about Phonograph Records—As We See Them." *RCA Victor News Letter* 4 (October): 1–4. [Box 9 / Folder 37, RCA Victor Camden / Frederick O. Barnum III collection (Accession 2069). Hagley Museum and Library, Wilmington, DE.]

Read, Oliver, and Walter Welch. 1976. *From Tin Foil to Stereo: Evolution of the Phonograph*. Indianapolis: Howard W. Sams & Co.

"A Real Captain of Industry." 1910. *Talking Machine World* 6(9): 24.

Reall, Jeannie. 2014. "Vinyl Records Refuse to Fade Out." *Plastics News* (18 November): online.

"Record Demand Steadily Expanding." 1920. *Talking Machine World* 16(4): 9.

"Record Growth: The Story Behind the Vinyl Comeback." 2014. *Compounding World* (April): 31–32, 34, 36.

"The Record-Setting Business of Records." 1961. *Bakelite Review* (January): 1–3.

Rehding, Alexander. 2017. "Discrete/Continuous: Music and Media Theory after Kittler." *Journal of the American Musicological Society* 70(1): 221–256.

Reilly, Lucas. 2017. "The Most Important Scientist You've Never Heard Of." *Mental Floss* (17 May): online.

Rekret, Paul. 2018. "The Head, the Hand, and Matter: New Materialism and the Politics of Knowledge." *Theory, Culture, and Society* 35(7–8): 49–72.

Reynolds, Simon. 2011. *Retromania: Pop Culture's Addiction to Its Own Past*. New York: Faber and Faber.

Richardson, John. 2016. "Ecological Close Reading of Music in Digital Culture." In *Embracing Restlessness: Cultural Musicology*, edited by Brigit Abels, 111–142. Hildesheim: Georg Olms Verlag.

Richardson, Tanya, and Gisa Weszkalnys. 2014. "Introduction: Resource Materialities." *Anthropological Quarterly* 87(1): 5–30.

Ríos, Kristofer. 2011. "In Age of Digital Music, Vinyl Gets Second Life in Brooklyn Factory." *New York Times* (17 April): online.

"Robbie Williams to Pave Chinese Roads." 2008. *NME* (16 January): online.

Robbins, Paul. 2012. *Political Ecology: A Critical Introduction*. Oxford: Wiley-Blackwell.

Rodgers, Tara. 2010. *Synthesizing Sound: Metaphor in Audio-Technical Discourse and Synthesis History*. PhD diss., McGill University.

Rodia, Carl. 1985. "CD Manufacturing: Trials and Tribulations." *One-to-One* (December): 28, 30.

Rondeau, René. 2001. *Tinfoil Phonographs: The Dawn of Recorded Sound*. Corte Madera: René Rondeau.

Rondeau, René. 2002. "Sweet Music: Stollwerck Phonographs Play Chocolate Records." *Journal of Mechanical Music* 48(2): 18ff.

Rossell, Deac. 1998. *Living Pictures: The Origins of the Movies*. Albany: State University of New York Press.

Rothenbuhler, Eric. 2012. "The Compact Disc and Its Culture: Notes on Melancholia." In *Cultural Technologies: The Shaping of Cultural in Media and Society*, edited by Göran Bolin, 36–50. New York: Routledge.

Rothenbuhler, Eric, and John Durham Peters. 1997. "Defining Phonography: An Experiment in Theory." *The Musical Quarterly* 81(2): 242–264.

Roy, Elodie. 2013. "Digital Wastelands: Materiality between Salvation and Oblivion." Presented at Music, Digitization, Mediation: Towards Interdisciplinary Music Studies, University of Oxford.

Roy, Elodie. 2014. "All the Memory in the World, All the Music in the World: Mediating Muscial Patrimony in the Digital Age." *Networking Knowledge: Journal of the MeCCSA Postgraduate Network* 7(2): online.

Roy, Elodie. 2015. *Media, Materiality, and Memory: Grounding the Groove*. Farnham: Ashgate.

Roy, Elodie. 2016–2017. "Shellac Shards." *The Drouth* 57: 31–36.

Roy, Elodie. Forthcoming. "Another Side of Shellac: Cultural and Natural Cycles of the Gramophone Disc." In *Audible Infrastructures: Music, Sound, Media*, edited by Kyle Devine and Alexandrine Boudreault-Fournier. New York: Oxford University Press.

Ruda, Joseph. 1977. "Record Manufacturing: Making the Sound for Everyone." *Journal of the Audio Engineering Society* 25(10–11): 702–711.

Rust, Brian. 1978. *The American Record Label Book*. New York: Da Capo Press.

Saito, Kohei. 2017. *Karl Marx's Ecosocialism: Capitalism, Nature, and the Unfinished Critique of Political Economy*. New York: Monthly Review Press.

Sale, Stephen, and Laura Salisbury. 2015. "Editors' Introduction." In *Kittler Now: Current Perspectives in Kittler Studies*, edited by Stephen Sale and Laura Salisbury, xiii–xxxix. Cambridge: Polity.

Sanders, Joseph. 1906. *Joseph Sanders' Diary, 1906*. Washington: Library of Congress.

Sanders, Joseph. 1907. *Joseph Sanders' Diary, 1907*. Washington: Library of Congress.

Sarlan, M.S. 1924. RCA Victor letter (5 Nov): 3pp. [Box 9 / Folder 48, RCA Victor Camden / Frederick O. Barnum III collection (Accession 2069). Hagley Museum and Library, Wilmington, DE.].

Savage, Mike, and Modesto Gayo. 2011. "Unravelling the Omnivore: A Field Analysis of Contemporary Musical Taste in the United Kingdom." *Poetics* 39: 337–357.

Savicky, Randy. 1987. "US Report." *One-to-One* (February): 10.

Scaping, Peter, ed. 1979. *BPI Year Book 1979: A Review of the British Record and Tape Industry*. Wadford: British Phonograph Industry.

Schack, William. 1946. "Pianos Adopt Plastics." *Plastics* 5(2): 15–18.

Schmidgen, Henning. 2014. *Bruno Latour in Pieces: An Intellectual Biography*. New York: Fordham University Press.

Schmidgen, Henning. 2018. "Successful Paranoia: Friedrich Kittler, Lacanian Psychoanalysis, and the History of Science." *Theory, Culture, and Society* 36(1): 107–131.

Scholz, Trebor. 2017. *Uberworked and Underpaid: How Workers Are Disrupting the Digital Economy*. Cambridge: Polity.

Schoop, Monika. 2017. *Independent Music and Digital Technology in the Philippines*. New York: Routledge.

Sears, Richard. 1980. *V-Discs: A History and Discography*. Westport: Greenwood Press.

Sedgewick, Augustine. 2014. "Against Flows." *History of the Present* 4(2): 143–170.

Sellen, Abigail, and Richard Harper. 2001. *The Myth of the Paperless Office*. Cambridge: MIT Press.

Shedden, Iain. 2015. "Vinyl Artisans Groove to a Record Revival." *Weekend Australian* (31 January): 3.

Shehabi, Arman, Ben Walker, and Eric Masanet. 2014. "The Energy and Greenhouse-Gas Implications of Internet Video Streaming in the United States." *Environmental Research Letters* 9: 1–11.

Shekhar, G.C. 1996. “A Record Collection.” *India Today* (15 November): online.

“Shellac for Talking Machine.” 1906. *Talking Machine World* 2(12): 60.

“Shellac High in Price.” 1903. *New York Times* (1 November): 26.

“Shellac Importers Are Worried.” 1919. *Talking Machine World* 15(12): 42.

“The Shellac Market—Conditions Affecting Supply.” 1920. *Talking Machine World* 16(4): 69.

Shepherd, John. 1982. “A Theoretical Model for the Sociomusicological Analysis of Popular Musics.” *Popular Music* 2: 145–177.

Shepherd, John. 1993. “Difference and Power in Music.” In *Musicology and Difference: Gender and Sexuality in Music Scholarship*, edited by Ruth Solie, 46–65. Berkeley: University of California Press.

Shepherd, John, and Kyle Devine. 2015. “Music and the Sociological Imagination—Pasts and Prospects.” In *The Routledge Reader on the Sociology of Music*, edited by John Shepherd and Kyle Devine, 1–26. New York: Routledge.

Shepherd, John, and Peter Wicke. 1997. *Music and Cultural Theory*. Cambridge: Polity.

Shiga, John. 2015. “Sonar and the Channelization of the Ocean.” In *Living Stereo: Histories and Cultures of Multichannel Sound*, edited by Paul Théberge, Kyle Devine, and Tom Everrett, 85–104. New York: Bloomsbury.

“Shortage of Shellac.” 1920. *Talking Machine World* 16(2): 219–213.

Shuker, Roy. 2010. *Wax Trash and Vinyl Treasures: Record Collecting as a Social Practice*. Farnham: Ashgate.

Siegert, Bernhard. 2003. “There Are No Mass Media.” In *Mapping Benjamin: The Work of Art in the Digital Age*, edited by Hans Ulrich Gumbrecht and Michael Marrinan, 30–38. Stanford: Stanford University Press.

Siegert, Bernhard. 2013. “Mineral Sound or Missing Fundamental: Cultural History as Signal Analysis.” *Osiris* 28(1): 105–118.

Siegert, Bernhard. 2015. *Cultural Techniques: Grids, Filters, Doors, and Other Articulations of the Real*. Stanford: Stanford University Press.

Siegert, Bernhard. 2017. "After the Media: The Textility of Cultural Techniques." In *Media Theory and Cultural Technologies: In Memoriam of Friedrich Kittler*, edited by Maria Teresa Cruz, 1–21. Newcastle upon Tyne: Cambridge Scholars Publishing.

Silvers, Michael B. 2018. *Voices of Drought: The Politics of Music and Environment in Northeastern Brazil*. Urbana: University of Illinois Press.

Singh, Ramesh. 2007. "Lac Culture." New Delhi: National Science Digital Library.

Sippel, John. 1973. "New Extender Is Seen as Relief to Shortage of PVC." *Billboard* (10 November): 1, 83.

Sippel, John, et al. 1974. "Plastic for Disks Still In Short Supply as Gas Lines Disappear." *Billboard* (4 May): 8, 62.

Sisario, Ben. 2015. "Vinyl LP Frenzy Brings Record-Pressing Machines Back to Life." *New York Times* (14 September): online.

Slade, Giles. 2006. *Made to Break: Technology and Obsolescence in America*. Cambridge: Harvard University Press.

"Slump in Demand for Shellac." 1921. *Talking Machine World* 17(1): 92.

Small, Christopher. 1998. *Musicking: The Meanings of Performing and Listening*. Middletown: Wesleyan University Press.

Smil, Vaclav. 2014. *Making the Modern World: Materials and Dematerialization*. Chichester: Wiley.

Smith, Casper Llewellyn. 2008. "A Record-Making Invention." *The Guardian* (20 July): online.

Smith, Jacob. 2011. *Spoken Word: Postwar American Phonograph Cultures*. Berkeley: University of California Press.

Smith, Jacob. 2015. *Eco-Sonic Media*. Berkeley: University of California Press.

Smith, Ted, David Sonnenfeld, and David Naguib Pellow, eds. 2006. *Challenging the Chip: Labor Rights and Environmental Justice in the Global Electronics Industry*. Philadelphia: Temple University Press.

Smith, Tim Leigh. 1985. "PR Records: Vinyl Pressing and CD Expansion." *One-to-One* (December): 18–20.

Snape, Carl. 1987. "The Opening of DADC Austria." *One-to-One* (November): 26–28.

Soghomonian, Talia. 2010. "Will We Ever Be Nostalgic For the CD?" *NME* (15 April): online.

Sousa, John Philip. 1906. "The Menace of Mechanical Music." *Appleton's Magazine* 8: 278–284.

Spiller, Henry. 2014. "Interdisciplinarity and Musical Exceptionalism." *Ethnomusicology* 58(2): 341–346.

Spitzer, Horton, et al. 1946. *Plastics: The Story of an Industry*. New York: Society of the Plastics Industry.

Spotify. 2017. *Sustainability Report*. Stockholm: Spotify.

Spotify. 2018. *Sustainability and Social Impact Report*. Stockholm: Spotify.

Stahl, Matt. 2013. *Unfree Masters: Recording Artists and the Politics of Work*. Durham: Duke University Press.

Stahl, Matt. 2015. "Popular Musical Labor in North America." In *The SAGE Handbook of Popular Music*, edited by Andy Bennett and Steve Waksman, 135–153. London: SAGE.

Stamm, Michael. 2018. *Dead Tree Media: Manufacturing the Newspaper in Twentieth-Century North America*. Baltimore: Johns Hopkins University Press.

Stanley, Bob. 2015. "Vinyl Revival: Is It Back For Good?" *The Guardian* (14 April): online.

Stanley, F.B. 1947. "Molded Vinyl Phonograph Records." *Modern Plastics* (July): 107–111.

Stanyek, Jason, and Benjamin Piekut. 2010. "Deadness: Technologies of the Intermundane." *TDR: The Drama Review* 54(1): 14–38.

Starosielski, Nicole. 2015. *The Undersea Network*. Durham: Duke University Press.

Starosielski, Nicole, and Janet Walker, eds. 2016. *Sustainable Media: Critical Approaches to Media and Environment*. New York: Routledge.

Steingo, Gavin. 2015. "Sound and Circulation: Immobility and Obduracy in South African Electronic Music." *Ethnomusicology Forum* 24(1): 102–123.

Steingo, Gavin. 2016. *Kwaito's Promise: Music and the Aesthetics of Freedom in South Africa*. Chicago: University of Chicago Press.

Steingo, Gavin. 2017. "Actors and Accidents in South African Electronic Music: An Essay on Multiple Ontologies." *Contemporary Music Review* (online pre-publication version): 1–21.

Steingo, Gavin. Forthcoming. "Electronic Music and the Problem of Electricity." In *Audible Infrastructures: Music, Sound, Media*, edited by Kyle Devine and Alexandrine Boudreault-Fournier. New York: Oxford University Press.

Steingo, Gavin, and Jim Sykes. 2019. "Introduction: Remapping Sound Studies in the Global South." In *Remapping Sound Studies*, edited by Gavin Steingo and Jim Sykes, 1–36. Durham: Duke University Press.

Stentiford, Claire, et al. 2007. *Ecological Footprint and Carbon Audit of Radiohead North American Tours, 2003 and 2006*. Oxford: Best Foot Forward.

Sterne, Jonathan. 2003a. *The Audible Past: Cultural Origins of Sound Reproduction*. Durham: Duke University Press.

Sterne, Jonathan. 2003b. "Bourdieu, Technique, and Technology." *Cultural Studies* 17(3–4): 367–389.

Sterne, Jonathan. 2006a. "What's Digital in Digital Music?" In *Digital Media: Transformations in Human Communication*, edited by Paul Messaris and Lee Humphreys, 95–109. New York: Peter Lang.

Sterne, Jonathan. 2006b. “The Death and Life of Digital Audio.” *Interdisciplinary Science Reviews* 31(4): 338–348.

Sterne, Jonathan. 2007. “Out with the Trash: On the Future of New Media.” In *Residual Media*, edited by Charles Acland, 16–31. Minneapolis: University of Minnesota Press.

Sterne, Jonathan. 2008. “The Preservation Paradox in Digital Audio.” In *Sound Souvenirs: Audio Technologies, Memory, and Cultural Practices*, edited by Karin Bijsterveld and José van Dijck, 55–65. Amsterdam: Amsterdam University Press.

Sterne, Jonathan. 2012. *MP3: The Meaning of a Format*. Durham: Duke University Press.

Sterne, Jonathan. 2014a. “There Is No Music Industry.” *Media Industries Journal* 1(1): 50–55.

Sterne, Jonathan. 2014b. “Media Analysis Beyond Content.” *Journal of Visual Culture* 13(1): 100–103.

Sterne, Jonathan. 2014c. “What Do We Want? Materiality! When Do We Want It? Now!” In *Media Technologies: Essays on Communication, Materiality, and Society*, edited by Tarleton Gillespie, Pablo Boczkowski, and Kirsten Foot, 119–128. Cambridge: MIT Press.

Sterne, Jonathan. 2015. “The Example: Some Historical Considerations.” In *Between Humanities and the Digital*, edited by Patrick Svensson and David Theo Goldberg, 17–33. Cambridge: MIT Press.

Sterne, Jonathan. 2016a. “Analog.” In *Digital Keywords: A Vocabulary of Information Society and Culture*, edited by Benjamin Peters, 31–44. Princeton: Princeton University Press.

Sterne, Jonathan. 2016b. “Afterword: Opera, Media, Technicity.” In *Technology and the Diva: Sopranos, Opera, and Media from Romanticism to the Digital Age*, edited by Karen Henson, 159–164. Cambridge: Cambridge University Press.

Sterne, Jonathan. 2017. “What Is an Intervention?” *Topia: Canadian Journal of Cultural Studies* 37: 5–14.

Sterne, Jonathan. 2019. "Spectral Objects: On the Fetish Character of Music Technologies." In *Sound Objects*, edited by James Steintrager and Rey Chow, 94–109. Durham: Duke University Press.

Sterne, Jonathan, and Joan Leach. 2006. "The Point of Social Construction and the Purpose of Social Critique." *Social Epistemology* 19(2–3): 189–198.

Stewart, Glen. 1951. "Music for Millions." *The Electrical Workers' Journal* (May): 40–55. [Box 3 / Folder 25, RCA Victor Camden / Frederick O. Barnum III collection (Accession 2069). Hagley Museum and Library, Wilmington, DE.]

Stiegler, Bernard. 1998. *Technics and Time, 1: The Fault of Epimetheus*. Stanford: Stanford University Press.

The Story of Shellac. 1913. New York: William Zinsser.

Stokes, Martin. 1994. "Introduction: Ethnicity, Identity, and Music." In *Ethnicity, Identity, and Music: The Musical Construction of Place*, edited by Martin Stokes, 1–27. Oxford: Berg.

Stokes, Martin. 2002. "Marx, Musicians, and Money." In *Music and Marx: Ideas, Practice, Politics*, edited by Regula Qureshi, 139–163. New York: Routledge.

Størvold, Tore. Forthcoming. "Ecomusicology in the Future Tense" (unpublished essay).

Strasser, Susan. 1999. *Waste and Want: A Social History of Trash*. New York: Holt.

Strauss, Neil. 1995. "Pennies That Add Up to $16.98: Why CDs Cost So Much." *New York Times* (5 July): online.

Straw, Will. 1999. "The Thingishness of Things." *Invisible Culture* 1(2): online.

Straw, Will. 1999–2000. "Music as Commodity and Material Culture." *Repercussions* 7–8: 147–172.

Straw, Will. 2000. "Exhausted Commodities: The Material Culture of Music." *Canadian Journal of Communication* 25(1): 175–185.

Straw, Will. 2007. "Embedded Memories." In *Residual Media*, edited by Charles Acland, 3–15. Minneapolis: University of Minnesota Press.

Straw, Will. 2009. "In Memoriam: The Music CD and Its Ends." *Design and Culture* 1(1): 79–92.

Straw, Will. 2010a. "Cultural Production and the Generative Matrix." *Cultural Sociology* 4(2): 209–216.

Straw, Will. 2010b. "Spectacles of Waste." In *Circulation and the City*, edited by Alexandra Boutros and Will Straw, 193–213. Montreal: McGill-Queen's University Press.

Straw, Will. 2010c. "The Circulatory Turn." In *The Wireless Spectrum: The Politics, Practices, and Poetics of Mobile Media*, edited by Barbara Crow, Michael Longford, and Kim Sawchuck, 17–28. Toronto: University of Toronto Press.

Straw, Will. 2011a. "The Small Parts, Small Players Dossier." *Screen* 52(1): 78–81.

Straw, Will. 2011b. "The Consecration of Musical Incoherence." *Kinephanos* 2(1): 89–94.

Straw, Will. 2012. "Music and Material Culture." In *The Cultural Study of Music: A Critical Introduction*, edited by Martin Clayton, Trevor Herbert, and Richard Middleton, 227–236. New York: Routledge.

Straw, Will. 2015. "Mediality and the Music Chart." *SubStance* 44(3): 128–138.

Straw, Will. 2016. "Twists and Turns: Splits, Snowballs, and Tweaks in Cultural Theory." *eTopia: Canadian Journal of Cultural Theory*: online.

Sturdy, W. Lionel. 1913. "From Our European Headquarters." *Talking Machine World* 9(3): 30–34.

Sturdy, W. Lionel. 1919a. "From Our European Headquarters." *Talking Machine World* 15(8): 165–170.

Sturdy, W. Lionel. 1919b. "From Our European Headquarters." *Talking Machine World* 15(11): 187–190.

Sturdy, W. Lionel. 1920a. "From Our European Headquarters." *Talking Machine World* 16(1): 196–200.

Sturdy, W. Lionel. 1920b. "From Our European Headquarters." *Talking Machine World* 16(2): 219–223.

Sturdy, W. Lionel. 1920c. "From Our European Headquarters." *Talking Machine World* 16(3): 232–235.

Sturdy, W. Lionel. 1920d. "From Our European Headquarters." *Talking Machine World* 16(5): 224–248.

Sturdy, W. Lionel. 1920e. "From Our European Headquarters." *Talking Machine World* 16(7): 165–170.

Sturdy, W. Lionel. 1921a. "From Our European Headquarters." *Talking Machine World* 17(3): 178–180.

Sturdy, W. Lionel. 1921b. "From Our European Headquarters." *Talking Machine World* 17(10): 172–175.

Sturdy, W. Lionel. 1921c. "From Our European Headquarters." *Talking Machine World* 17(12): 161–164.

Subotnik, Rose Rosengard. 1991. *Developing Variations: Style and Ideology in Western Music*. Minneapolis: University of Minnesota Press.

Sundaram, Ravi. 2010. *Pirate Modernity: Delhi's Media Urbanism*. Abingdon: Routledge.

"Tape Industry Shortage Eases; Benefits Gained." 1974. *Billboard* 86: 3, CES-12–13.

Taussig, Michael. 1993. *Mimesis and Alterity: A Particular History of the Senses*. New York: Routledge.

Taylor, Timothy. 2007a. "The Commodification of Music at the Dawn of the Era of 'Mechanical Music.'" *Ethnomusicology* 51(2): 281–205.

Taylor, Timothy. 2007b. *Beyond Exoticism: Western Music and the World*. Durham: Duke University Press.

Taylor, Timothy. 2012. *The Sounds of Capitalism: Advertising, Music, and the Conquest of Cool*. Chicago: University of Chicago Press.

Taylor, Timothy. 2016. *Music and Capitalism: A History of the Present*. Chicago: University of Chicago Press.

Terranova, Tiziana. 2013. "Free Labor." In *Digital Labor: The Internet as Playground and Factory*, edited by Trebor Scholz, 33–57. New York: Routledge.

Théberge, Paul. 1997. *Any Sound You Can Imagine: Making Music / Consuming Technology*. Middletown: Wesleyan University Press.

Théberge, Paul. 2004. "The Network Studio: Historical and Technological Paths to a New Ideal in Music Making." *Social Studies of Science* 34(5): 759–781.

Théberge, Paul. 2013. "Visualizing Music and Sound in the Digital Doman." Presented at Music, Digitization, Mediation: Towards Interdisciplinary Music Studies, University of Oxford.

Théberge, Paul. 2015. "Digitalization." In *The Routledge Reader on the Sociology of Music*, edited by John Shepherd and Kyle Devine, 329–338. New York: Routledge.

Thomas, Larry. 1980. "Pressing Matters: The Manufacturers and the Issues." *The Mix* 4(2): 17.

Thomas, William, and Dorothy Thomas. 1928. *The Child in America: Behavior Problems and Programs*. New York: Knopf.

Thompson, Emily. 1995. "Music, Machines, and the Quest for Fidelity: Marketing the Edison Phonograph in America, 1877–1925." *Musical Quarterly* 79(1): 131–171.

Thompson, Marie. 2017. "Whiteness and the Ontological Turn in Sound Studies." *Parallax* 23(3): 266–282.

Thompson, Michael. 1979. *Rubbish Theory: The Creation and Destruction of Value*. Oxford: Oxford University Press.

Thompson, Richard, Shanna Swan, Charles Moore, and Frederick vom Saal. 2009. "Our Plastic Age." *Philosophical Transactions of the Royal Society B: Biological Sciences* 364(1526): 1973–1976.

Tomlinson, Gary. 1993. "Musical Pasts and Postmodern Musicologies: A Response to Lawrence Kramer." *Current Musicology* 53: 18–24, 36–40.

Tomlinson, Gary. 1999. "Vico's Songs: Detours at the Origins of (Ethno) musicology." *Musical Quarterly* 83(3): 344–377.

Tomlinson, Gary. 2015. *A Million Years of Music: The Emergence of Human Modernity*. New York: Zone Books.

Toth, James. 2018. "Perfect Sound for a Little Longer: In Defence of the CD." *The Quietus* (5 June): online.

Toynbee, Jason. 2003. "Fingers to the Bone or Spaced Out on Creativity? Labor Process and Ideology in the Production of Pop." In *Cultural Work: Understanding the Cultural Industries*, edited by Andrew Beck, 39–55. London: Routledge.

Traiman, Stephen. 1979. "Tape Products Rocked by Higher Oil Costs." *Billboard* (14 April): 1, 80.

Traiman, Steve. 1995. "Confronting the Cost Demon." *Billboard* (11 March): 74, 90.

Trippett, David. 2017. "Towards a Materialist History of Music: Histories of Sensation." *Framklin Humanities Institute*: online.

Tschmuck, Peter. 2017. "Warum Sony wider Vinyl presst." *Zeit Online* (5 August): online.

Tsing, Anna. 2005. *Friction: An Ethnography of Global Connection*. Princeton: Princeton University Press.

Tsing, Anna. 2009. "Supply Chains and the Human Condition." *Rethinking Marxism* 21(2): 148–176.

Türk, Volker, Vidhya Alakeson, Michael Kuhndt, and Michael Ritthoff. 2003. *The Environmental and Social Impacts of Digital Music: A Case Study with EMI*. Brussels: Digital Europe.

"US Vinyl Suppliers Struggling to Keep up with Demand from Pressing Plants." 2014. *FACT* (15 December): online.

Vágnerová, Lucie. 2017. "'Nimble Fingers' in Electronic Music: Rethinking Sound through Neo-colonial Labour." *Organised Sound* 22(2): 250–258.

Valiquet, Patrick. 2017. "A Managed Risk: Mediated Musicianships in a Networked Laptop Orchestra." *Contemporary Music Review* (online prepublication version): 1–20.

Valiquet, Patrick. 2018. "Technologies of Genre: Digital Distinctions in Montreal." In *The Routledge Companion to Electronic Music: Reaching Out with Technology*, edited by Simon Emerson, 96–112. London: Routledge.

VanCour, Shawn, and Kyle Barnett. 2017. "Eat What You Hear: Gustasoinc Discourses and the Material Culture of Commercial Sound Recording." *Journal of Material Culture* 22(1): 93–109.

Vanderbilt, Byron. 1971. *Thomas Edison, Chemist*. Washington: American Chemical Society.

Vera, Hector. 2016. "Rebuilding a Classic: *The Social Construction of Reality* at 50." *Cultural Sociology* 10(1): 3–20.

Victor Talking Machine Company. 1924–1928. Managing Committee Regular Meeting. [Box 6, RCA Victor Records (Accession 2658). Hagley Museum and Library, Wilmington, D.E.]

Waksman, Steve. 2018. "Reconstructing the Past: Popular Music and Historiography." In *The Routledge Companion to Popular Music History and Heritage*, edited by Sarah Baker, Catherine Strong, Lauren Istvandity, and Zelmarie Cantillon, 55–66. New York: Routledge.

Walker, Percy, and Lawrence Steele. 1922. "Shellac." *Technological Papers of the Bureau of Standards* 17: 277–296.

Wallenberg, Björn. 2017. "Han skriver en bok om Spotify: 'Det var från början en pirattjänst.'" *DiGITAL* (7 May): online.

Wallerstein, Immanuel. 2004. *World-Systems Analysis: An Introduction*. Durham: Duke University Press.

Walton, Benjamin. 2015. "Quirk Shame." *Representations* 132: 121–129.

Warrender, W.T. 1947. "How Records Are Made." *Radio Age* 6(3): 11–13, 31.

Wasson, Haidee. 2015. "Formatting Film Studies." *Film Studies* 12: 56–61.

Weber, Christopher, Jonathan Koomey, and Scott Matthews. 2010. "The Energy and Climate Change Implications of Different Music Delivery Methods." *Journal of Industrial Ecology* 14(5): 754–769.

Weber, William. 1975. *Music and the Middle Class: The Social Structure of Concert Life in Paris, London, and Vienna*. London: Croom Helm.

Weheliye, Alexander. 2005. *Phonographies: Grooves in Sonic Afro-Modernity*. Durham: Duke University Press.

Weisberg, H. 1979. "Visit with Akzo Chemi Nederland." Unpublished RCA Internal Correspondence. [Box M&A 881 / Folder 28, David Sarnoff Research Center Records (Accession 2464.09). Hagley Museum and Library, Wilmington, DE.]

Western, Tom. 2015. *National Phonography: Field Recording and Sound Archiving in Postwar Britain*. PhD diss., University of Edinburgh.

Whitman, Mark. 1987. "New Research into Polycarbonate." *One-to-One* (November): 42, 46.

"Why South African Millennials Are Buying More Vinyl Records Online?" 2016. *TechFinancials* (6 May): online.

Whyte, Bert. 1979. "Behind the Scenes." *Audio* (August): 29–31.

Wile, Raymond. 1990. "Etching the Voice: The Berliner Invention of the Gramophone." *ARSC Journal* 21(2): 2–22.

Wile, Raymond. 1990. "The Development of Sound Recording at the Volta Laboratory." *ARSC Journal* 21(2): 208–225.

Wile, Raymond. 1992. "Cylinder Record Materials." *ARSC Journal* 26(2): 162–177.

Wile, Raymond. 1993. "The Launching of the Gramophone in America, 1890–1896." *ARSC Journal* 24(2): 176–192.

Williams, Raymond. 1977. *Marxism and Literature*. Oxford: Oxford University Press.

Williams, Raymond. 1989. "Culture Is Ordinary." In *Resources of Hope: Culture, Democracy, Socialism*. London: Verso.

Williamson, John, and Martin Cloonan. 2007. "Rethinking the Music Industry." *Popular Music* 26(2): 305–322.

Williamson, John, and Martin Cloonan. 2013. "Contextualising the Contemporary Recording Industry." In *The International Recording Industries*, edited by Lee Marshall, 11–29. Abingdon: Routledge.

Williamson, John, and Martin Cloonan. 2016. *Players' Work Time: A History of the British Musicians' Union, 1893–2013*. Manchester: Manchester University Press.

Wilson, Sheena, Imre Szeman, and Adam Carlson. 2017. "On Petrocultures: Or, Why We Need to Understand Oil to Understand Everything Else." In *Petrocultures: Oil, Politics, Culture*, edited by Sheena Wilson, Adam Carlson, and Imre Szeman, 3–19. Montreal: McGill-Queen's University Press.

Winner, Lewis. 1944. "Shellac and Development of Substitutes." *Plastics* 1(2): 55–56, 96.

Winseck, Dwayne. 2011. "The Political Economies of Media and the Transformation of the Global Media Industries." In *The Political Economies of Media and the Transformation of the Global Media Industries*, edited by Dwayne Winseck and Dal Yong Jin, 3–48. New York: Bloomsbury.

Winters, Paul. 2016. *Vinyl Records and Analog Culture in the Digital Age: Pressing Matters*. Lanham: Lexington Books.

Winthrop-Young, Geoffrey. 2011a. *Kittler and the Media*. Cambridge: Polity.

Winthrop-Young, Geoffrey. 2011b. "Krautrock, Heidegger, Bogeyman: Kittler in the Anglosphere." *Thesis Eleven* 107(1): 6–20.

Winthrop-Young, Geoffrey. 2014. "The Kultur of Cultural Techniques: Conceptual Inertia and the Parasitic Materialities of Ontologization." *Cultural Politics* 10(3): 376–378.

Winthrop-Young, Geoffrey. 2015. "Siren Recursions." In *Kittler Now: Current Perspectives in Kittler Studies*, edited by Stephen Sale and Laura Salisbury, 71–94. Cambridge: Polity.

Winthrop-Young, Geoffrey. 2017. "The Kittler Effect." *New German Critique* 44(3): 205–224.

Winthrop-Young, Geoffrey. 2018. "Recursive Innovation." In *The Technological Introject: Friedrich Kittler between Implementation and the Incalculable*, edited by Jeffrey Champlin and Antje Pfannkucken, 193–208. New York: Fordham University Press.

Witkin, Jim. 2011. "A Virtuous (and Fun?) Way to Trade in Old CDs." *New York Times* (12 September): online.

Witt, Stephen. 2015. *How Music Got Free: The Inventor, the Mogul, the Thief*. London: Vintage.

Wittchen, Samantha. 2012. "Recycling Challenge: Vinyl Records." *Grid Magazine* 43: 7.

Wong, Deborah. 2014. "Sound, Silence, Music: Power." *Ethnomusicology* 58(2): 347–353.

"WPB Announce No New Shellac After November." 1942. *Billboard* 54(46): 20.

"WPB Sharply Curtails Music Industry." 1942. *Music Trades* 90(2): 5.

Yamamoto, Tokugen. 1977. "Far East—Problems and Growth Potential." *Journal of the Audio Engineering Society* 25(10–11): 800–801.

York, Richard. 2006. "Ecological Paradoxes: William Stanley Jevons and the Paperless Office." *Human Ecology Review* 13(2): 143–147.

Young, Liam Cole. 2017. "Innis's Infrastructure: Dirt, Beavers, and Documents in Material Media Theory." *Cultural Politics* 13(2): 227–249.

Index